RIPLEY & THE GOLDEN VALLEY

THROUGH TIME

Jill Armitage

AMBERLEY PUBLISHING

Acknowledgements

I would like to thank all who have shared ideas, given information and made suggestions to make this book possible.

My most grateful thanks goes to the individuals, organisations and libraries whose old photographs I was able to copy for inclusion. Some of the period illustrations have come from obscure sources, making it difficult to credit the originators, or the people who have preserved the images. To them all, I give my sincere thanks.

First published 2013

Amberley Publishing
The Hill, Stroud, Gloucestershire, GL5 4EP
www.amberley-books.com

ISBN 978 1 4456 3290 2 (print)
ISBN 978 1 4456 3299 5 (ebook)

British Library Cataloguing in Publication Data.
A catalogue record for this book is available from the British Library.

Typesetting by Amberley Publishing.
Printed in Great Britain.

Introduction

The Armorial Bearings of Ripley gives a pictorial story of its history. The green background symbolises the Royal Forest of Duffield, which stretched across to Ripley from the hills of Heage, represented by the yellow chevron. The horseshoes are from the arms of the Ferrers family, who gave this area to the monks of Darley Abbey. The fleur-de-lis is from the seal of Darley Abbey. In the Domesday Book, Ripley and Pentrich were linked, and this early association is shown with the stag heads of the Cavendish family, who later owned Pentrich.

The Ripley region owes its growth to the area's natural resources of coal and iron, the rather unexpected find of oil, and the rich band of clay on which the celebrated Denby pottery was founded. With such a concentrated abundance of riches, this previously insignificant locale on the Derbyshire/Nottinghamshire border was given the name 'The Golden Valley'.

The unicorn's head is adapted from the crest of the Wright family, early ironmasters with interests in the world-famous Butterley Company, who later used the crest. The Butterley Company ran a vast engineering, iron-making and mining empire that was centred here. So many industries moved to the area that at the start of the twentieth century, it had taken on an industrial character. The rising flames in the arms of Ripley represent the heavy local industry. The black chevron represents the coal seams lying beneath the ground, and the black walled crown acknowledges Ripley as a mining town. Villages like Denby, Codnor, Marehay, Waingroves, Riddings, Swanwick and Somercotes were sucked together, and at the centre was Ripley. Alongside the ancient villages, new towns like Ironville were built, a name that leaves no doubt as to what the growth of the town was built on.

The contribution that Ripley and the surrounding area made to the economy of Britain in the centuries up to recent times is colossal, but the post-war period saw a running down of the traditional industries and the closure of the pits and iron foundries. Now there is a greater diversity of occupations. Ripley is progressive but still retains its weekly outdoor market that dates back to 1251. It can boast of having one of the first co-operatives, while its shopping centre is compact, convenient and modern.

It also has its personalities. Barnes Wallis, the inventor of the bouncing bomb, was born in Ripley. There is a tradition that a Mr Taylor of Ripley created a soft drink, but finding no success in Britain he took his idea to America. The drink became Coca-Cola. John Flamsteed, the eminent Astrologer Royal, was born at Denby Old Hall. More recently, there are celebrities like John Flanagan, actor and writer, who appeared in such television epics as *The Sweeney* and *Shipman*, and Andy Sneap, musician and guitarist of Sabbat.

At the base of the Armorial Bearings is the quotation *Ingenium Industria Alitur,* which translates as 'ability thrives on industry', a fitting tribute to the energy and resourcefulness of the people of Ripley and The Golden Valley.

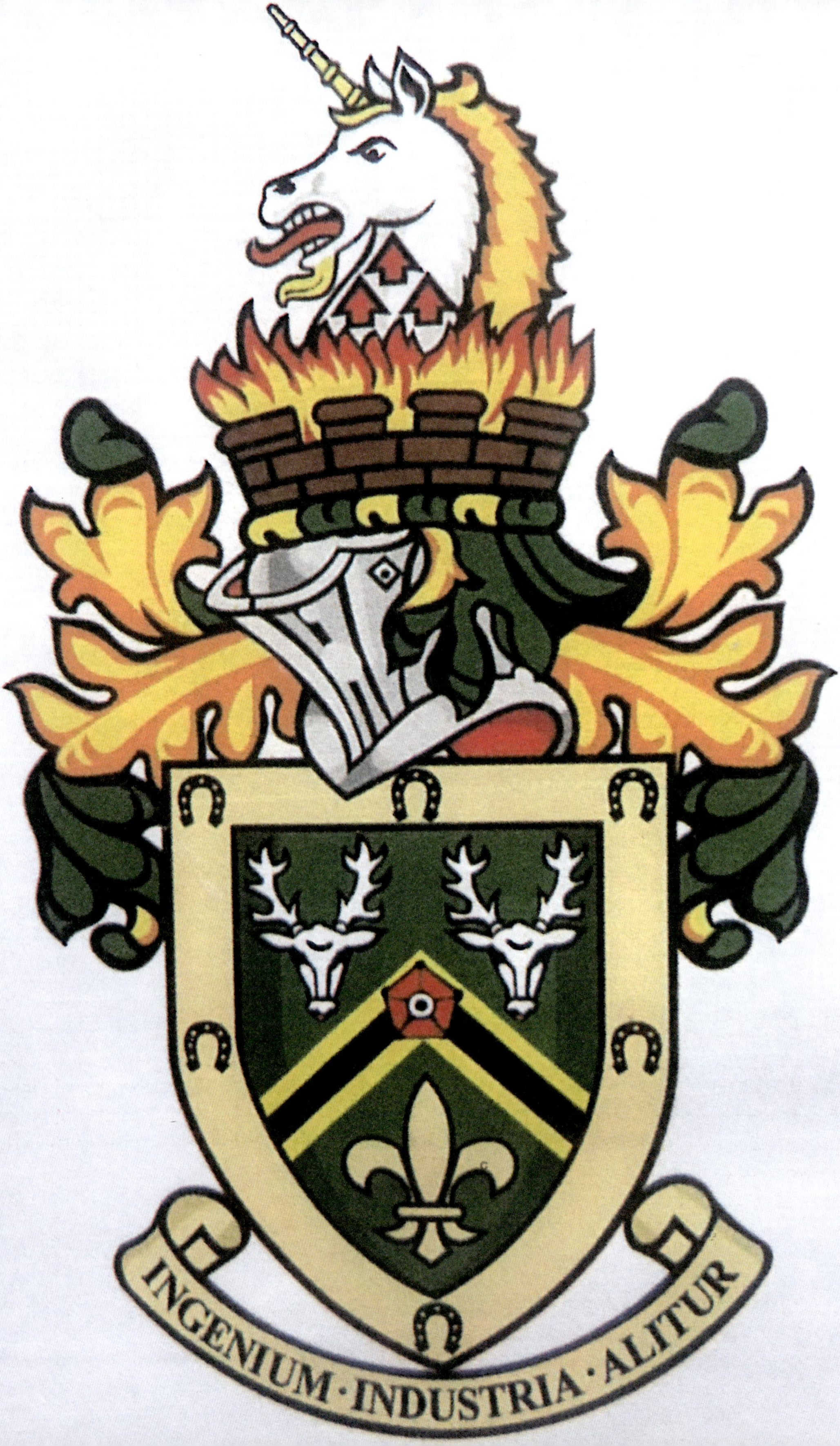
INGENIUM · INDUSTRIA · ALITUR

Rykneld Road

Ripley's early history is linked firmly with its neighbour Pentrich, which covered a much larger area and became the principle village. This was probably due to the Roman Rykneld Road that went straight through the region from north to south. The long, straight stretch called Street Lane still runs north from Denby, until its course disappears beside the A38 at Ripley. The name 'street' is derived from the Anglican 'stret', meaning a Roman paved road. Rykneld Road then continued through Hartshay and Pentrich, where a Roman fort was built on the elevated site called Castle Hill, currently occupied by Coneygrey Farm. Although now just a heap of stones incorporated into a field wall, as the photograph below shows, the views are far-reaching, with South Wingfield Manor in the middle distance. This Roman fort would have been a busy hub at the intersection of many tracks and coal ways. Archaeologists have found that the Romans mined the local coal (or got the natives to mine it for them) and used the compacted slack for road building throughout this area. For centuries, Rykneld Road continued in use as a major commercial highway, offering good trading opportunities long after the Romans left.

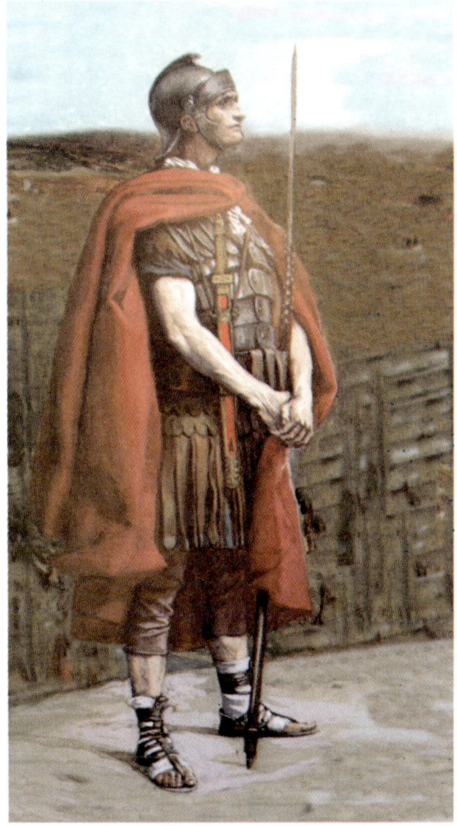

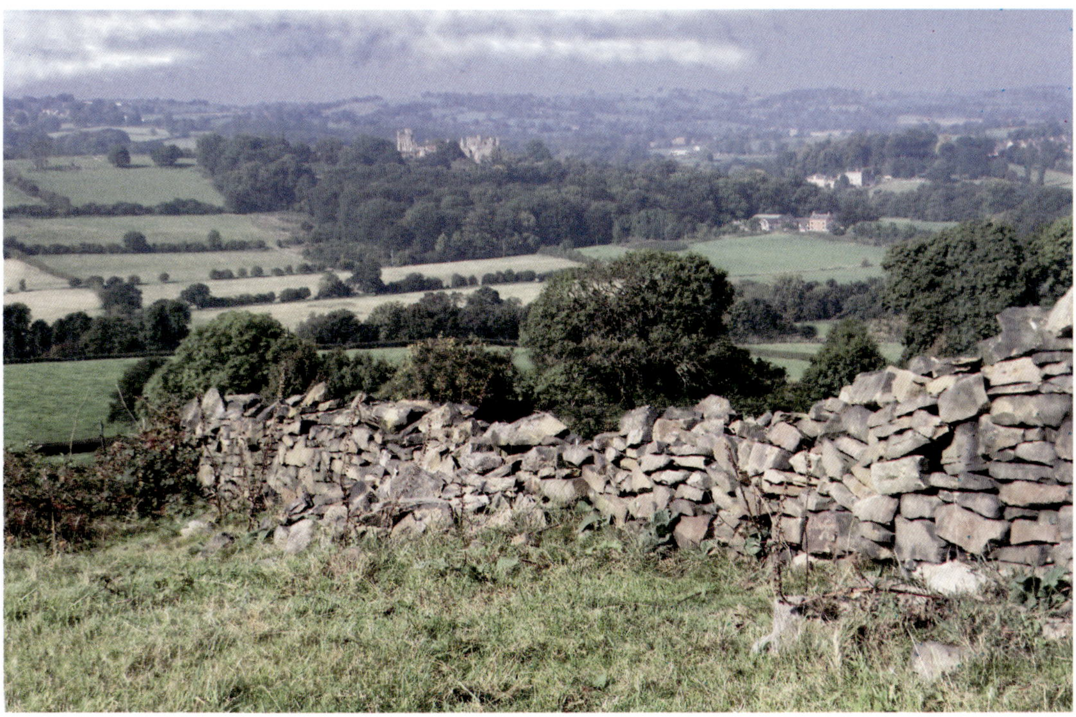

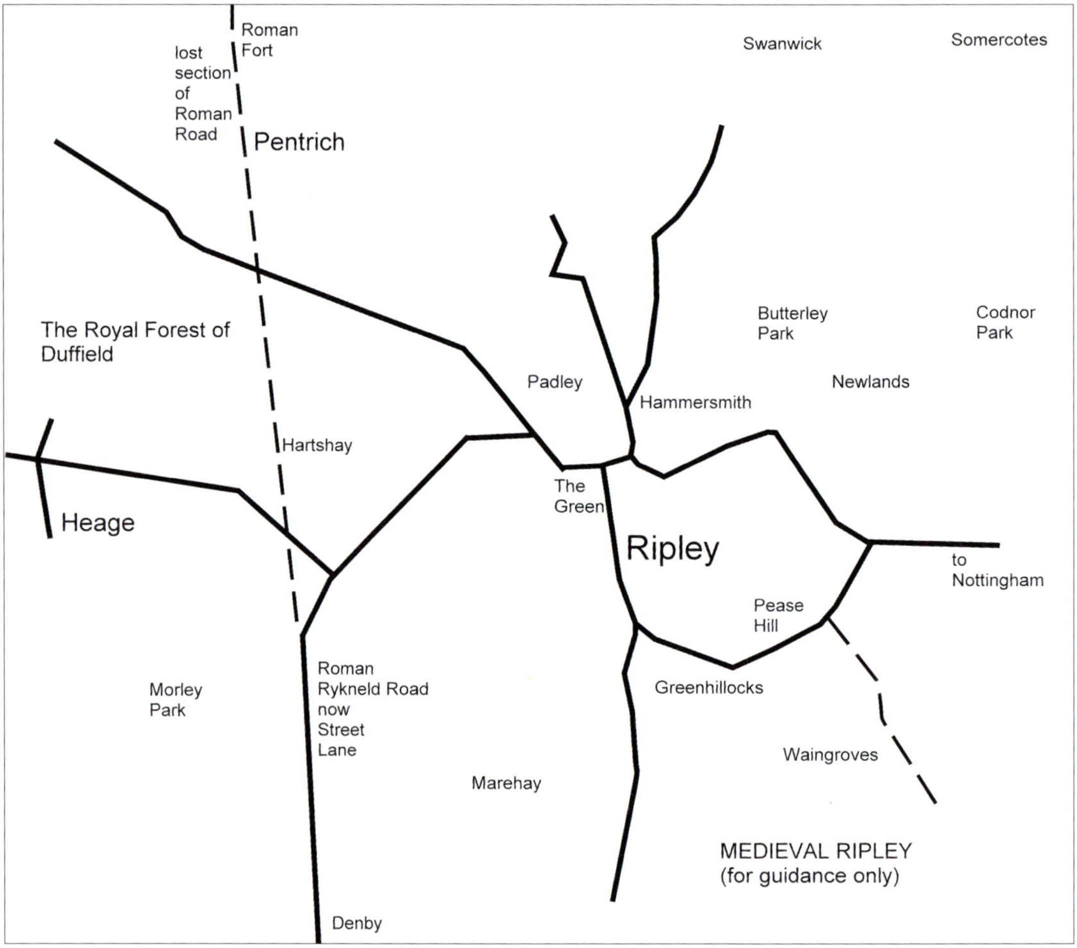

The Domesday Book

In the Domesday Book of 1068, the hamlets of Ripelie (Ripley) and Pentric (Pentrich) were surveyed together and valued at £4. The land was held by a man called Levenot, and sixteen families lived in the two hamlets set on neighbouring hills. They worked the fields and tended livestock in the valley of the River Amber. When William the Conqueror gave the land to Ralph Fitzhubert, the villagers had to swear fealty to their Norman lord, who in turn handed over the Pentrich and Ripley lands to Darley Abbey. In 1291, there is reference to two watermills with fish ponds in Ripley owned by the Abbot of Darley. All corn was ground at these mills, and the monks visited the farms and cottages to collect the tithes of wool, hemp, flax, pigs and geese. Tithes were one tenth of the peasants' agricultural produce levied as a tax for the support of the church, and the feudal dues exacted by the King. The charters that were drawn up by the monks during this time are in the British Museum, and are full of references to local places like Paddel (Padley), Lowes, Botleyam (Butterley), Witeleg (Whiteley), Salterwode (Salterwood) and Hertshay (Hartsay).

Until the nineteenth century, there was an ancient, stone-built farm on Cromford Road, Ripley, called Abbey Farm. It was believed that the tithe barns where local produce was stored by the Abbey – a picturesque reminder of monastic rule – were situated here.

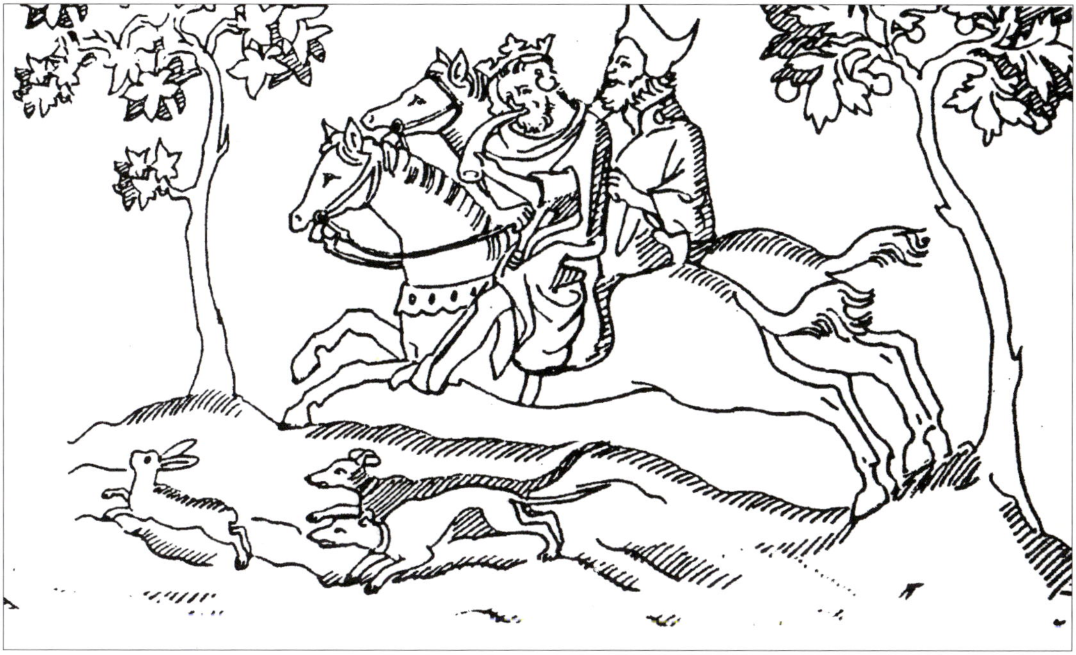

Ripley, Once Part of the Royal Forest

The association between the villages of Ripley and Pentrich lasted for eight centuries. Their neighbour Highledge, now Heage, was always a straggling village on the periphery of Ripley, its houses and farms stretching over a wide area of hilly countryside, with field paths descending to the valley of the River Amber. In medieval times, Heage was part of the Royal Forest of Duffield, which stretched into the outlying woodlands and parks of Hartshay and Buckland, Butterley Park and Salterwood. The latter probably took its name from a 'saltaria' or 'deer leap', designed to keep the King's deer in and the peasants out. Royal forests were strictly for the hunting pleasure of the crown, with harsh forest rules and severe penalties for anyone caught poaching or stealing deer. This was the time of Robin Hood, and as Ripley and its environs stretch over the Nottinghamshire border, the infamous outlaw could very probably have frequented this area.

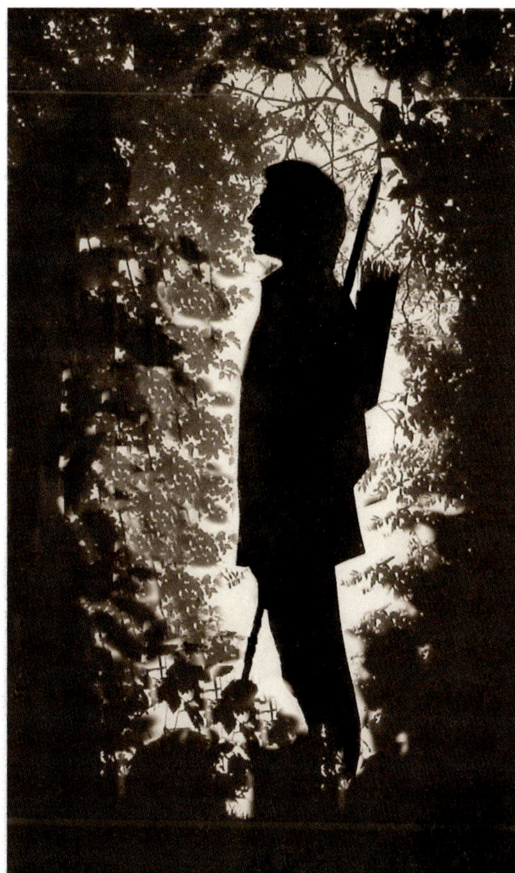

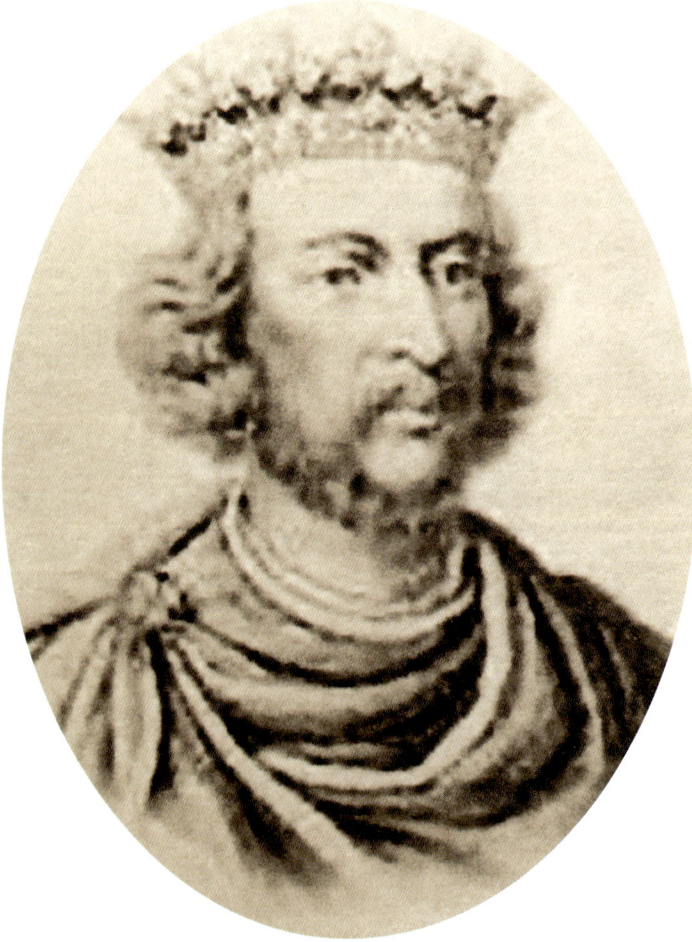

Ripley's Market Charter

In 1251, while staying with the Abbot of Darley Abbey during a hunting session at Duffield Forest, Henry III granted a market charter for 'one market, one day a week on Wednesday at the manor of Ryppeleg, and one fair each year, lasting three days on the Vigil Day and Morrow of St Helen'. The fair attracted large numbers of horse dealers, and drovers who guided their cattle and flocks for long distances along the country lanes to Ripley Green. There was a brisk trade in young ponies, and the photograph below shows a line-up of pit ponies in the market place. Later, market day was changed to Saturday and a Friday market was added. Ripley market is still a feature of the town.

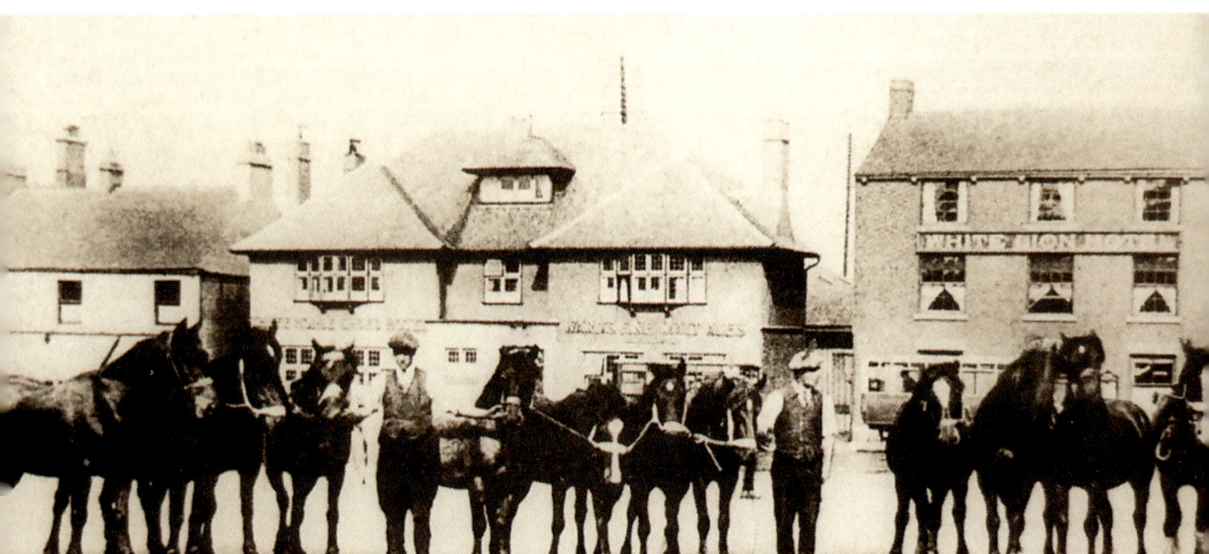

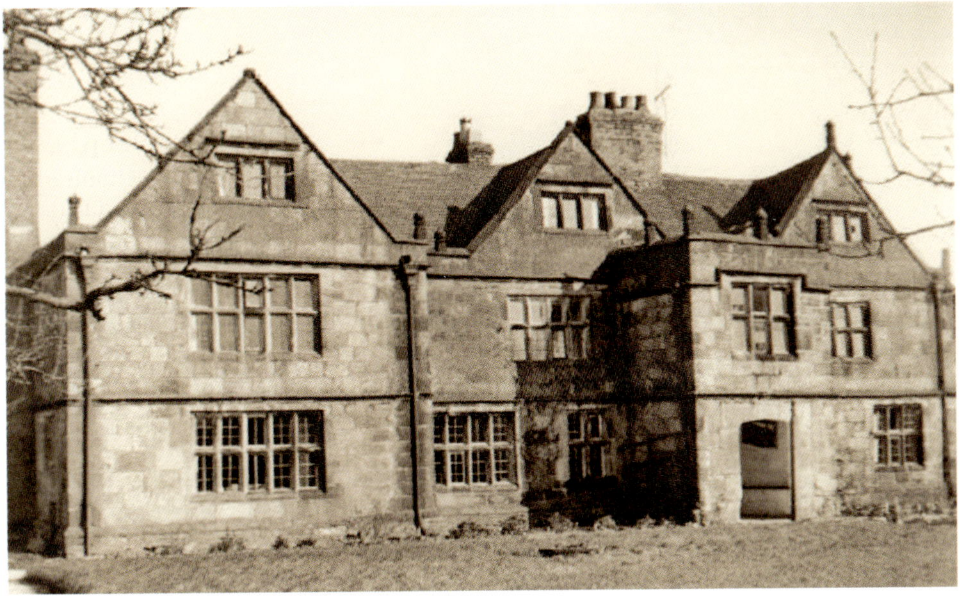

Padley Hall

Padley Hall is a delightful, Elizabethan Grade II-listed manor house, believed to be the oldest building in the Ripley area. It is mentioned in the Darley Chartulary as Paddel. It retains many features dating back to the late fifteenth century, including the half-timbered cross-wing hall built on the site, but the visible façade dates from the mid-seventeenth century, with nineteenth-century additions. There is substantiation that the family at Padley Hall was in sympathy with the Parliamentarians during the Civil War and, along with other distinguished Parliamentary leaders, Oliver Cromwell is believed to have stayed here when the siege of Wingfield Manor was in progress.

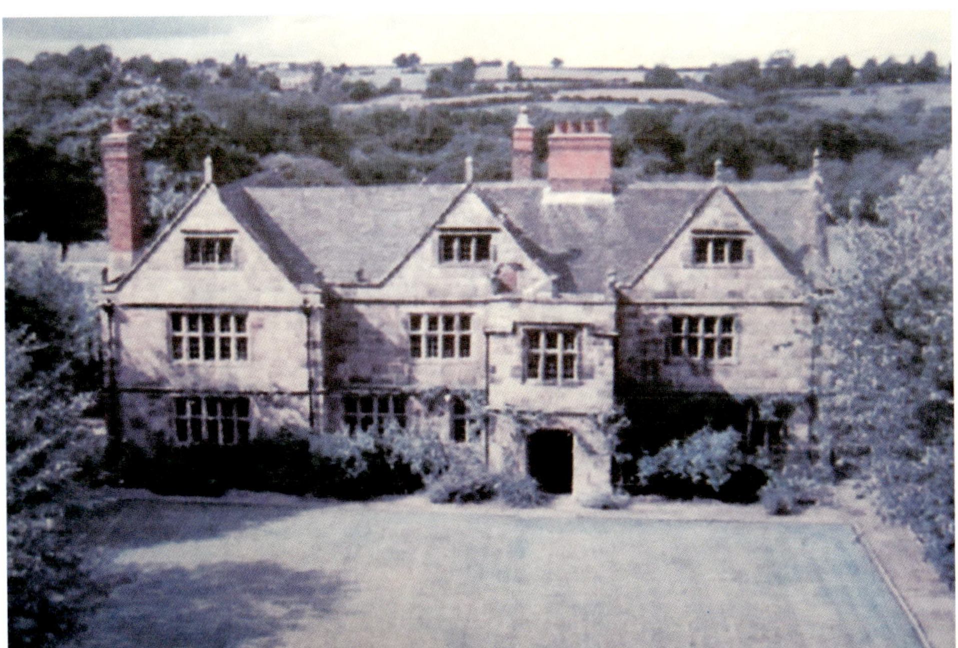

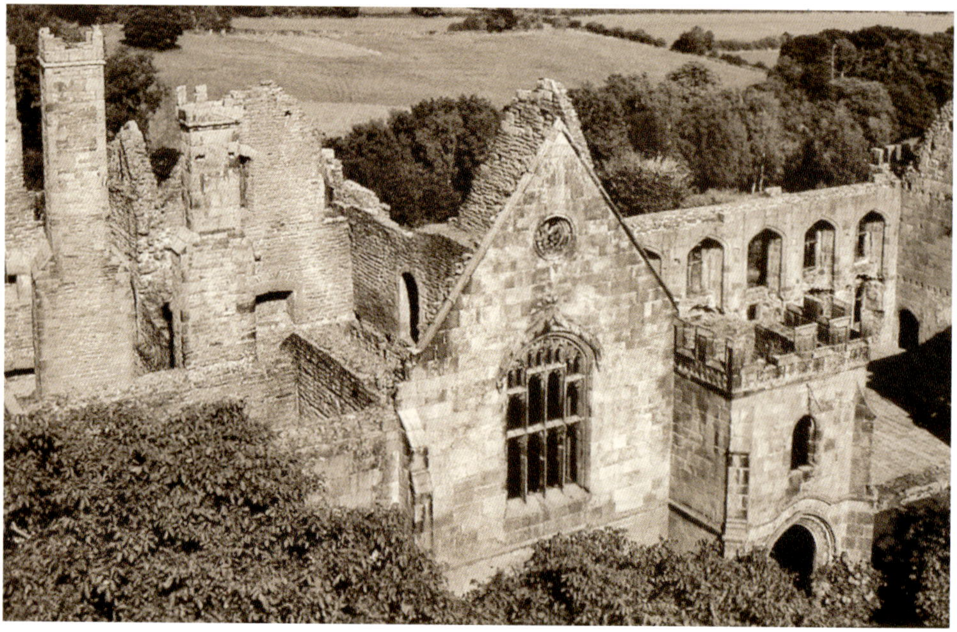

South Wingfield Manor

Wingfield was originally called Winfield, and probably derived its name from the quantity of win or gorse that grew wild in the locality. There is no record of a dwelling house until Wingfield Manor was built by Sir Ralph Cromwell. Two hundred years later, it was razed by order of Oliver Cromwell. In that period, it was little known until its then owner, the Earl of Shrewsbury, was made gaoler of Mary, Queen of Scots. When the siege at South Wingfield Manor was taking place during the Civil War, the canon that battered the manor was set up on the site of the old Roman camp, 1,200 yards away. Finding the range was too far to cause a total breach of the walls, the canon was moved to Wingfield Park gates on 14 August 1643. After a three-hour attack, South Wingfield Manor was surrendered. Like many castles that were needlessly destroyed at this time, South Wingfield Manor was never rebuilt. The ruined castle, now in the ownership of English Heritage, can only be viewed by appointment.

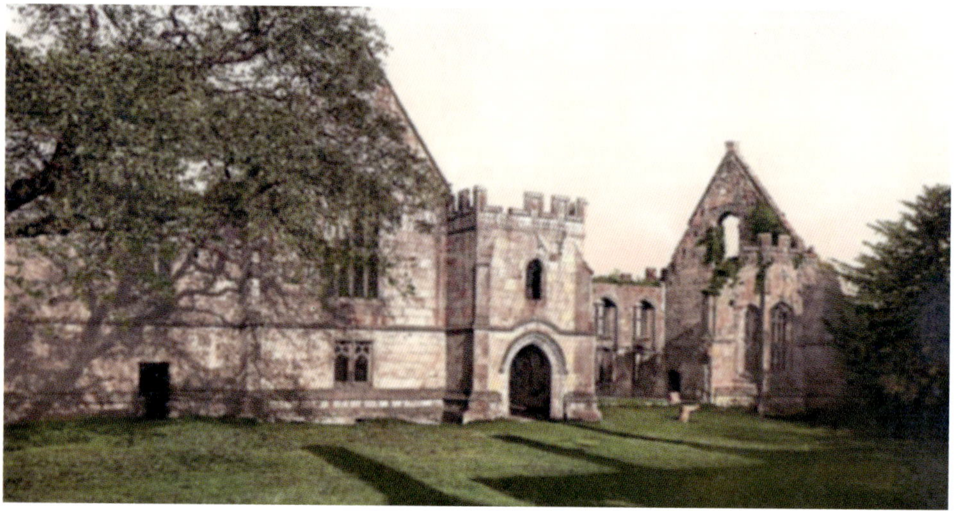

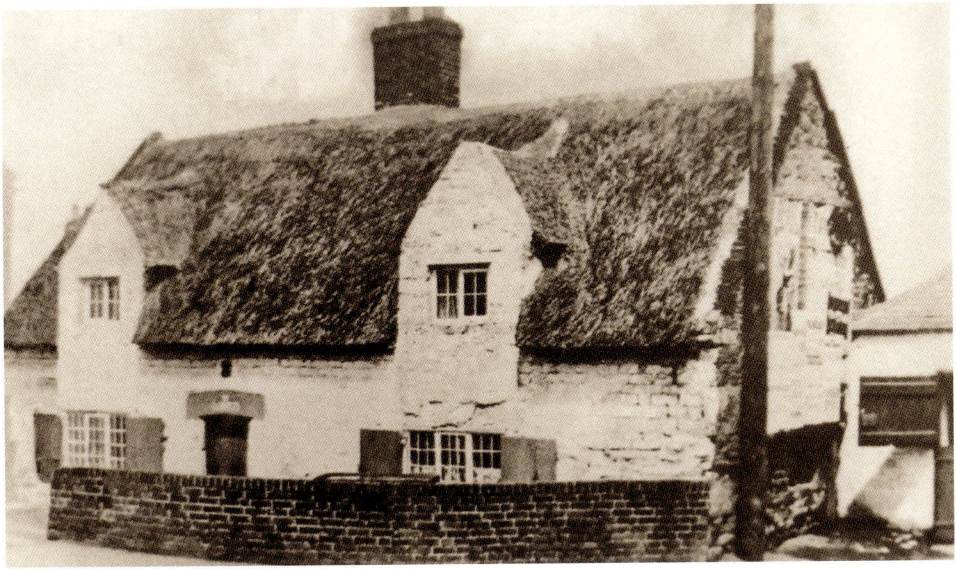

Early Ripley

At the sixteenth-century dissolution of the monasteries, all monastic land went into private ownership. The Cavendish family of Chatsworth took Pentrich, and the Zouche family of Codnor took Ripley. The latter soon sold their manor to the yeoman farmers and individuals who became Ripley's leading citizens. Early Ripley consisted of a few stone cottages centred around the village green, where the market was held. The photograph above shows a thatched cottage that stood on the corner of Chapel Street and Church Street, with a date stone of 1675. The small settlements and farmsteads around Ripley were linked by rough roads and tracks, crossing open fields and commons. There was a hostel of the order of St John of Jerusalem, a form of the Knight's Hospitallers at the area of Ripley known as Waingroves, prepared to offer shelter and help to travellers. The photograph below shows a stone plaque of uncertain age depicting a rural scene mounted in the wall of the seventeenth-century Waingroves Hall.

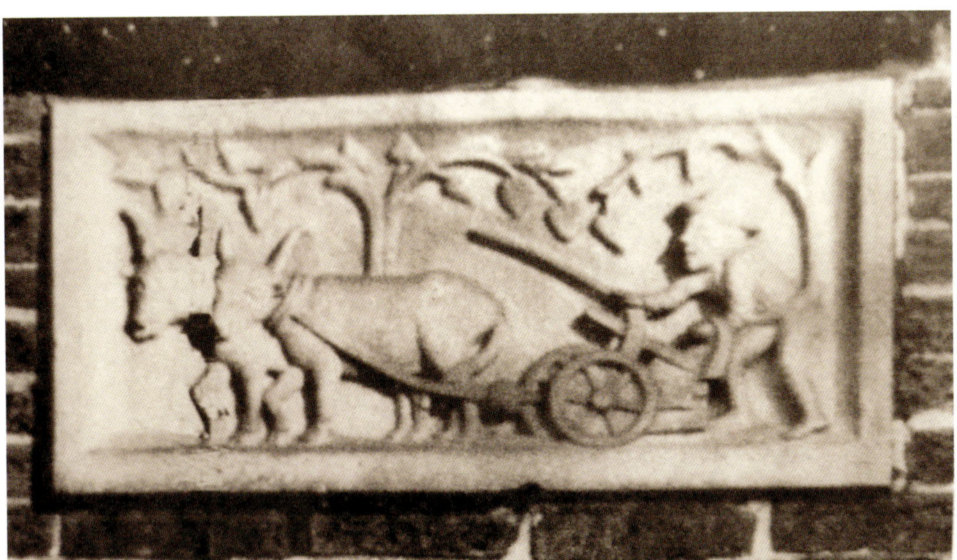

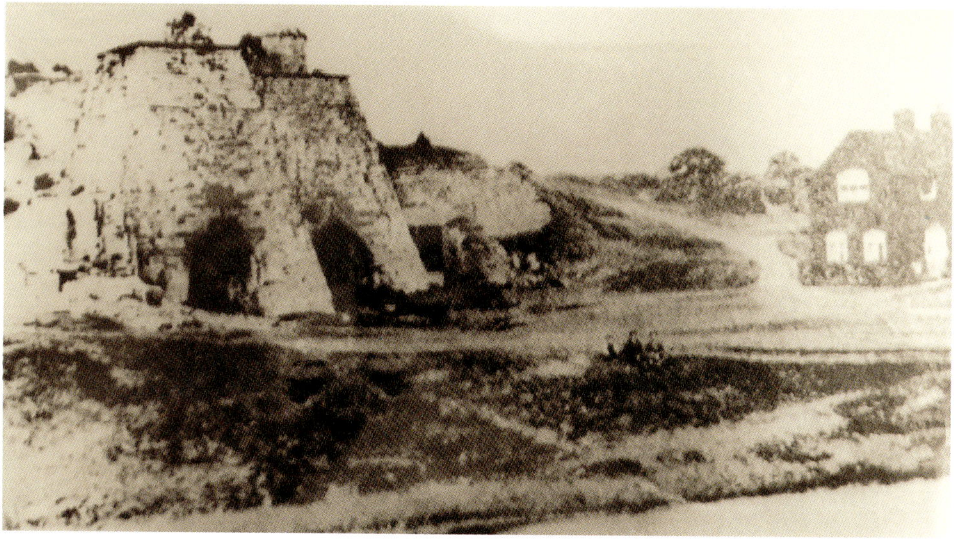

Morley Park Ironworks

Coal and iron had been dug from local opencast workings long before the sixteenth-century transference of monastic mineral-bearing land into private ownership. The site of Morley Park Ironworks has been worked for coal and ironstone since at least 1372. Its position on the side of the Roman road now called Street Lane would indicate that the Romans mined the iron here too. Few traces now remain, except this fine pair of cold blast, coke-fired iron smelting furnaces standing in a field. These furnaces were erected by Francis Hurt of Alderwasley, the first proprietor of Morley Park Ironworks, which was later worked by C. & J. Mold. The older furnace was probably the first of its type in Derbyshire, and dates from 1780. The other dates from 1818. They are both square in plan and built of grit stone in the form of truncated pyramids, roughly 40 feet high and surmounted by cupolas. Being built against a hill would have facilitated loading from the top, allowing the metal to drop into the bottle-shaped kiln. In 1846, the Morley Park Ironworks had 400 employees and 300 horses, but was last in blast around 1875.

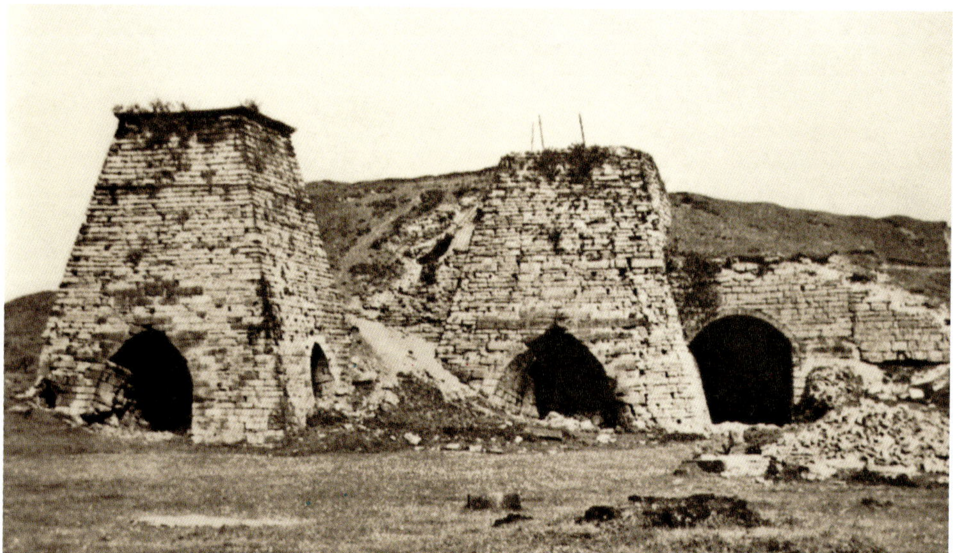

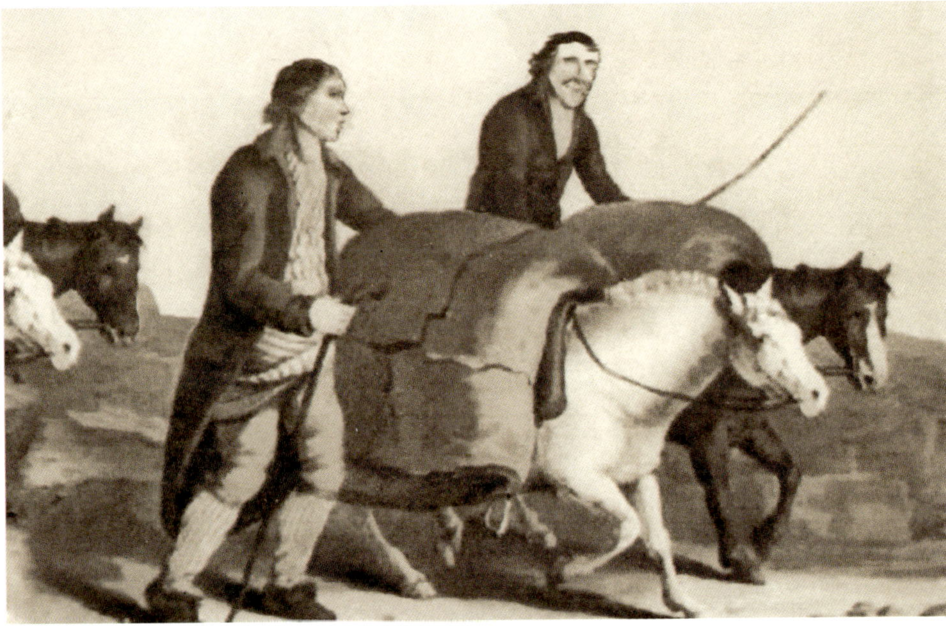

Packhorse Trails

After the Romans left Derbyshire, the roads became neglected, and although kinder to unshod hooves, the unpaved dirt roads hindered transportation. During the Middle Ages, roads became increasingly uncared for and centuries of use wore down sections to form sunken lanes, often referred to as holloways, especially on the steeper climbs out of the valleys. With the additional hazards of foot pads, potholes and highwaymen, road travel was fraught with problems. The perilous conditions of these narrow tracks could not accommodate wheeled vehicles, so raw materials and goods were transported by convoys of packhorses tended by jaggers. The photograph below shows a packhorse bridge in the Golden Valley, just wide enough for the pack-loaded animals, and paved down the centre to prevent wear.

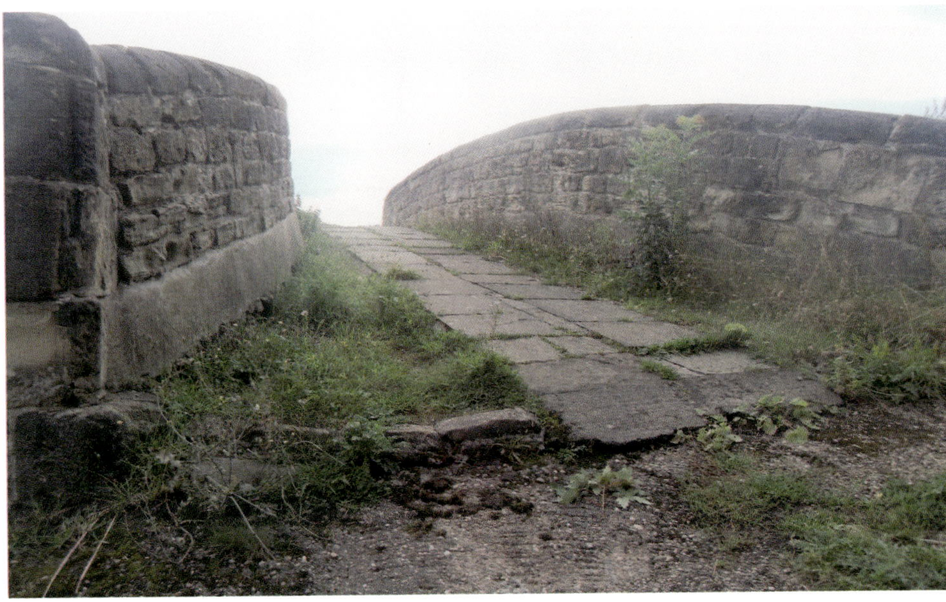

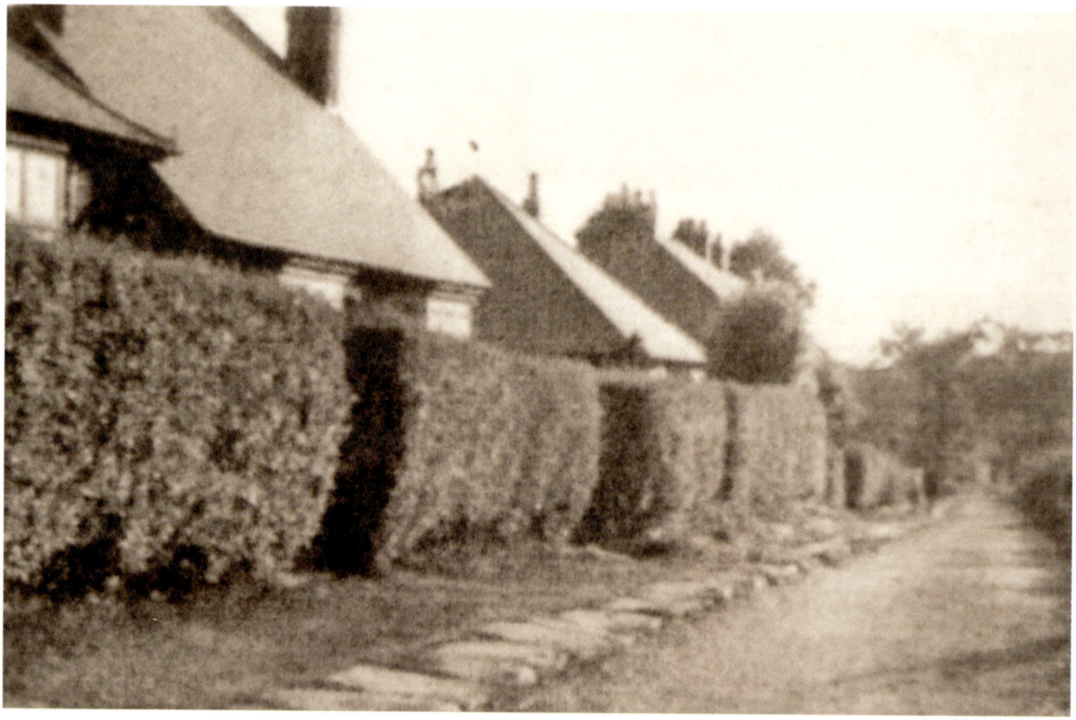

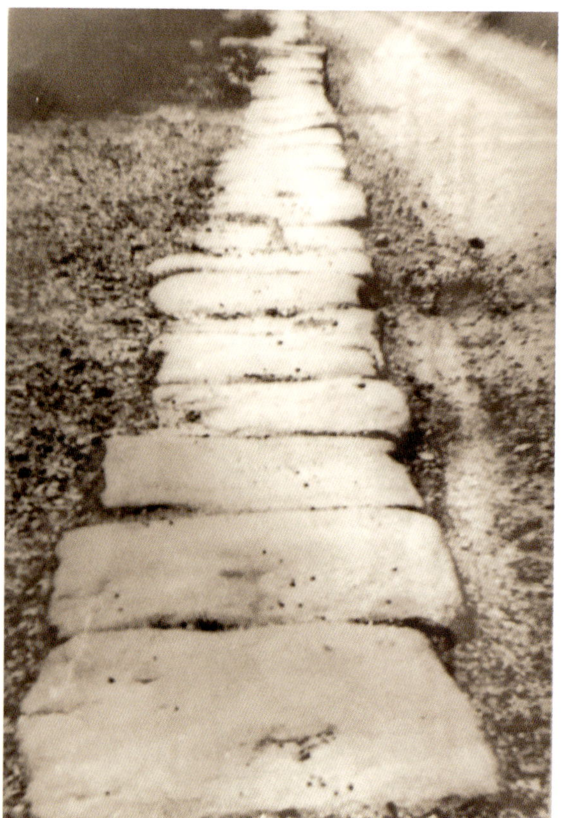

The Remains of a Packhorse Trail Along Sandham Lane

In 1555, the repair of the highways was made the responsibility of each parish, with every parishioner performing four days labour on the roads each year as his statute duty. Although this was later increased to six days, and landowners whose land exceeded £50 in value had to provide a horse and cart, this form of maintenance was not effective. The crude methods of construction and repair became inadequate as wheeled carts and wagons replaced packhorses, and roads deteriorated under the heavier use. The photographs show the remains of a packhorse track on Sandham Lane, which passed through Ripley. Sandham Lane now goes past the hospital and continues south-west as a footpath to join the old Roman road, Street Lane. This packhorse trail would then continue to Morley Park Furnaces. The slabs on Sandham Lane (*left*) were taken up in April 1973 and transported to the council depot on Derby Road. They were supposed to be laid as a feature in the market place but disappeared.

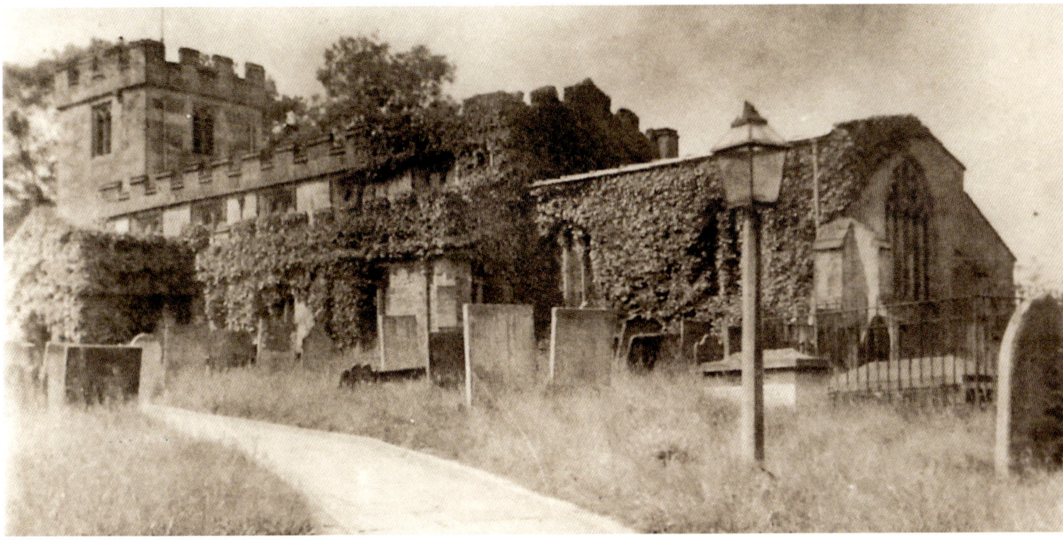

Pentrich Church

Because the ecclesiastical parish of Ripley was part of the larger parish of Pentrich, for centuries the people of Ripley trudged along the lanes to the parish church of St Matthew for worship. Dating back to the twelfth century, Pentrich church was possibly built on the site of an earlier and smaller church from pre-Norman times. The Norman tower is a stronghold, with walls over a metre thick, enclosing a space almost three metres square. The nave has Norman pillars, but the aisles, the clerestory and the chantry are later additions. Although there is a date of 1662 on the font, it is believed to be Norman and this date is when it was restored.

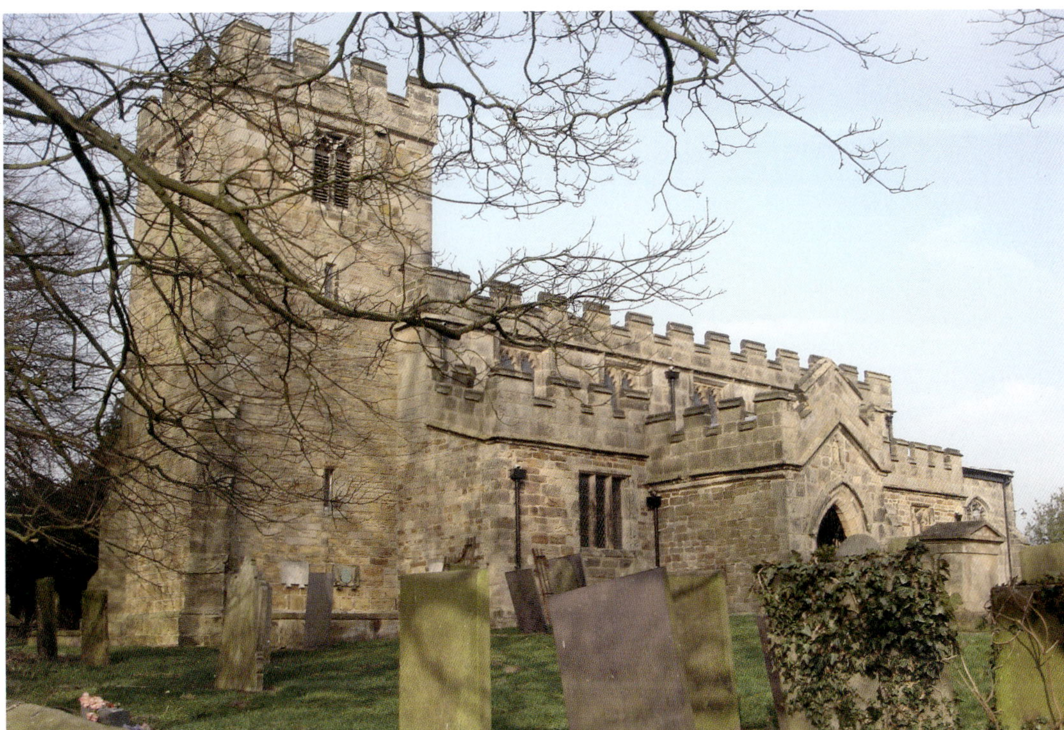

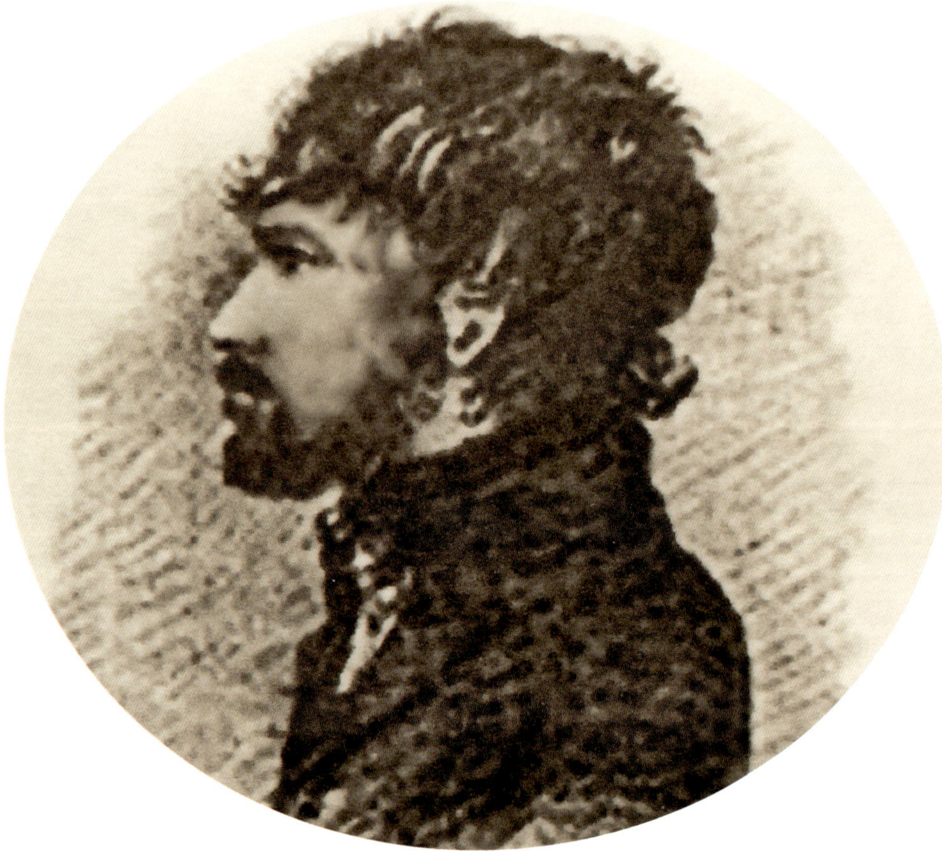

The Years of Discontent and the Pentrich Revolution

When the Napoleonic wars came to an end in 1815, thousands of men were released from the forces, but, unable to find work, discontentment grew. The following year in Derbyshire, it was cold and wet, with snow as late as June. Crops failed and, as a consequence, a third of the working population were thrown out of work and became paupers. The knock-on effect was disastrous. The workhouses were overflowing, crime increased fourfold and prisons were overcrowded.

In Pentrich, where many relied upon the struggling hosiery industry, Jeremiah Brandreth, a twenty-seven-year-old framework knitter proposed to march to London to voice their discontent. Because of Brandreth's strong personality and commanding presence, coupled with his promise of a better life after their victory, very few hesitated and, on 9 June 1817, around 400 men and boys set off from Pentrich. Unfortunately, at a farm in Wingfield Park, turmoil broke out and an innocent manservant was killed. Suddenly, the undertaking had taken a disturbingly reckless new turn. As they marched on to Ripley, there was a feeling of uncertainty, and despite the addition of a large party of men from Swanwick, the men's morale was flagging. When they arrived at Langley Mill and heard that soldiers from Nottingham were on their way, panic set in, and many of the men ignored Brandreth's pleading and threats and quickly dispersed. Around forty men were arrested and sent to gaol. Trials began on 15 October and lasted for ten days. Most of the insurrectionists were pardoned, twenty of the men were transported, but the three ringleaders, Brandreth, Ludlam and Turner, were executed at Derby on 7 November 1817. The poet Shelley had witnessed the gory execution and under a *nom de plume* published an indignant pamphlet referring to 'the corpse of British liberty'.

The High Price to Pay for Treason

Although this was a fight against injustice, not everyone was sympathetic. Ripley was still part of the ecclesiastical parish of Pentrich, but for the convenience of Ripley folk, there was a chapel of ease at Ripley. The then vicar of Pentrich, John Wood, stated sanctimoniously that 'the smallness of the church accommodation at Ripley has occasioned a neglect of religious duties and morals, the lamentable effects of which during the last two years are but too well known, and have rendered it an imperious duty upon the well-disposed inhabitants to take some means of stemming the torrent of irreligion and disaffection'. The 'well-disposed inhabitants' obviously felt obliged to take note of this pious view and, as a result, the parish church of All Saints Ripley was built in 1821.

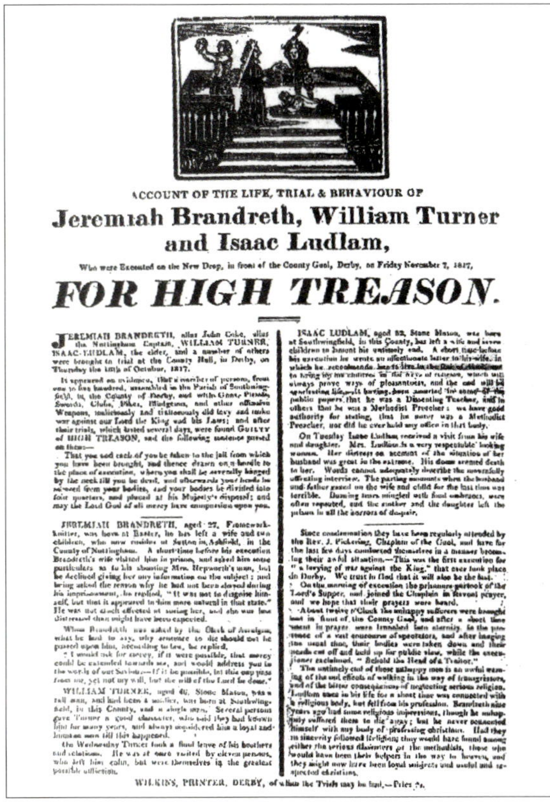

ACCOUNT OF THE LIFE, TRIAL & BEHAVIOUR OF

Jeremiah Brandreth, William Turner and Isaac Ludlam,

Who were Executed on the New Drop, in front of the County Gaol, Derby, on Friday November 7, 1817,

FOR HIGH TREASON.

JEREMIAH BRANDRETH, alias John Coke, alias the Nottingham Captain, WILLIAM TURNER, ISAAC LUDLAM, the elder, and a number of others were brought to trial at the County Hall, in Derby, on Thursday the 16th of October, 1817.

It appeared on evidence, that a number of persons, from one to five hundred, assembled in the Parish of Southwingfield, in the County of Derby, and with Guns, Pikes, Swords, Clubs, Pikes, Bludgeons, and other offensive Weapons, maliciously and traitorously did levy and make war against our Lord the King and his Laws; and after their trials, which lasted several days, were found GUILTY of HIGH TREASON, and the following sentence passed on them:—

That you and each of you be taken to the jail from which you have been brought, and thence drawn on a hurdle to the place of execution, where you shall be severally hanged by the neck till you be dead, and afterwards your heads be severed from your bodies, and your bodies be divided into four quarters, and placed at his Majesty's disposal; and may the Lord God of all mercy have compassion upon you.

JEREMIAH BRANDRETH, aged 27, Framework-knitter, was born at Exeter, he has left a wife and two children, who now reside at Sutton in Ashfield, in the County of Nottingham. A short time before his execution Brandreth's wife visited him in prison, and asked him some particulars as to his shooting Mrs. Hepworth's man, but he declined giving her any information on the subject; and being asked the reason why he had not been shaved during his imprisonment, he replied, "It was not to disguise himself, but that it appeared to him more natural in that state." He was not much affected at seeing her, and she was less distressed than might have been expected.

When Brandreth was asked by the Clerk of Arraigns, what he had to say, why sentence to die should not be passed upon him, according to law, he replied,

"I would ask for mercy, if it were possible, that mercy could be extended towards me, and would address you in the words of our Saviour,—If it be possible, let this cup pass from me, yet not my will, but the will of the Lord be done."

WILLIAM TURNER, aged 46, Stone Mason, was a tall man, and had been a soldier, was born at Southwingfield, in this County, and a single man. Several persons gave Turner a good character, who said they had known him for many years, and always considered him a loyal and humane man till this happened.

On Wednesday Turner took a fond leave of his brothers and relations. He was at once visited by eleven persons, who left him calm, but were themselves in the greatest possible affliction.

ISAAC LUDLAM, aged 52, Stone Mason, was born at Southwingfield, in this County, has left a wife and seven children to lament his untimely end. A short time before his execution he wrote an affectionate letter to his wife, in which he recommends her to live in the fear of God and to bring up the children in the ways of religion, which will always prove ways of pleasantness, and the end will be everlasting life. It having been asserted in some of the public papers that he was a Dissenting Teacher, and in others that he was a Methodist Preacher: we have good authority for stating, that he never was a Methodist Preacher, nor did he ever hold any office in that body.

On Tuesday Isaac Ludlam received a visit from his wife and daughter. Mrs. Ludlam is a very respectable looking woman. Her distress on account of the situation of her husband was great in the extreme. His doom seemed death to her. Words cannot adequately describe the mournfully affecting interview. The parting moments when the husband and father gazed on the wife and child for the last time was terrible. Burning tears mingled with fond embraces, were often repeated, and the mother and the daughter left the prison in all the horrors of despair.

Since condemnation they have been regularly attended by the Rev. J. Pickering, Chaplain of the Gaol, and have for the last few days conducted themselves in a manner becoming their awful situation.—This was the first execution for "a levying of war against the King," that ever took place in Derby. We trust in God that it will also be the last.

On the morning of execution the prisoners partook of the Lord's Supper, and joined the Chaplain in fervent prayer, and we hope that their prayers were heard.

About twelve o'Clock the unhappy sufferers were brought out in front of the County Gaol, and after a short time spent in prayer, were launched into eternity, in the presence of a vast concourse of spectators, and after hanging the usual time, their bodies were taken down and their heads cut off and held up for public view, while the executioner exclaimed, "Behold the Head of a Traitor."

The untimely end of these unhappy men is an awful warning of the sad effects of walking in the way of transgressors, and of the bitter consequences of neglecting serious religion. Ludlam once in his life for a short time was connected with a religious body, but fell from his profession. Brandreth nine years ago had some religious impressions, though he unhappily suffered them to die away; but he never connected himself with any body of professing christians. Had they in sincerity followed Religion, they would have found among either the serious dissenters or the methodists, those who would have been their helpers in the way to heaven, and they might now have been loyal subjects and useful and respected christians.

WILKINS, PRINTER, DERBY, of whom the Trials may be had,—Price 2s.

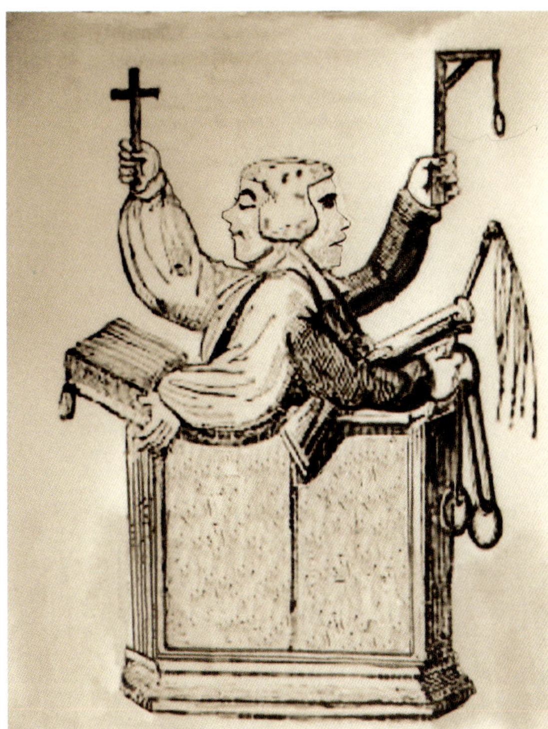

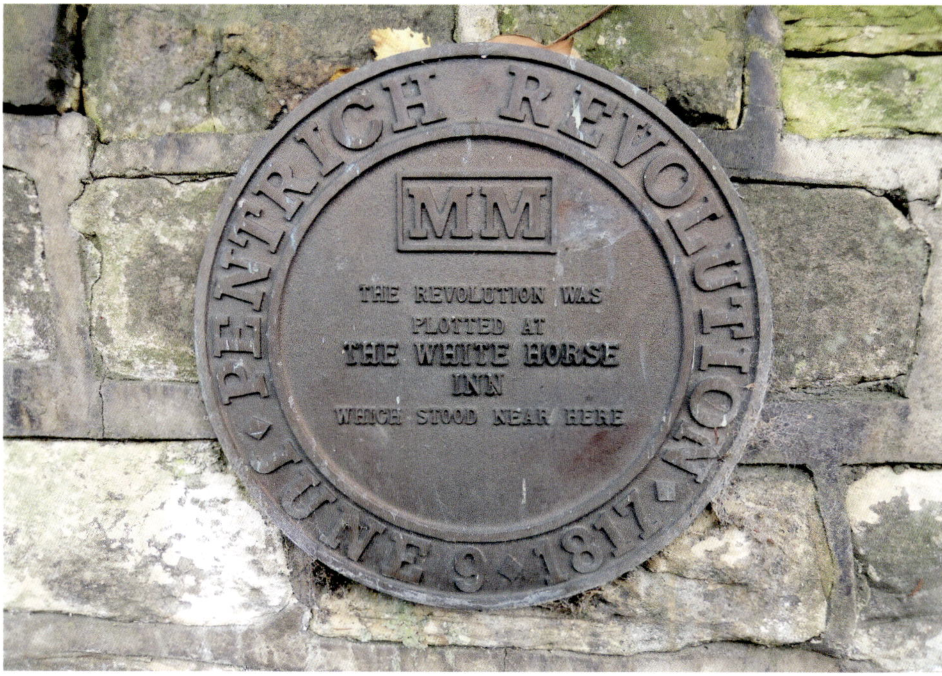

The Aftermath

The heartless Duke of Devonshire, who owned Pentrich, had the homes of the protestors razed to the ground, making the revolutionaries and their families even worse off than before. There are now a few plaques around the village commemorating the revolution. Shown here are two: one positioned where the White Horse Inn stood, stating that the revolution was plotted there, and one on the wall of the old water mill that reads, 'Pentrich Revolution June 9th 1817. Booth's Hovel. Hiding place of Thomas Bacon was near here.'

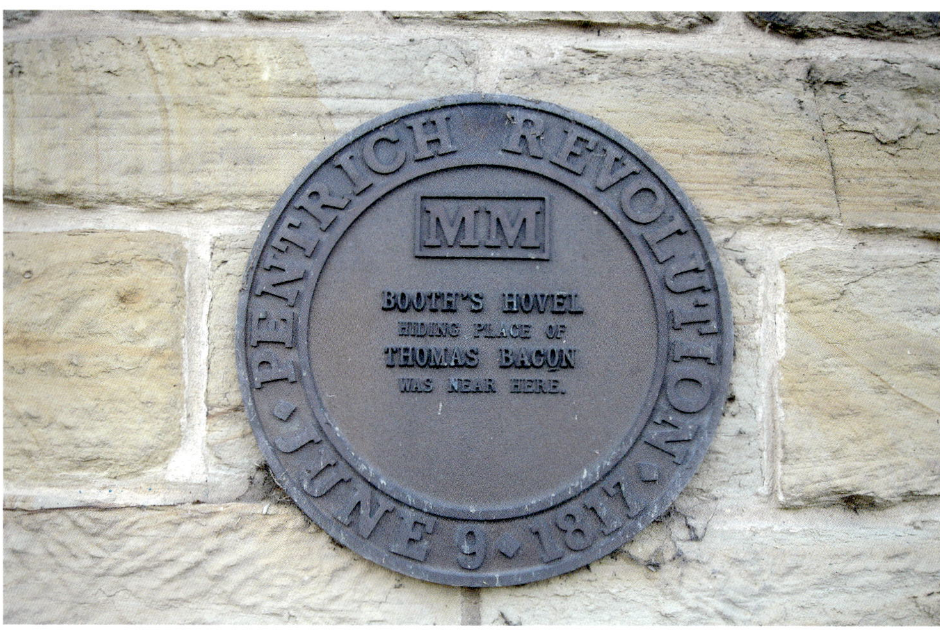

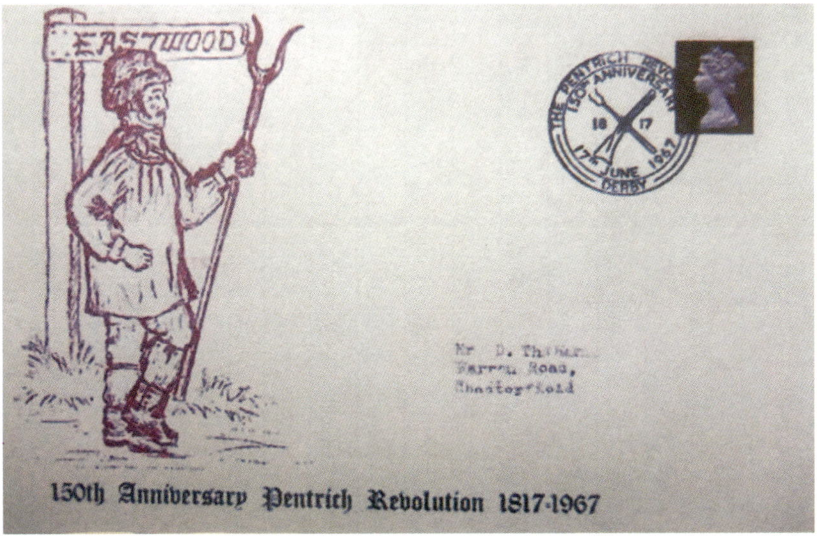

The Aftermath

The Pentrich Revolution was England's last revolution, but it has not found its rightful place in history. A First Day Commemorative Cover was produced in 1967 to mark the 150th anniversary of the Pentrich Revolution, and a local brewery named ASD has produced a bespoke beer named Pentrich Revolution, Best Bitter.

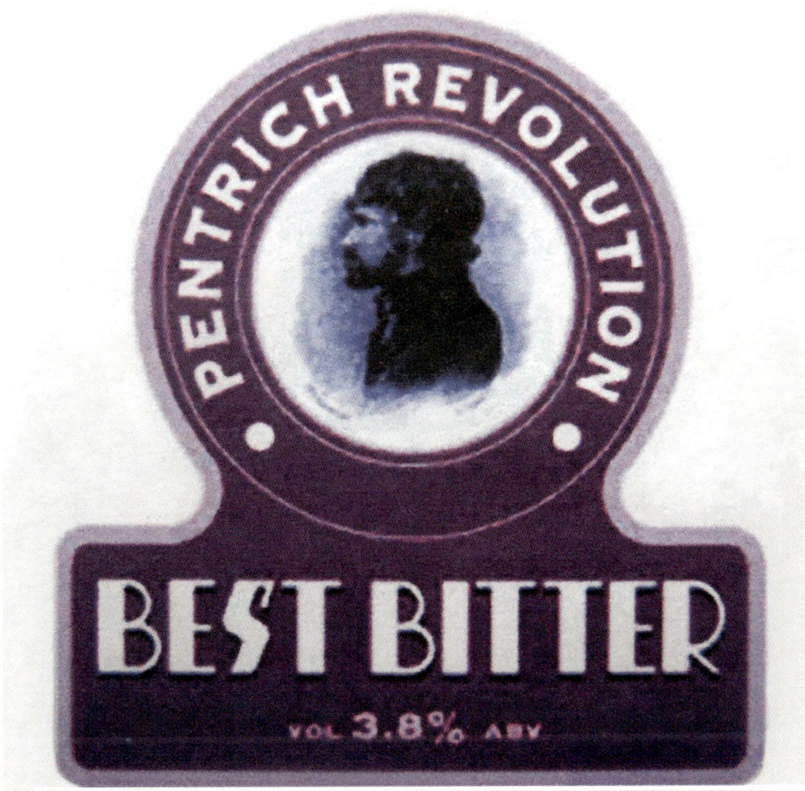

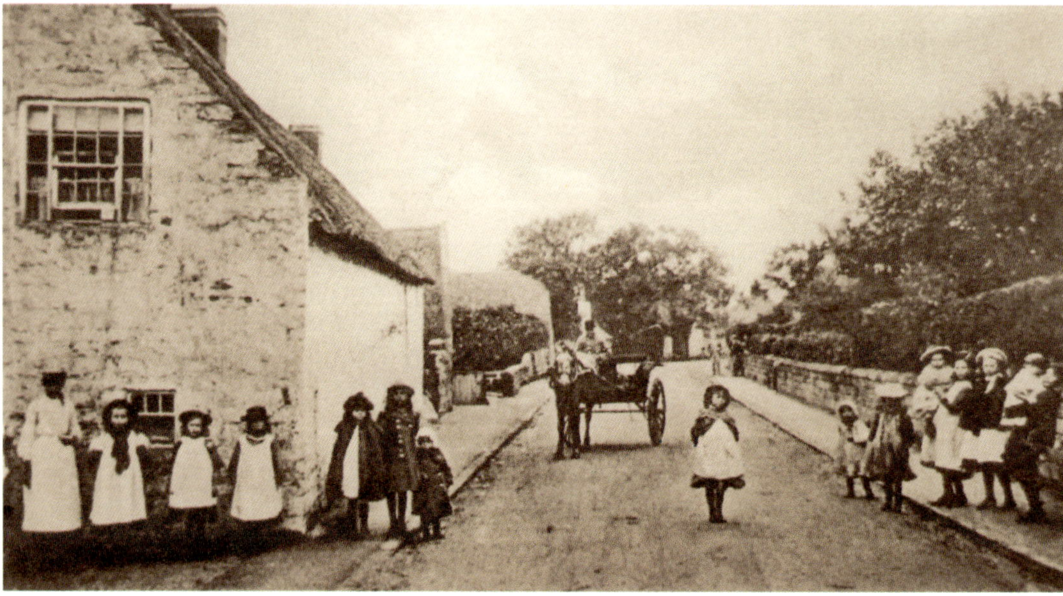

Pentrich's Legacy

Despite their early connection, Ripley and Pentrich are now totally separate. Ripley has expanded into a town, while Pentrich is still a village and has retained its quiet country ideal, as our photographs show. It will always be synonymous with the Pentrich Revolution, but as Clarence Daniel, the Derbyshire historian, wrote, 'The Derbyshire rising was a short chapter in the long story of the class struggle in which the working man has repeatedly pressed his claim for fairer wages and better living conditions. It was a revolt against hunger, poverty and unemployment. It was a pathetic and ill-timed protest against the tyranny, inhumanity and misrule of a government entirely out of sympathy with the labouring classes.'

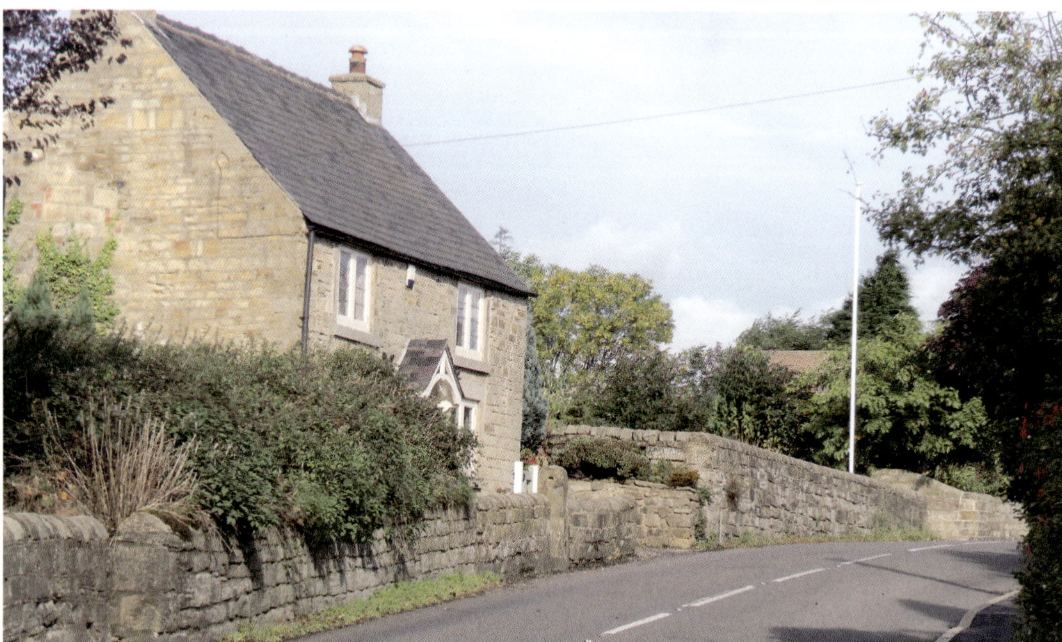

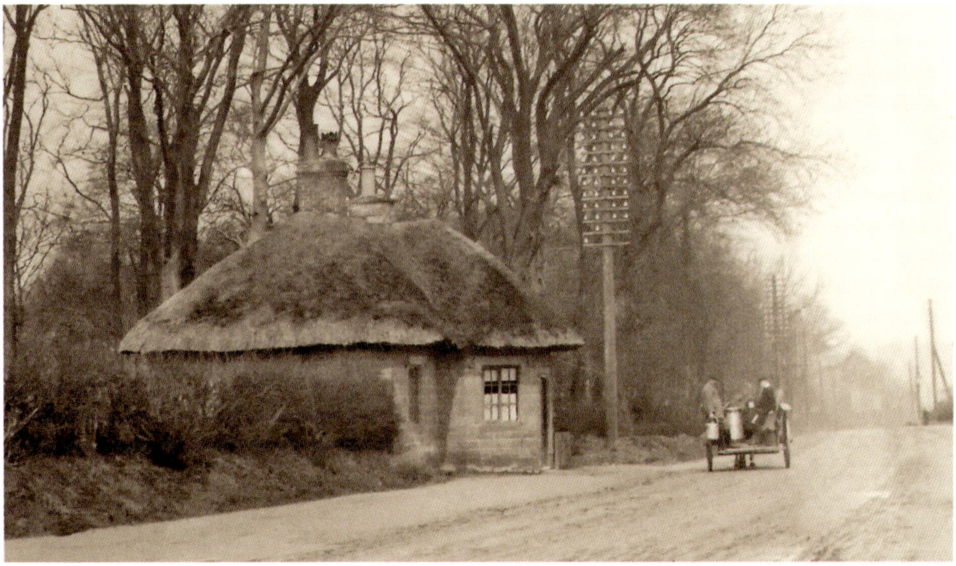

Turnpike Roads

In 1706/07, the first turnpike trusts were authorised, transferring the responsibility of maintaining roads from the parishioners to the users, who paid a toll. The Cromford to Langley Mill Turnpike was formed in 1766, but it wasn't until forty years later on 5 July 1807 that the Alfreton to Derby turnpike, which ran through Ripley, opened. It went across Alfreton common where, at the junction of Sleetmoor Lane, stood the toll bar cottage (*above*). The road continued through Swanwick Green and the ancient enclosed lands on the west side of the Butterley Foundry and Works, entering Ripley via Butterley Hill. The wider turnpike roads enabled goods to be carried on wheeled vehicles pulled by horses, which were far more economical for conveying bulky loads like coal and iron ore. A wagon able to carry 3 tons needed eight horses, whereas the same weight carried on the backs of packhorses required thirty horses. As motor power, like this charabanc parked on Beighton Street in the 1918 photograph, took over from horsepower, turnpike roads were abolished, and the responsibility for upkeep passed to the local government.

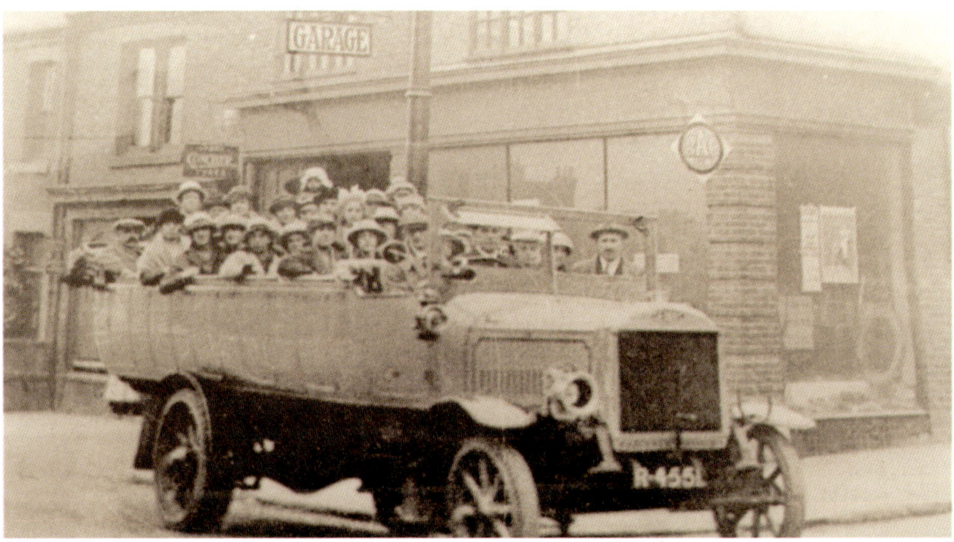

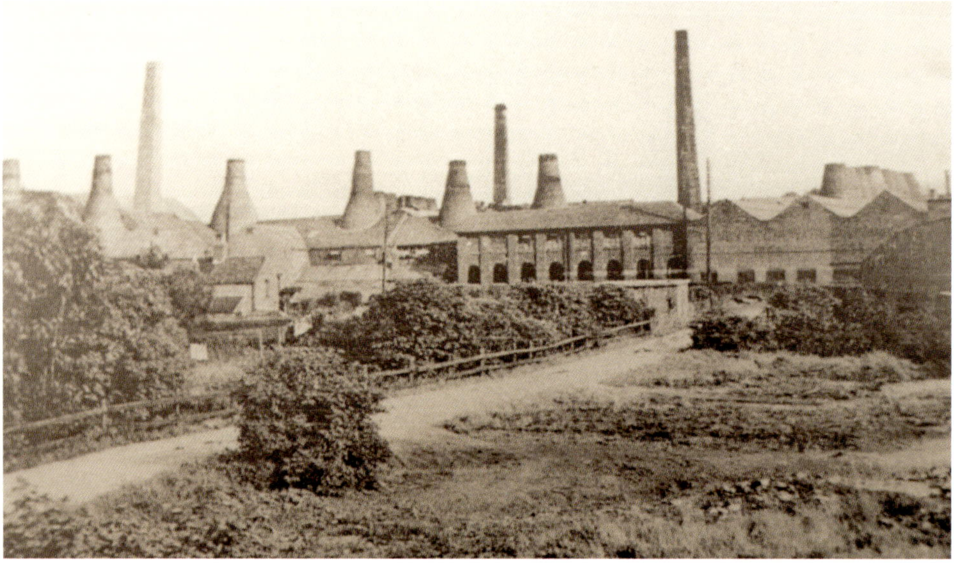

Denby Pottery

It was during the construction of the new turnpike road between Alfreton and Derby in 1806 that a bed of the finest stone-ware clay in Europe was uncovered just south of Ripley. That clay bed was leased by William Bourne and, through his son Joseph Bourne, the rights have passed to the famous Denby pottery, which the latter founded in 1809. The pottery began producing the finest salt-glaze pottery of its time, and is now celebrating two hundred years of tradition and craftsmanship. Not only does the company produce table and oven ware, they produce a variety of commercial containers, telegraphic insulators and other electrical stoneware. During the war, they produced many thousands of articles, including rum jars for our forces all over the world. Brick and earthenware manufacturing was stimulated by the coal industry in two ways: coalmining unearthed large quantities of clay of varying qualities, and the 'slack' or unsaleable coal was used in the kilns.

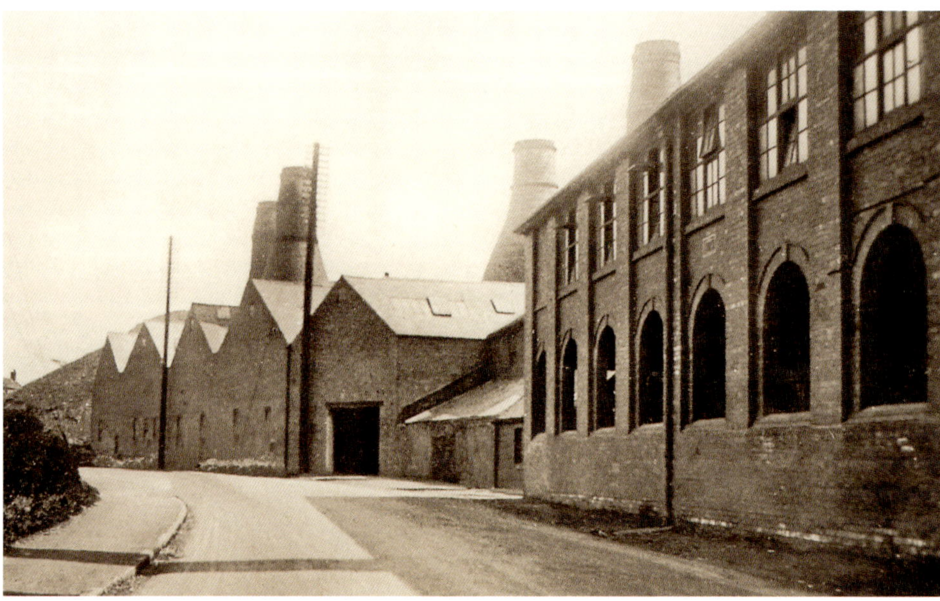

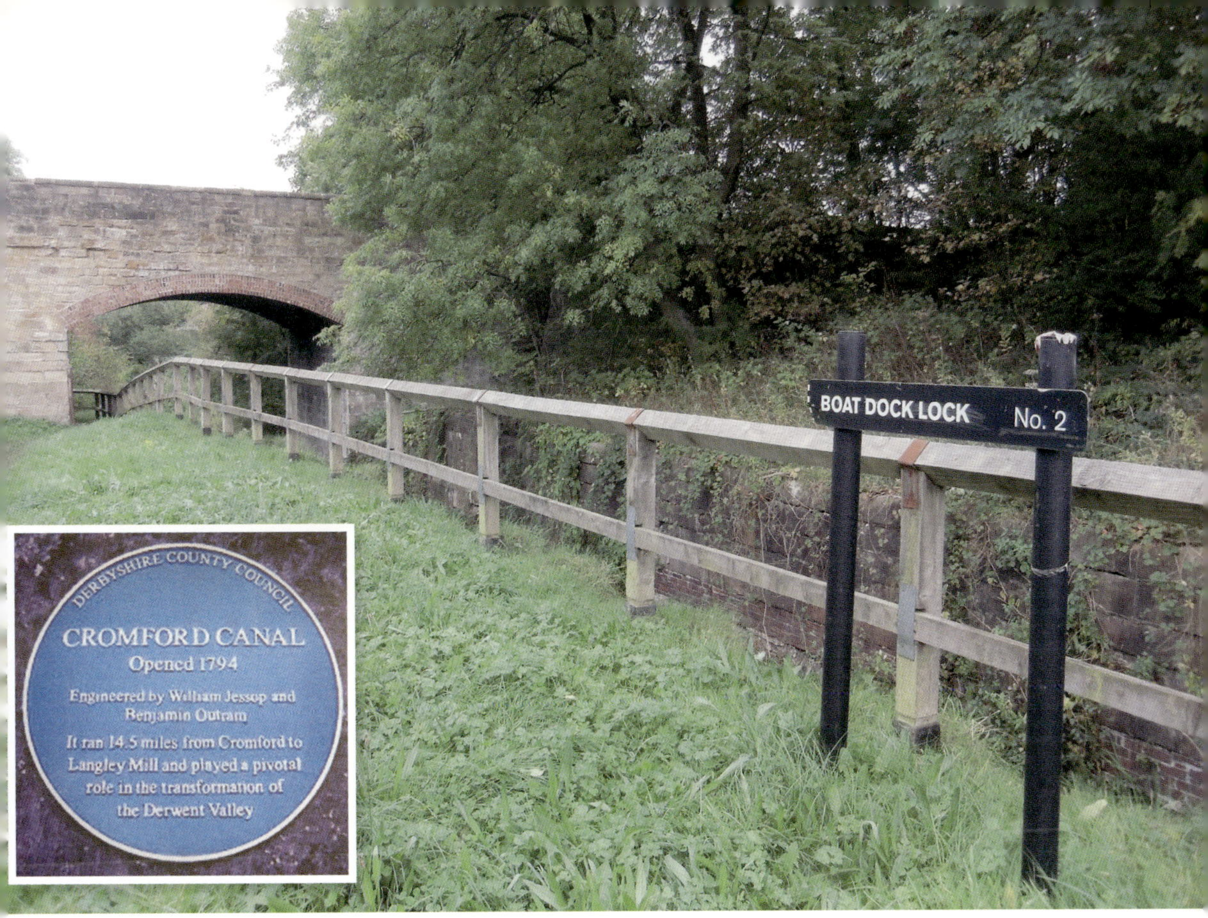

Canals

The first canal in England was the Fossdyke from Torksey on the Trent, built by the Romans for navigation as well as drainage, but seemingly the idea didn't catch on. The building of inland waterways really began in earnest because the growth of trade was being hindered by inadequate roads. In 1757, the pioneering efforts of James Brindley from Wormhill in Derbyshire led the way. On his death in 1772, his successors were Telford, Rennie, Outram and Jessop.

In July 1779, after the opening of the 11¾ mile Erewash Canal, which linked up with the Loughborough Navigation along the Soar, it was suggested that an extension should run north through Derbyshire, but this was declined by the canal company. Undeterred and anxious to develop the area, local businessmen representing interests in the commodities that would be carried on the canal – iron, coal, limestone, lead and cotton – decided to go ahead on their own and asked William Jessop, assisted by Benjamin Outram, to design a canal from Cromford to link with the Erewash Canal at Langley Mill on the Derbyshire/Nottinghamshire border.

Cromford Canal was authorised by an Act of Parliament in December 1788. When William Jessop submitted his plans and an estimate of £42,697, (the equivalent of £3,910,000 in today's money), half the sum was raised immediately and the rest within two weeks. In its simplest form, a canal is a long, watertight trough. To achieve this, the sides and bottom were spread with clay as much as 45cm (18 inches) thick. In areas subject to leakage through earth movement or subsidence, the canal bottom was lined with oak timbers corked with clay or, in extreme cases, concrete.

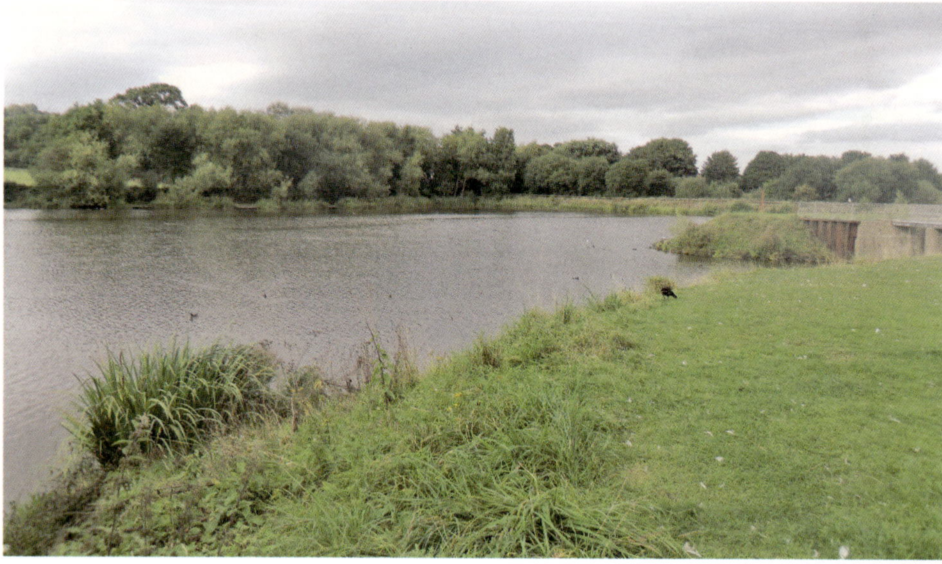

Cromford Canal

Jessop's cost predictions proved to be rather optimistic – the final cost was £80,000 – but the canal was an amazing realisation. It was 23.45 km (14½ miles) long, with three aqueducts, four tunnels and fourteen locks. Not only was it necessary to pay for the routine construction and engineering works, there was also the compulsory purchase of land, and fencing off from the local farms. Then there was the cost of water. In the canal age, water was a very valuable commodity. It was a power source, driving mills for all kinds of agricultural and industrial purposes, and the canal builders got their water rights only after much opposition from mill owners. Sometimes the canal companies had to pay the millers for the water, sometimes they even had to buy the mills. At the Cromford end, the canal was supplied with sough water (drainage from mines), while further along, three large reservoirs were formed to hold water. Butterley Park Reservoir was drained in the 1930s, while Butterley and the Golden Valley reservoirs remain as shown in our photographs.

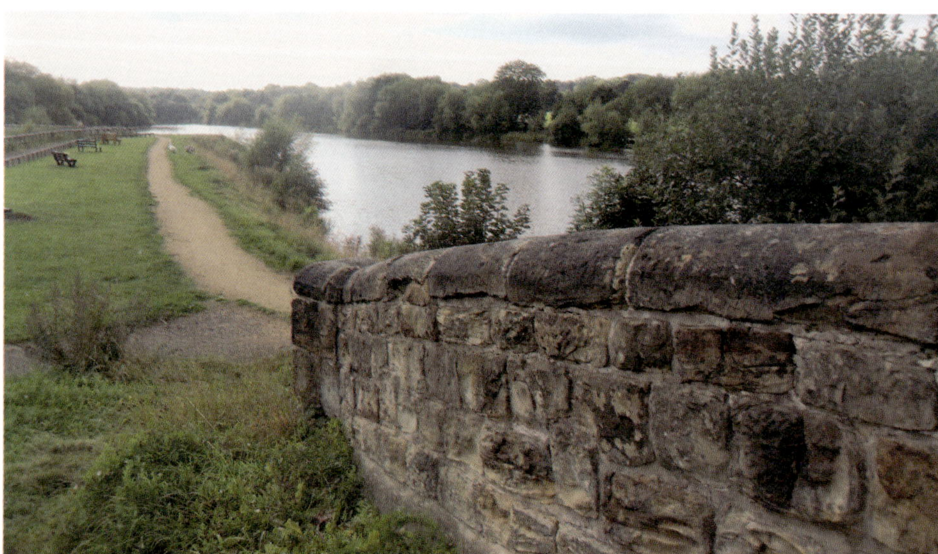

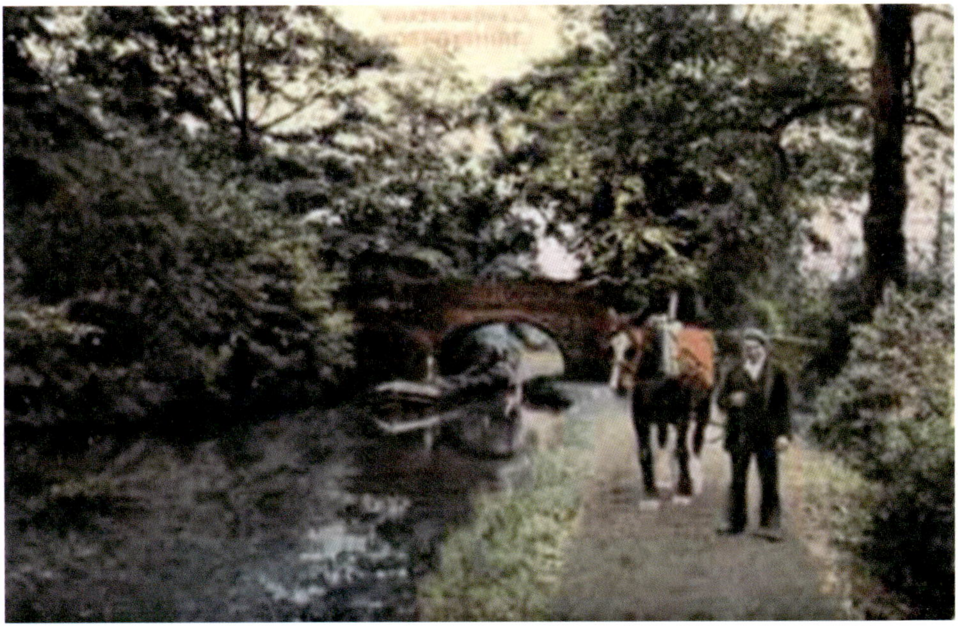

Canal Traffic

The opening of the Cromford Canal in 1793 connected the area with a network of waterways all over the country, thus giving better transportation and fresh impetus to the local coal and iron industries, and encouraging new enterprises. In 1802, the canal carried over 150,000 tons, which doubled in the next forty years. In the early days of the canals, horsepower was still the norm, but in comparison to a packhorse that was limited to a 100kg load, or a carthorse that could pull one tonne on a road, a horse could pull 25 tons on water. Although traffic was mainly commercial, in September 1779, a short-term passenger service operated between Cromford and Nottingham three times a week. Canal boats were scrubbed out and fitted with seats to carry passengers for these market boats as they were termed. They were also used for the occasional church outing on the canal, when people from Ripley went to Cromford and vice-versa, as the photograph below shows.

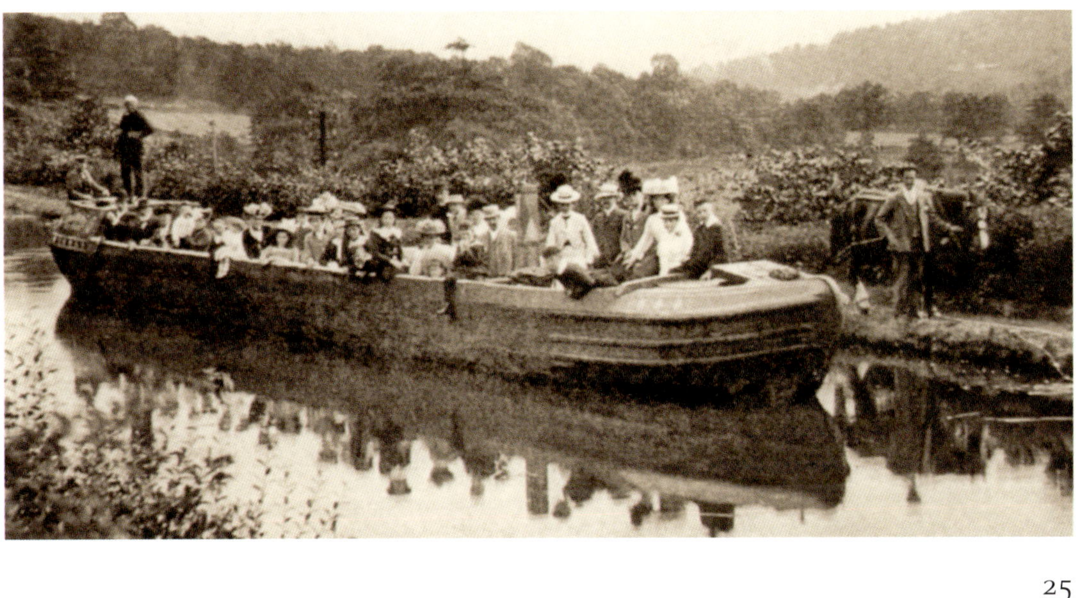

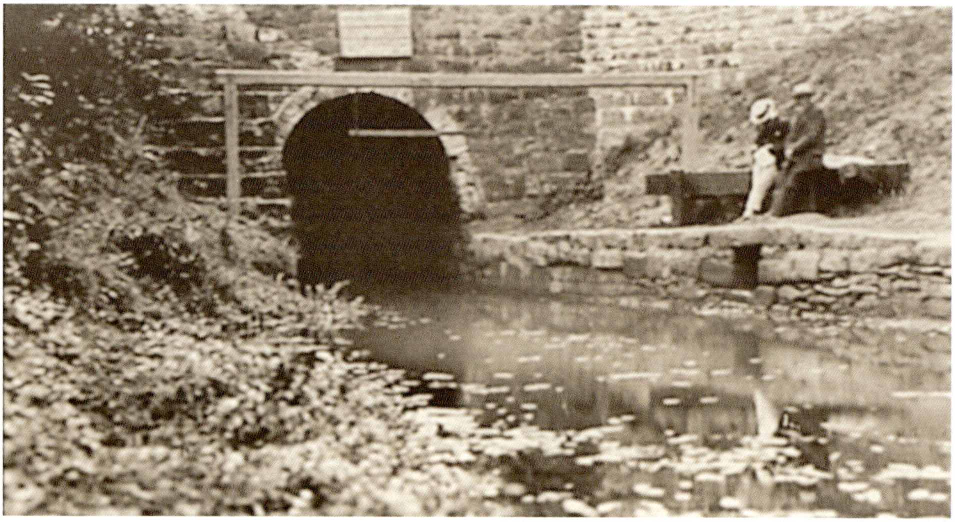

Butterley Tunnel

From Cromford basin, the canal's course stretched along the Derwent Valley and then turned east to run through the Amber Valley for four miles, until it reached Ripley and a range of hills that could not be negotiated. Because of this, it was necessary to dig the Butterley Tunnel, a fine feat of engineering for its time. Thirty-three shafts were sunk along its length to drive the tunnel, supply ventilation and act as escape routes. It was excavated through soft shale, which meant it was necessary to line it with bricks for much of the 2,966 yards, at a cost of £7 per yard. Until subsidence caused problems in the late 1800s, it had remained unsupported by any other means. Numbered markers in cast iron or wood were placed at intervals of one chain (66 feet) along its dark, murky length. After completion, only four shafts were left open, and now it is possible to trace the tunnel above ground by going along Tunnel Road and locating the air ducts, like this half-hidden shaft behind Butterley Hall.

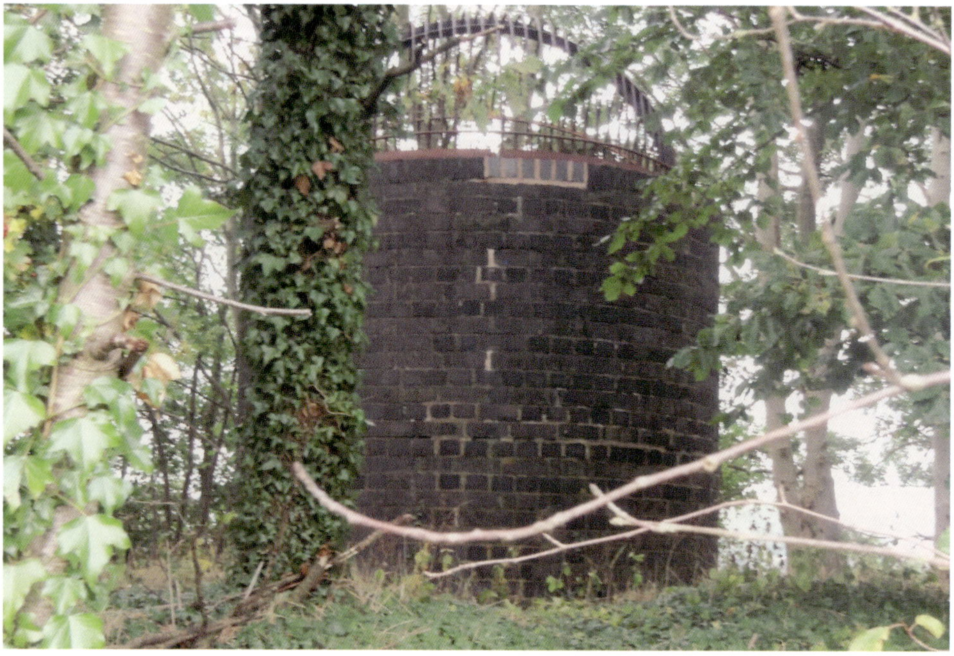

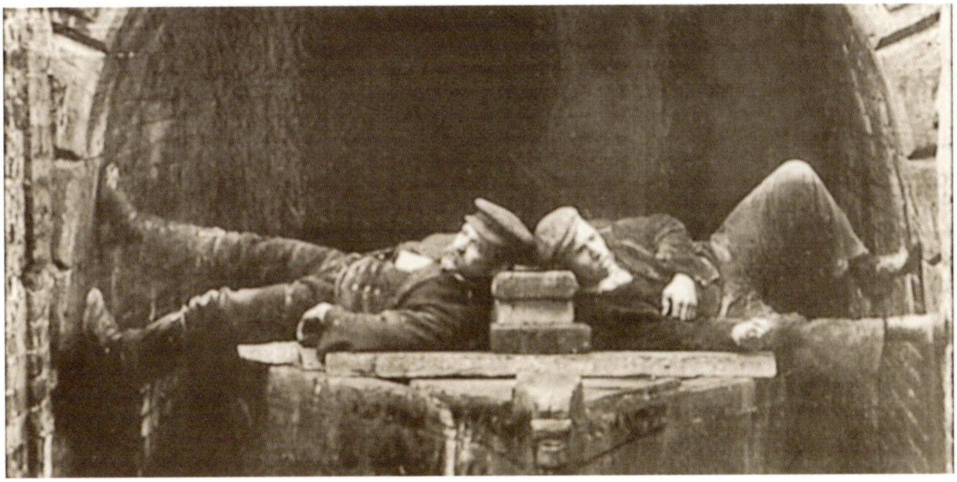

Legging it Through the Tunnel

The tunnel was 9 feet (2.7m) wide by 8 feet (2.4m), above the water level, so the horse-drawn boats were, of necessity, only 7 feet (2.1m) wide, but with no towpath through the tunnel, the only method of propulsion was poling or legging. This was timely, exhausting and dangerous. The bargemen propelled their craft through the tunnel's darkness by pushing against the walls or roof with the barge pole, or pushing with their feet on the sides of the tunnel in a walking movement. Some carriers would hire men for legging. These men would congregate at the public houses in Hartshay near the western portal, and at the Newlands Inn at Golden Valley by the eastern portal. There were strict rules for boats entering the tunnel, with a maximum of three hours being allowed for the journey. It would not be possible for a boat to cover the inbound journey, load and return to the same end within that time without breaking the rules that were displayed on boards above the tunnel entrances. These were quite pointless as few boatmen could read, but that was no excuse. The rules were enforced and fines imposed.

NOTICE.

Extract from the Rules, Byelaws and Orders made By the Cromford Canal Company: 30th May 1804

No boat shall enter Butterley Tunnel at the East end except between the hours of Five and Six in the Morning, One and Two in the Afternoon and Nine and Ten at Night and no boat shall enter the West end thereof, except between the hours of One and Two in the morning, Nine and Ten in the Forenoon and Five and Six at Night, and every boat shall make its passage through the same with all possible despatch and on no account exceed three hours after such entry. And if any Person or Persons having the care of any boat, shall offend in any of the particulars aforesaid, he or they shall forfeit for every such offence Forty Shillings and shall also turn back on meeting another boat in the said tunnel.

Seal of the Cromford Canal Company

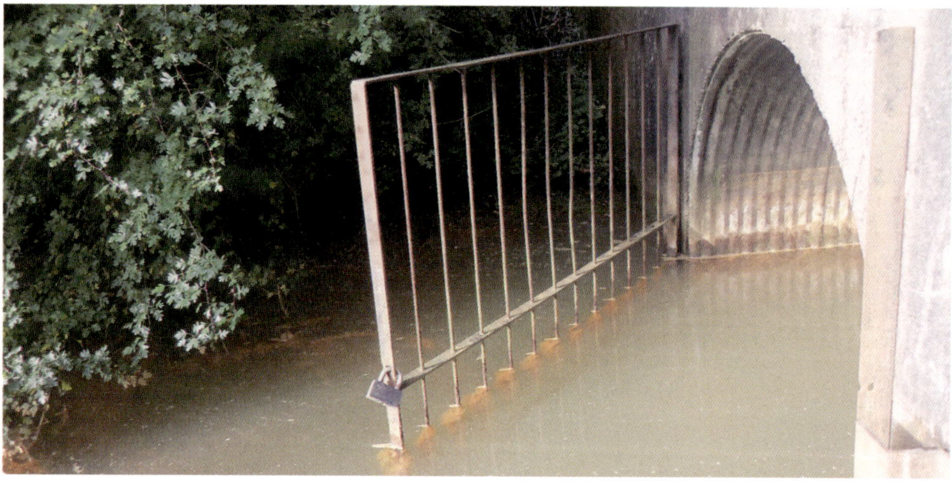

The Tunnel with a Unique Wharf

The tunnel ran under Benjamin Outram & Co., ironworks, later to become the Butterley Company, and here was a very rare, if not unique, feature; two vertical shafts 7 feet (2.1m) in diameter, sunk to a loading wharf on the canal 100 feet (30m) below. Details in the Canal Company's November 1791 minute book outline the details of the wide hole to be constructed by Outram & Co. beneath their property. The wide hole or underground wharf was between 15 foot and 16 foot (4.5m and 4.8m) wide, and capable of mooring two of the 7 foot (2.1m) wide boats for loading and unloading, without impeding through traffic. Raw materials from the company's mines and quarries could be hoisted up, and finished iron goods lowered down into the waiting canal boats standing in the wharf. It was used between 1794 and the 1860s, but then in 1889, the tunnel was closed due to a partial collapse. After repairs, which cost £7,364, and an extension to the western end in 1890 to facilitate the railway, the 3,063-yard tunnel reopened in 1893. Some 180 boats per year then used it, carrying between 3,000 and 4,000 tons, but a further collapse on 6 June 1900 closed it again. A survey in 1909 said it was beyond economic repair. In 1915, the wharf was narrowed and the loading shafts at the Butterley works were capped. In 1976, the tunnel was extended another 20 yards for the A38 dual carriageway, which is why the given length of the tunnel varies. Because the original western portal is now under the A38, the photographs show a gated entrance on the canal where it disappears under the A38 embankment, and a towpath beside the canal under a road bridge at Hartshay.

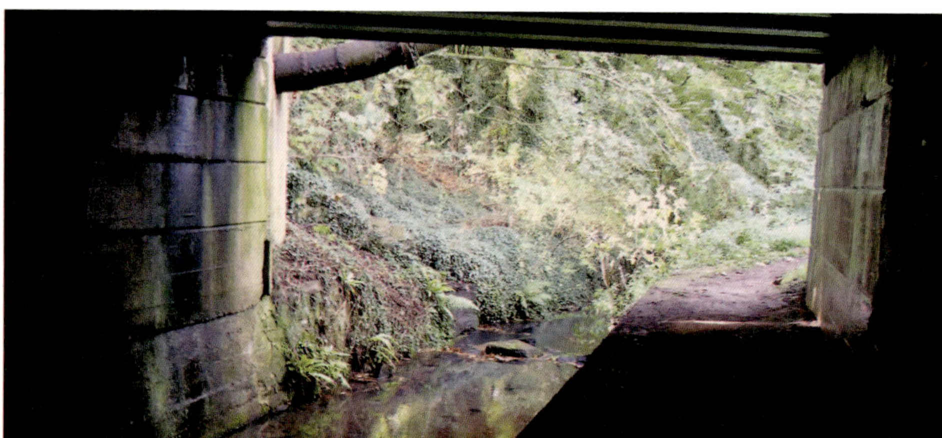

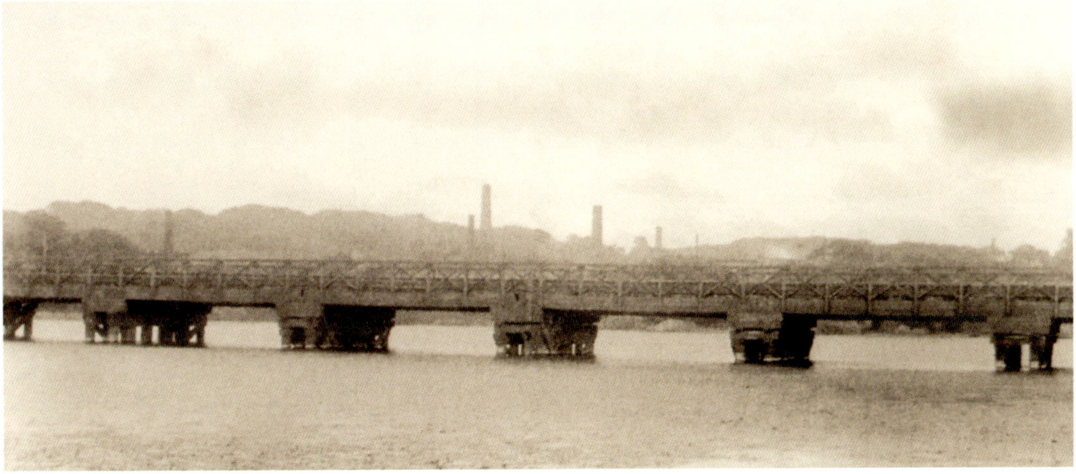

The Bridge Over Butterley Reservoir

When the railway line was constructed from Pye Bridge to Ambergate, it followed the line of the Cromford Canal, but climbed over the range of hills in the region of the tunnel. However, it was necessary to build a wooden trestle bridge of twenty spans to carry the line across the 103,000,000-gallon Butterley Reservoir. Coal was by far its principle traffic, and trains crossing the bridge were restricted to 20 mph. In an attempt to provide a direct and rapid through service between Nottingham and Manchester, the London, Midland & Scottish Railway (LMS) decided to strengthen the bridge. In 1927/28, 60,000 cubic yards of stone were used to infill the bridge to form a causeway, as the later photograph shows. The only intermediate station on the line was Swanwick, which opened on 1 May 1875, but as neither Ambergate nor Pye Bridge were large population centres, local passenger service was never frequent and the line was uneconomical.

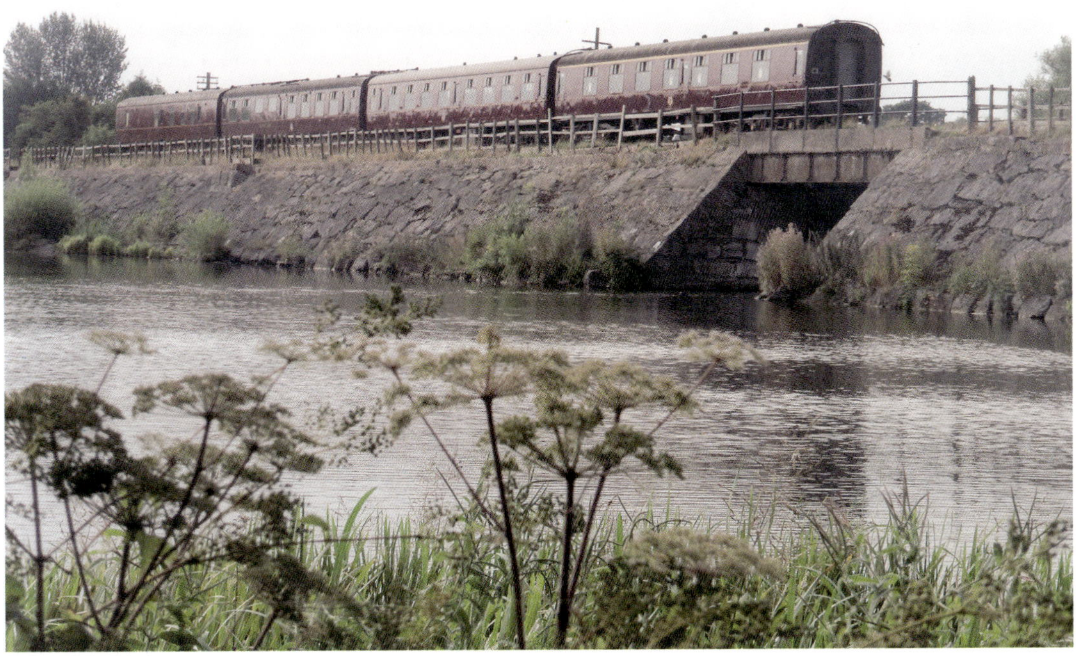

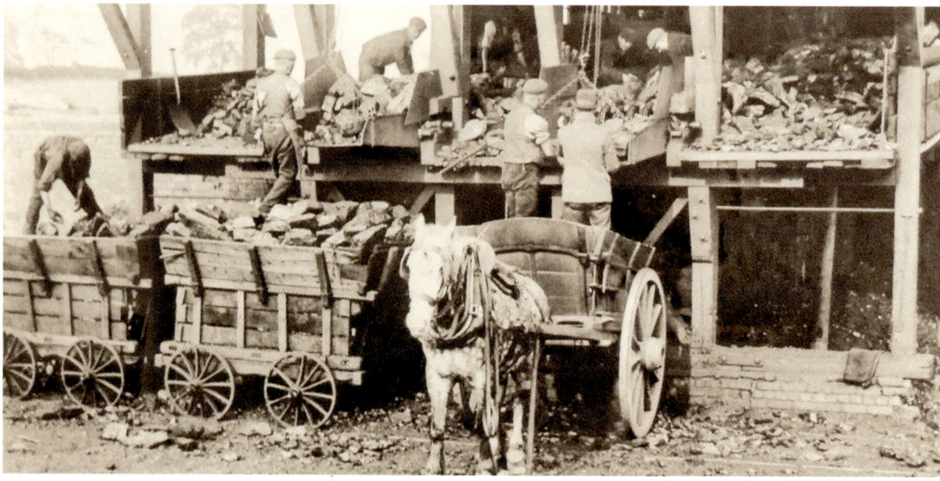

The Benjamin Outram & Co. Ironworks

Digging the tunnel revealed substantial mineral deposits, which prompted twenty-four-year-old Benjamin Outram of Alfreton to form the Benjamin Outram & Co. ironworks. It began trading in 1790 and the following year, William Jessop, a Nottingham banker named John Wright and Benjamin became partners, and the name was changed to the Butterley Company. The company expanded, bringing enormous change to the local landscape. As Benjamin Outram and William Jessop were well-respected canal engineers, amongst many other things, the company built the first cast-iron aqueduct carrying the Derby canal over the River Derwent. Benjamin Outram was also experimenting in mechanical engineering, with a special interest in the building of early railways and tramways known locally as gangways. The name 'tram' is believed to originate from Outram, who became a leading advocate in their construction. After he built the first gangway in May 1795, the district became crossed by a web of rails to transport the coal and iron from the mines and foundries to the canal. The photograph above shows two methods: a horse-drawn cart that was to be superseded by the wheeled wagons on the left that ran on rails. The wagon bodies that were removable from the wheels were known as boxes, as they could be craned into the waiting canal boats complete with their loads. This cut down on handling and cost, and was the earliest form of containerisation. The company also made cast-iron rails to replace the wooden tramways and flanged wagon wheels to fit on the rails, like this museum piece on display outside Butterley railway station.

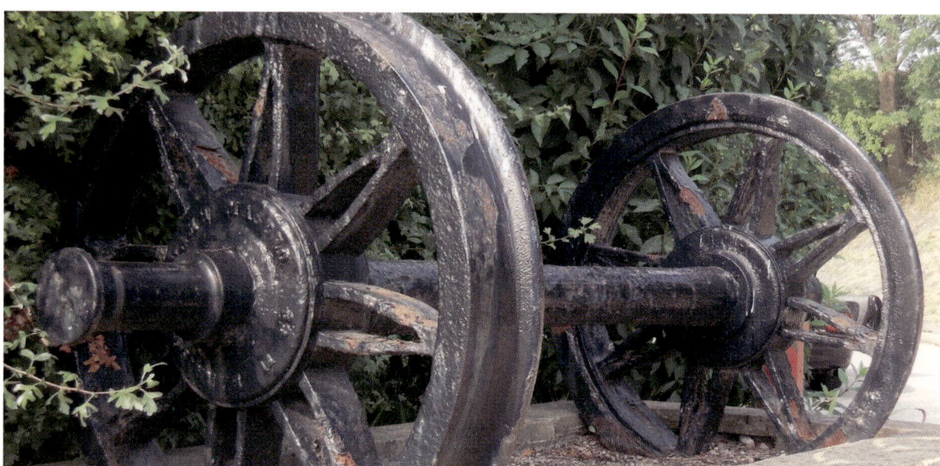

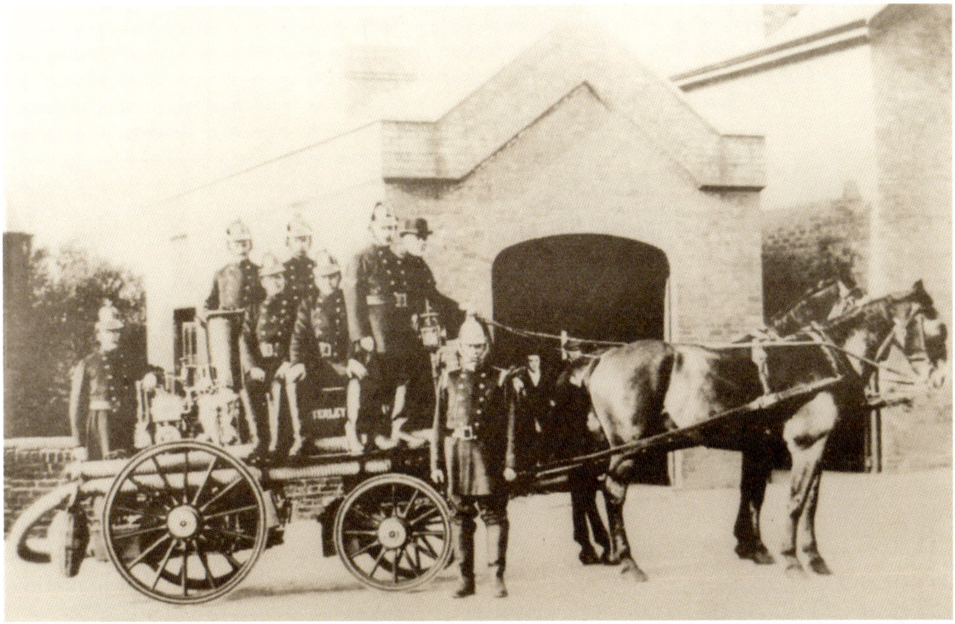

Butterley Fire Service

At the works just off Butterley Hill, the company had a fire station that also served the community. The stables were next door, and when the horse-drawn appliance was replaced by a Leyland, a solid-tyre machine, the stables became the firemen's changing room and equipment store. The service continued with a more up-to-date appliance until the end of the war in 1945. This 1903 photograph shows the men with their horse-drawn appliance turned out in their splendid brass helmets and uniforms. The crowd in the photograph below, of a similar vintage, have turned out to watch the fire at a thatched cottage at Newlands. The thatched roof is still ablaze but the crowd seem more interested in the photographer.

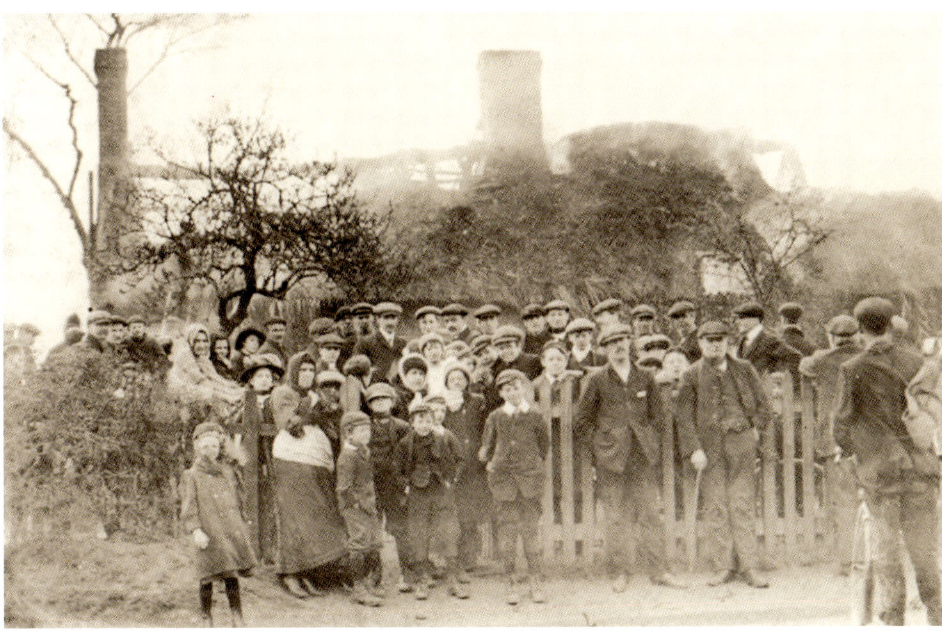

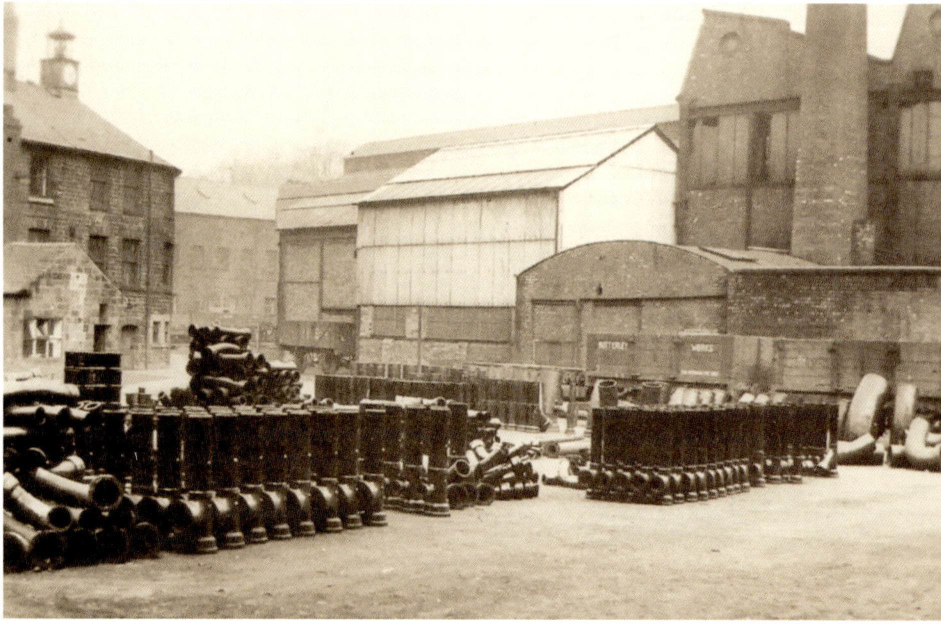

Extras

There were some rather opportune uses for the by-products of the Butterley Company. Prior to the building of the turnpike road from Butterley through Ripley to their pits in Denby, the company provided foundry slag as road surfacing. Many of the walls around here are not built of stone, but of blast furnace slag or clinkers, as seen in the photograph below. The finished pipes in this photograph in the Butterley works yard are a reminder that earlier cast-iron pipes made in the foundry were dipped in tar to protect them against rust. If a local child had a chesty cough, mothers used to take them to breathe the fumes from the tar in the belief that it had a curative effect.

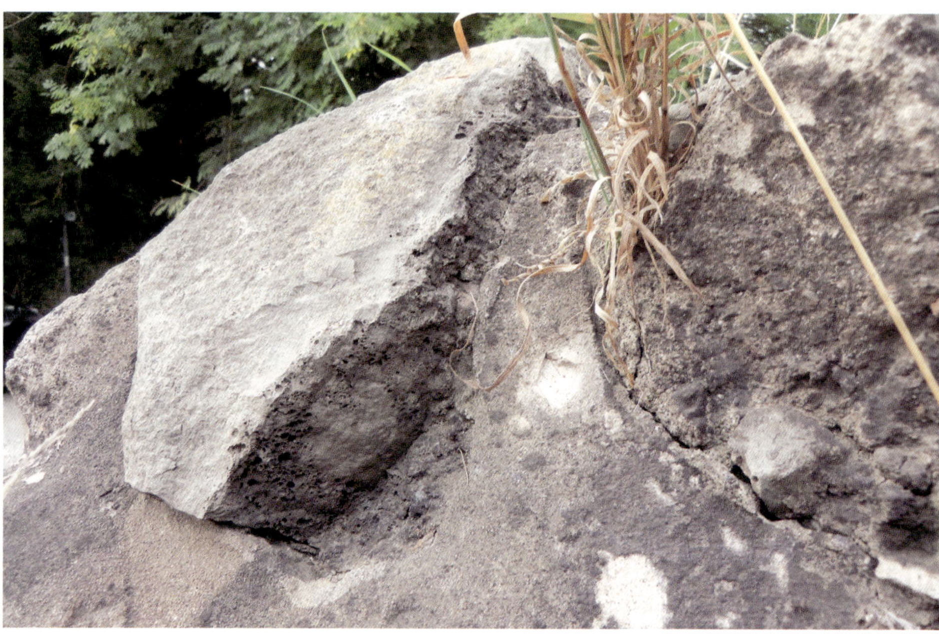

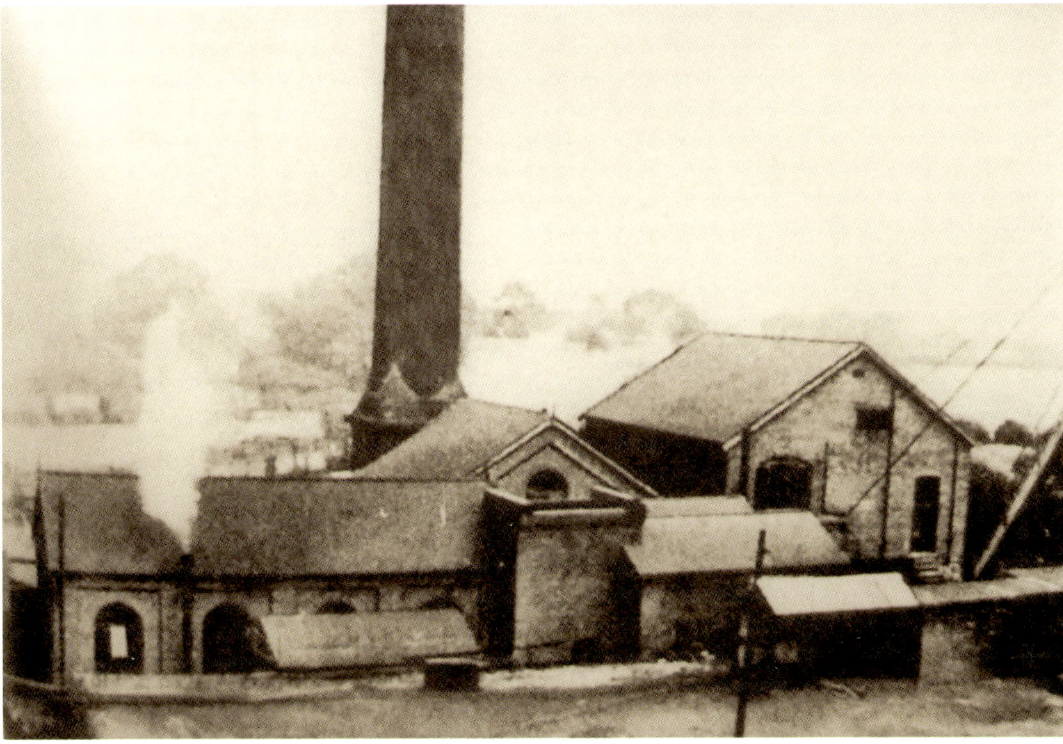

Butterley Company Coalmines

The Butterley Company needed coal in great quantities to feed their furnaces, so numerous mines were sunk around the extensive Butterley estates to supplement the earlier mines known as pits. By 1800, the company had eleven mines within a 3-mile radius of the works. Throughout its 217 years, Butterley owned and operated 40 local small mines, each with a workforce of under 600, and 15 to 18 larger mines, each with a workforce of over 600. At the time of Nationalisation in 1948, Butterley mines and works were employing 14,500 men.

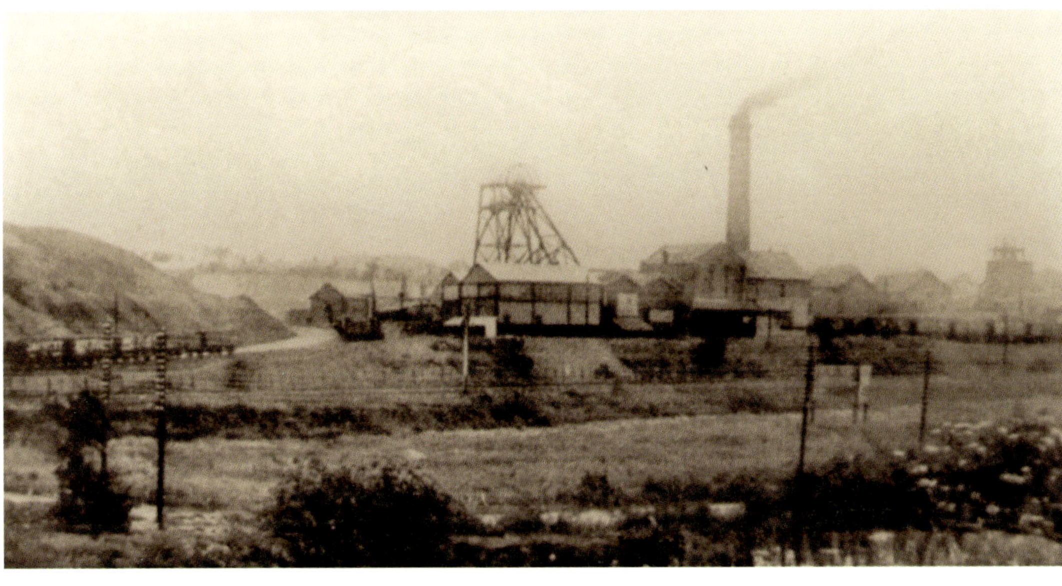

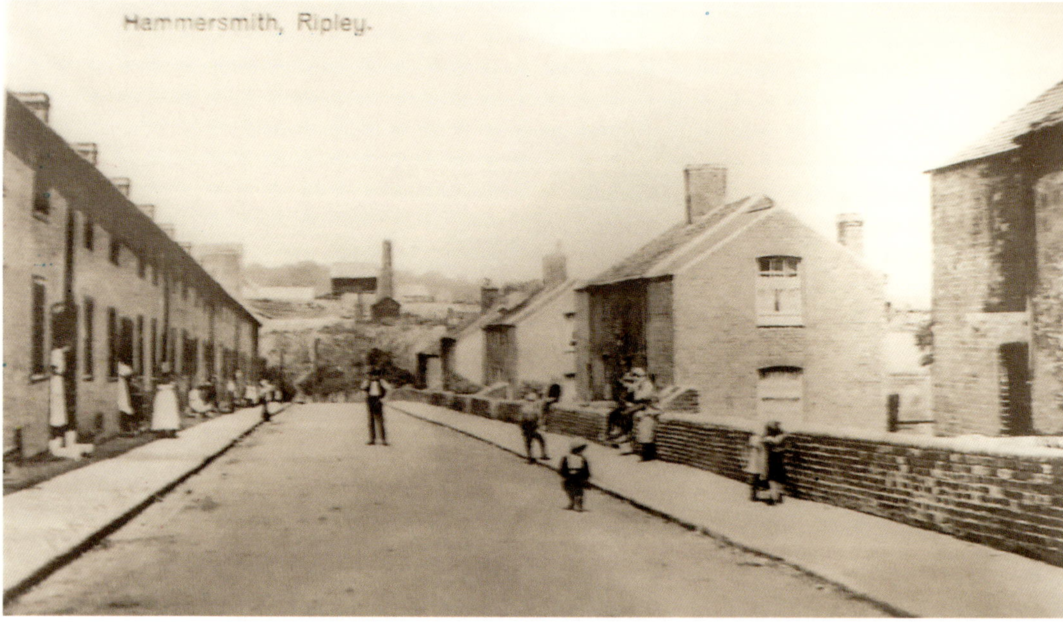

Poker Row, Hammersmith

The name Hammersmith, part of the ancient region of Padley, was not used until the Butterley Company built semi-detached houses here for their staff in 1820, followed a few years later by a row of terrace houses. These were known as Poker Row because, according to the legend, the occupants would pick up a poker and knock on the dividing walls to alert their neighbours the rent collector was coming, and to lock their doors and stay out of sight until the all clear was given. The street is still recognisable, but the photograph of around 1910 looks down the street to the Cinder Breaker on Cinder Bank, which is now woodland.

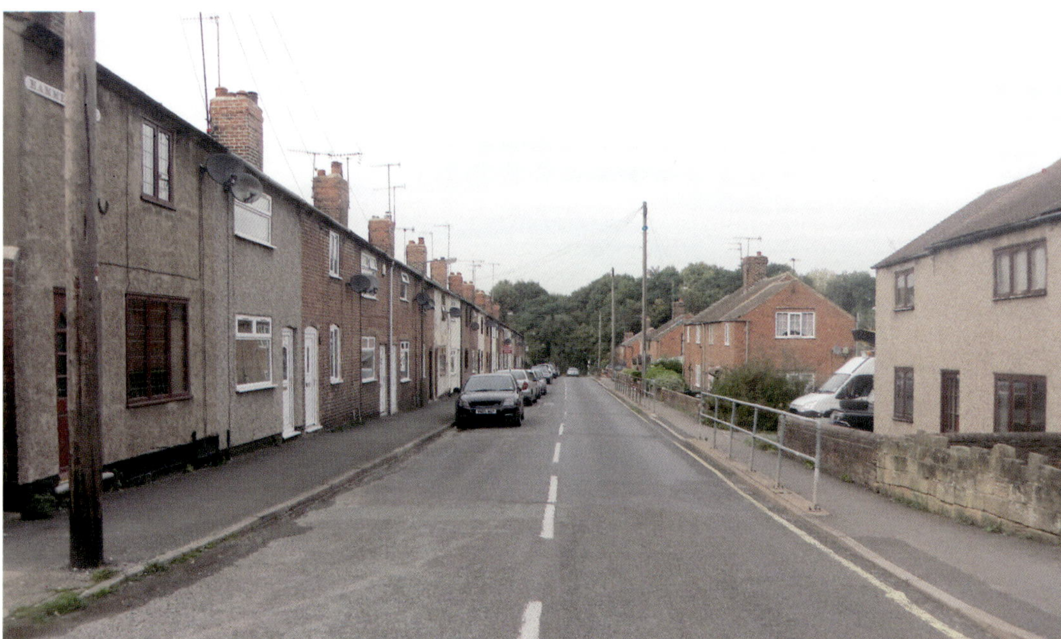

The Monks of Butterley Hall

It was while the Butterley tunnel was being driven that the neighbouring eighteenth-century Butterley Hall and its 200-acre estate came on the market. In 1175, Butterley Park, like much of the land around here, was given to the Canons of Darley Abbey, and a medieval chapel, probably a private chapel for the lay owners of Butterley Park, stood on the site of Butterley Hall. In November 1999, some of the original stones that once formed a window were set in the grass hillside beside the main entrance. Alongside is a sculpture of a crying monk by David Kent, a symbolic link with the past, reminding us that the monks were turned out and persecuted in the sixteenth century Dissolution of the Monasteries when all monastic land went into private ownership. In the eighteenth century, Butterley Hall was a pleasant country house with delightful open views in the possession of the Horne family, early coal owners. The dam in the field by the hall is still known as Horne's Dam. William Horne was executed in 1724 at the age of seventy-four for the gruesome murder of a child. His restless spirit is said to haunt the hall to this day.

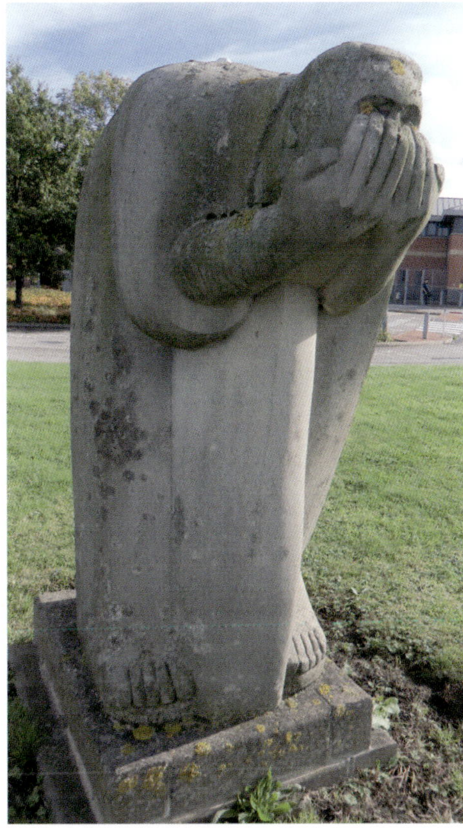

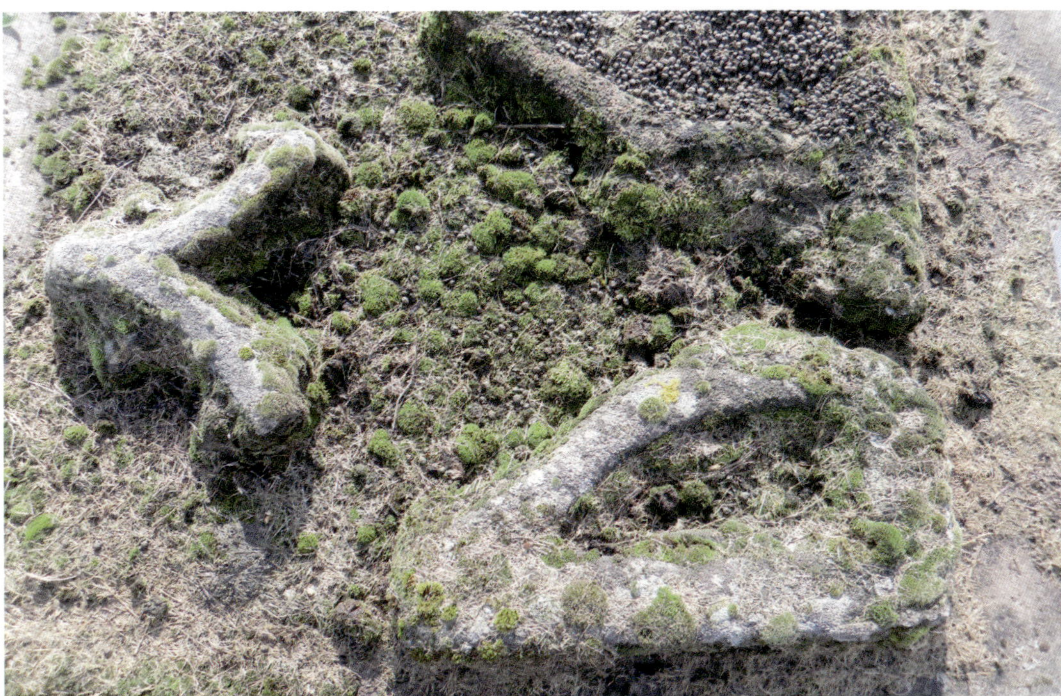

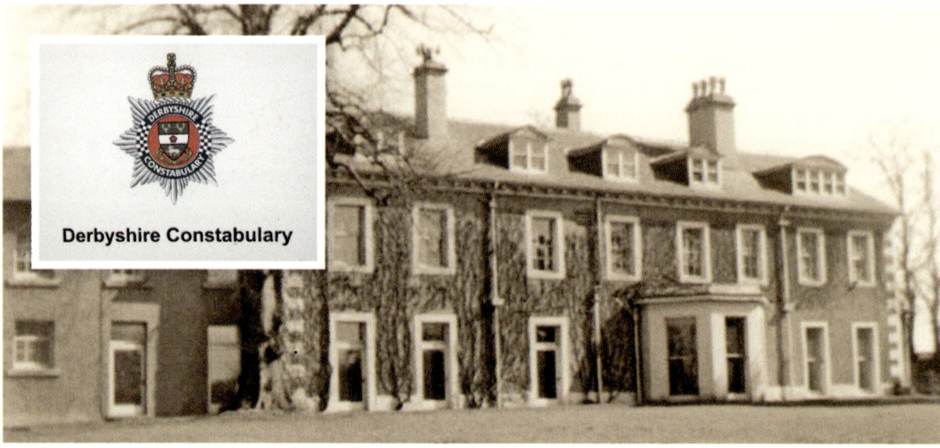

Butterley Hall is Acquired by the Canal Company

The estate was restored to Horne's heir, E. T. Warren, who sold it in 1790 to Francis Beresford, solicitor to the canal company. He bought the freehold of the hall and estate, which he leased on a moiety to Benjamin Outram until the latter had acquired enough capital for a 50 per cent holding. This became the Outram family home. Benjamin Outram enlarged it and modernised it, putting in bathrooms, which were almost unheard of at that time. On 22 May 1805, Benjamin Outram died of a stroke while visiting London, leaving his wife and five young children, but no will. He had invested heavily, so his untimely death at the age of forty-one found his widow Margaret almost penniless until his liabilities could be settled through court. Outram's old business partner William Jessop moved into Butterley Hall in 1814, followed by Leslie Wright in 1892. The Wright family of Nottingham were wealthy ironmongers, who founded a bank around 1760. Francis Wright was a director of the Butterley Company and a local JP, in addition to his other business interests. He married Selina, daughter of Sir Henry FitzHerbert of Tissington Hall, and built The Hayes at Swanwick for his son FitzHerbert. In 1938, the Wrights were succeeded by Butterley director A. P. Coote. It then became the headquarters of the Butterley Company before being acquired by Derbyshire Police, becoming their headquarters in 1969.

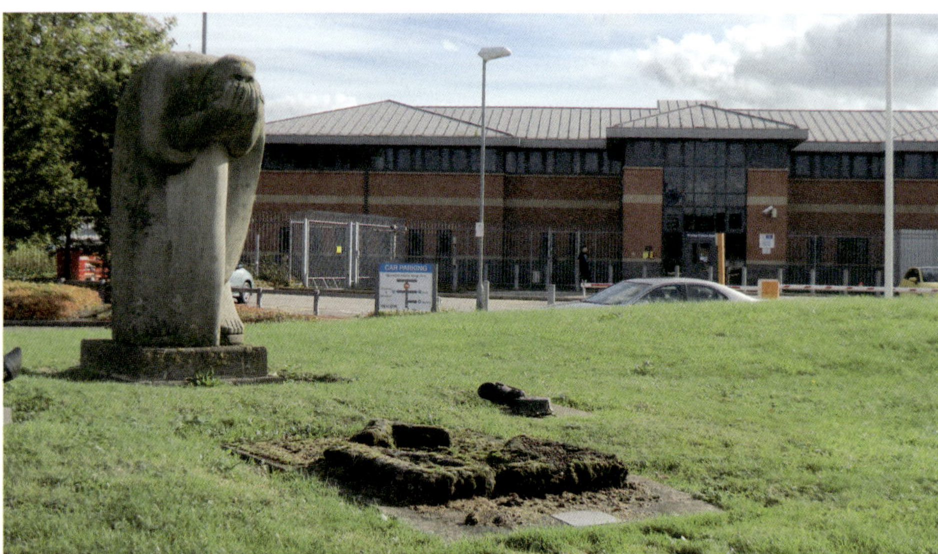

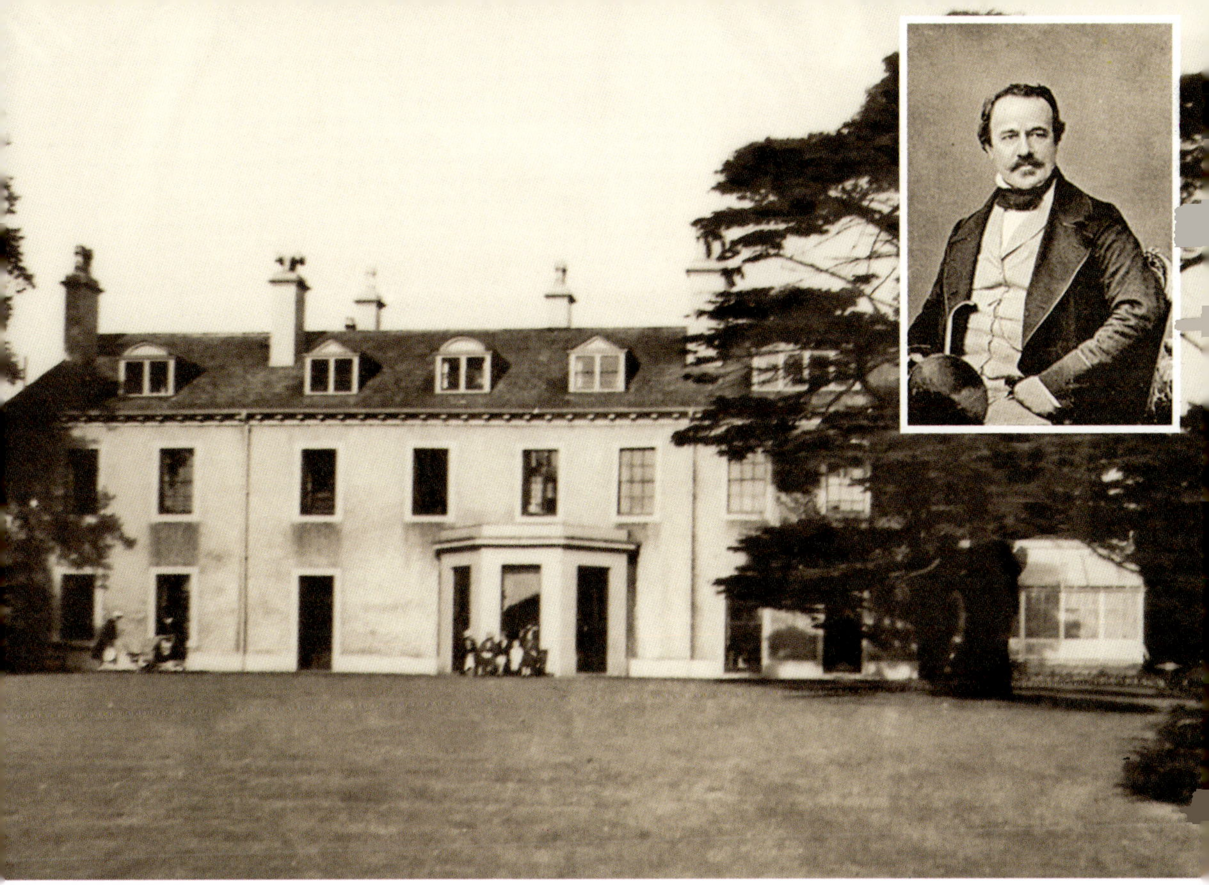

Sir James Outram (1803–1863)

The second son in a family of five children, James Outram was born at Butterley Hall on 29 January 1803. His father, Benjamin Outram, was the eminent civil engineer who started the Butterley Company, but died when James was only two years old. When James was five, the family moved to Scotland and, although not a studious boy, James excelled at every kind of sport. His chosen career was the army and in 1819, he was awarded a cadetship and sailed to India to join the 23rd Regiment of the Bombay Native Infantry. He soon became a lieutenant, then adjutant. He was sent to suppress a number of uprisings, which he carried out with skill and enthusiasm. He heroically defended the British Residency in Hyderbad against 8,000 native troops, yet was vigorously outspoken when exposing the bribery and corruption practiced by British officials. He gave his life to India as a soldier, diplomat and statesman.

James Outram was given the highest political office in India, but when trouble broke out in Persia, he was sent there, where he defeated the Persians and was knighted as a result. In recognition of these and his many successful exploits in India, he was promoted to lieutenant-general, and on his return to London, was created a baron and granted the Freedom of the City of London. By 1858, his health was poor and he was obliged to resign office. He was too ill to attend the various functions held in his honour, and in 1861, he was created one of the Founder Knights of the Star of India. He died on 3 March 1863, and was buried in Westminster Abbey with full military honours. His bust is in the south side of the nave and a statue of Sir James was erected on the Thames embankment.

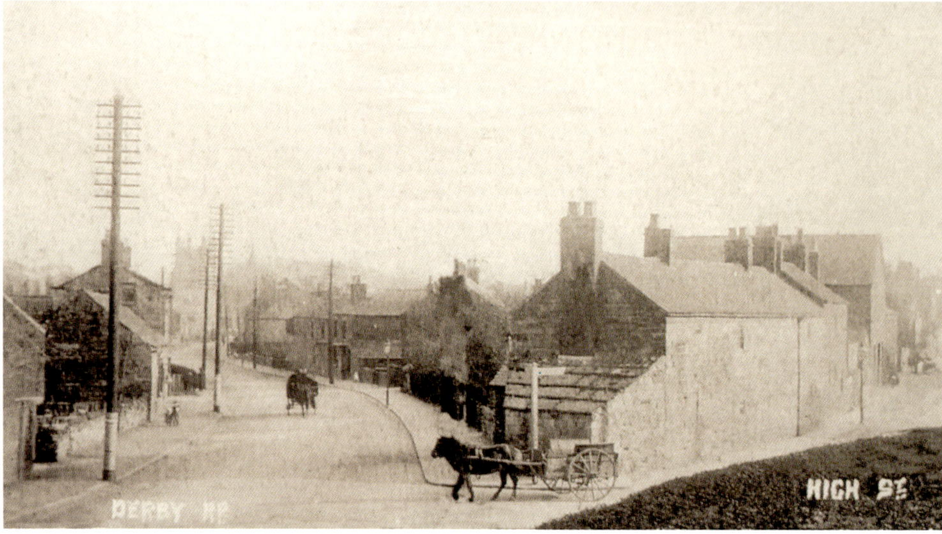

Swanwick

Swanwick (pronounced Swonnick) borders the Butterley land to the north. The name is composed of two Old English words: 'swana' meaning herdsman, and 'wic', a group of buildings or a farm, so the meaning could be 'farm of the herdsman', another reference to the area's rich farmland. There is a reference from 1368 to coal mining at Swanwick at The Delves, a name meaning 'diggings'. Swanwick was part of the monastic estate of Beauchief Abbey, founded in 1175. The monks were not only farmers and foresters, they extracted the minerals – coal, clay, stone, lead and iron – and the Beauchief Canons became noted ironmasters. It was this natural wealth that formed the basis of the area's industrial growth, as depicted in this memorial stone in Brewster's Garden, crafted by Carole Kirsopp, depicting the past, present and future of Swanwick.

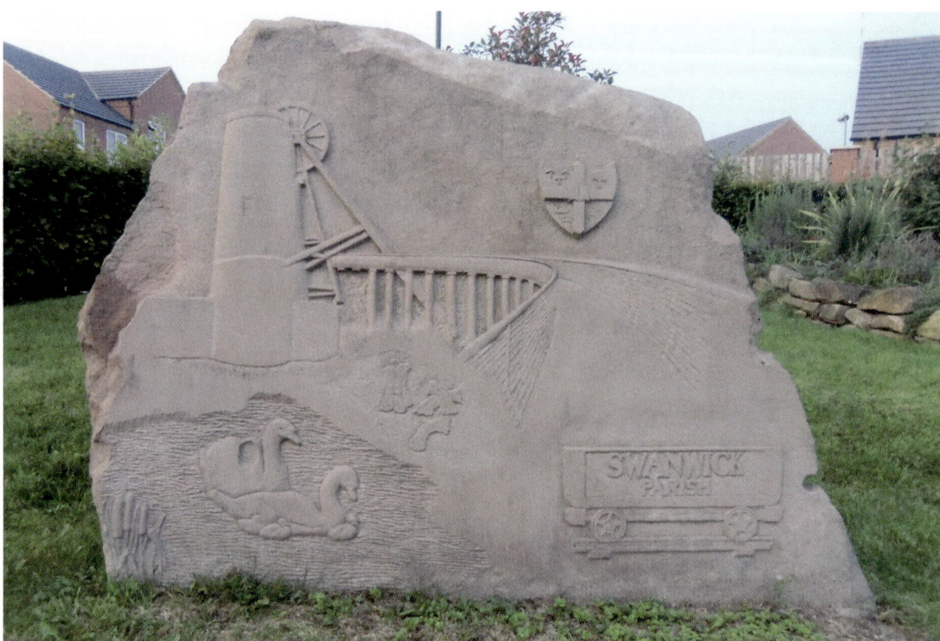

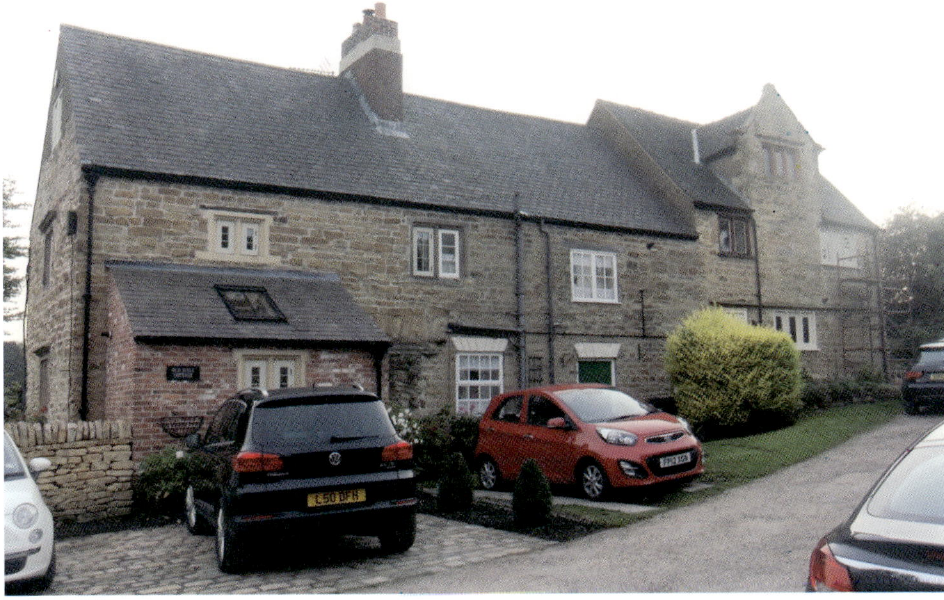

Swanwick Hall and Old Hall

The Wood family were major landowners in Swanwick, and can be traced back to the mid-sixteenth century. They built the original hall as shown here; it was a substantial yeoman's residence and has a date stone of 1678 high up on the dormer gable. Although too worn to decipher clearly, the date is incorporated into the crest adopted by the Wood family. It was given the name Old Hall around 1690 when John Turner built what we now know as Swanwick Hall. Hugh Turner is credited with rebuilding the hall between 1771 and 1782 to produce the present impressive building, which was purchased by the Derbyshire County Council and opened as a secondary school in 1922.

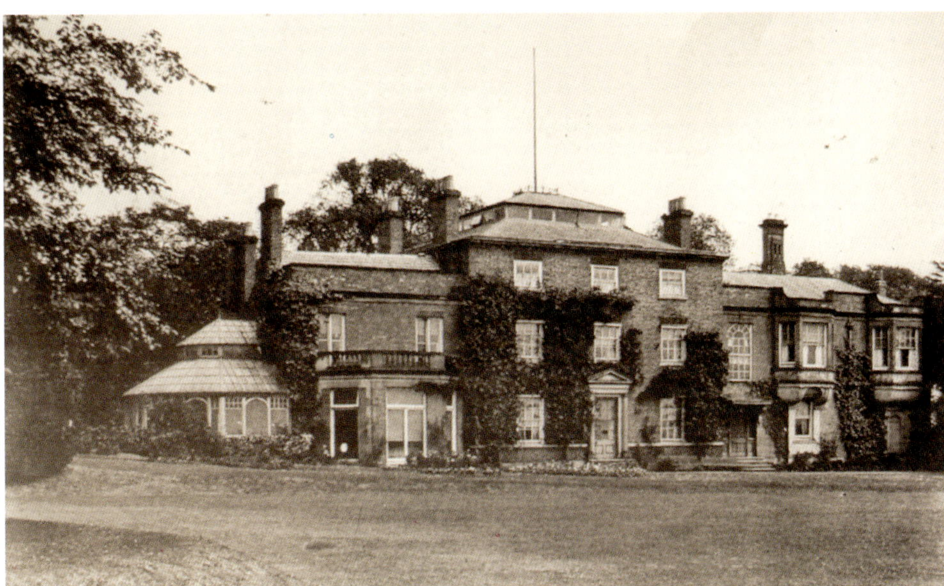

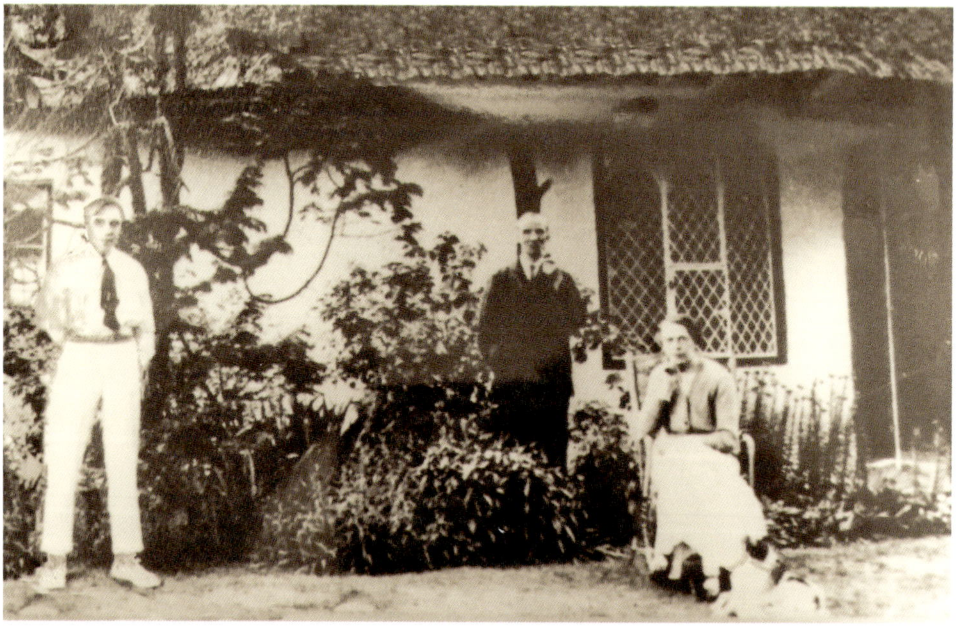

The Early Village

Like many of the local villages, for centuries Swanwick's industries consisted of coalmining, farming, framework knitting and footwear. Swanwick became renowned for quality silk stockings, reputedly worn by Queen Victoria and the Royal Family, a business begun by the Elliot family as a cottage industry around 1740. It continued into the twentieth century in cottages like this thatched dwelling in Yellow Yard, which is one of the oldest parts of the village. The Turners of Swanwick Hall made Swanwick coal well known in the seventeenth and eighteenth centuries, but there are now no signs of mining except for the renovated mining cars filled with flowers on the road between Swanwick and Ripley.

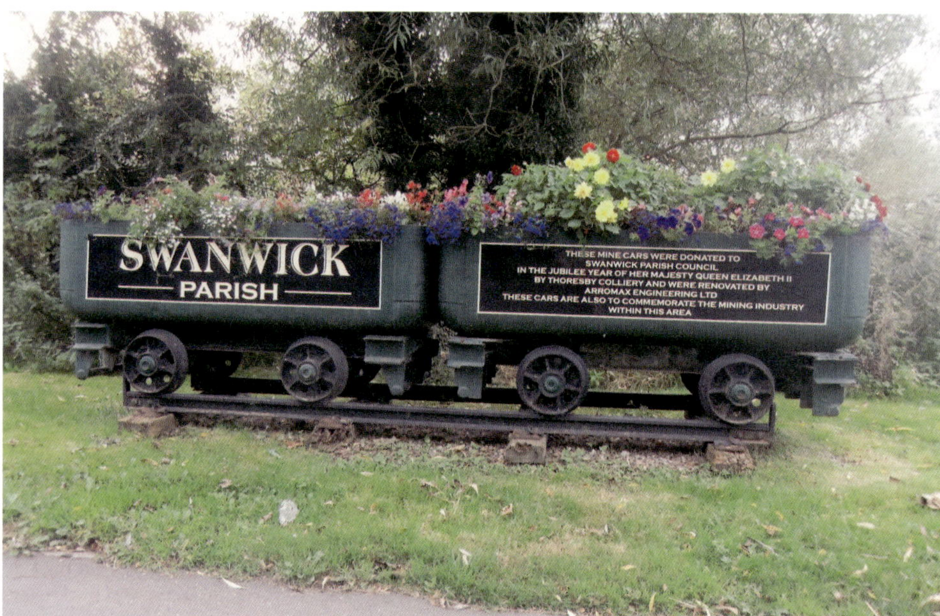

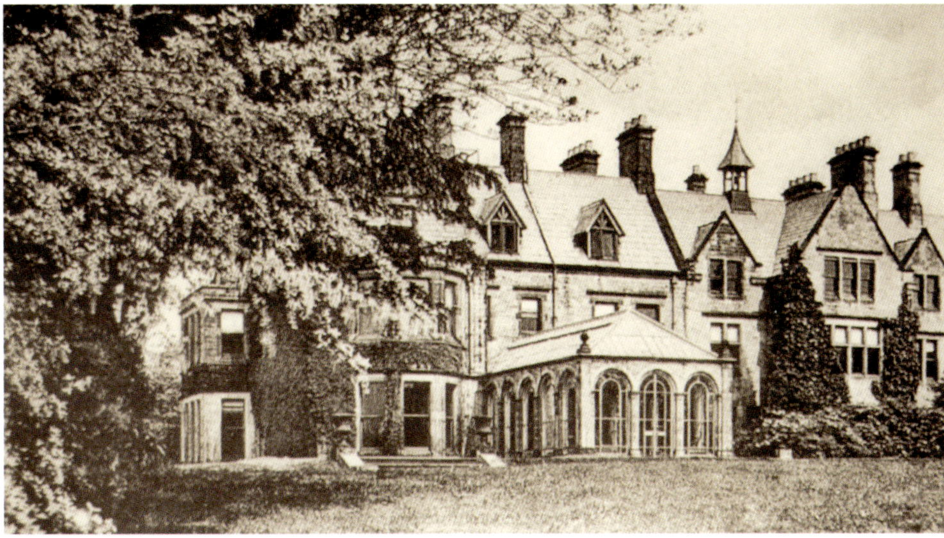

Swanwick Hayes

In 1860, Francis Wright of Butterley Hall built a mansion on land called The Hayes as a wedding present for his son FitzHerbert and his German-born wife, Louise Charlotte Rudolphine von Beckmann, daughter of a German pastor. The census of 1871 shows FitzHerbert Wright residing at The Hayes with his wife, three children and eleven servants. One of his great, great-granddaughters is Sarah Ferguson, who married HRH Prince Andrew. In 1910, The Hayes was purchased by First Conference Estate Ltd for £11,500, about a fifth of its original cost of construction. Plans were made to erect a sleeping block to hold 200 people, a dining room for 300, to turn the stables into bedrooms and to build a conference hall. The alterations cost £10,240, and the first conferences were held in 1912, with men sleeping in tents within the grounds and ladies accommodated indoors. One hundred years later, The Hayes offers first class facilities for all and is world renowned.

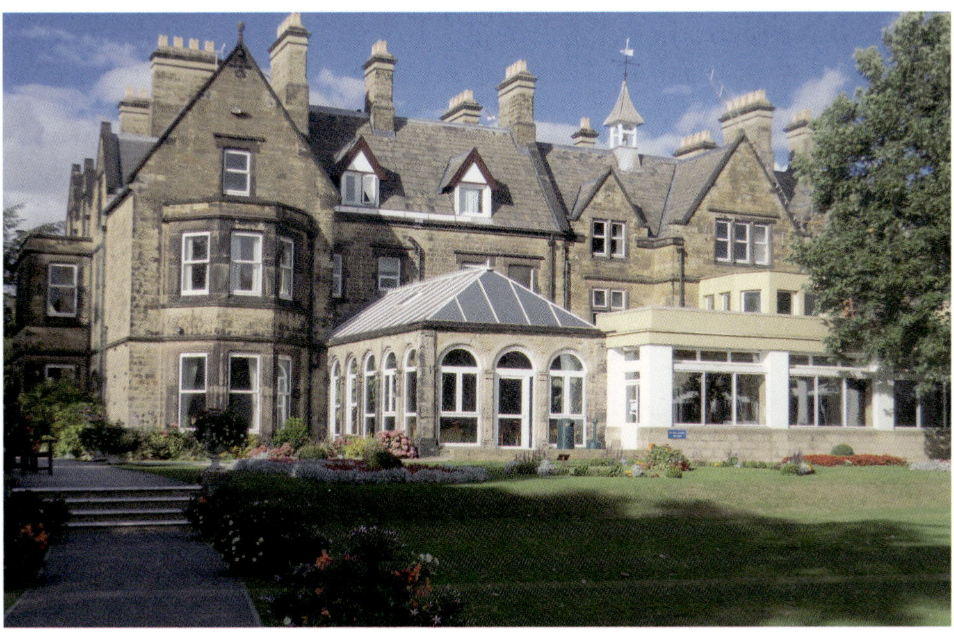

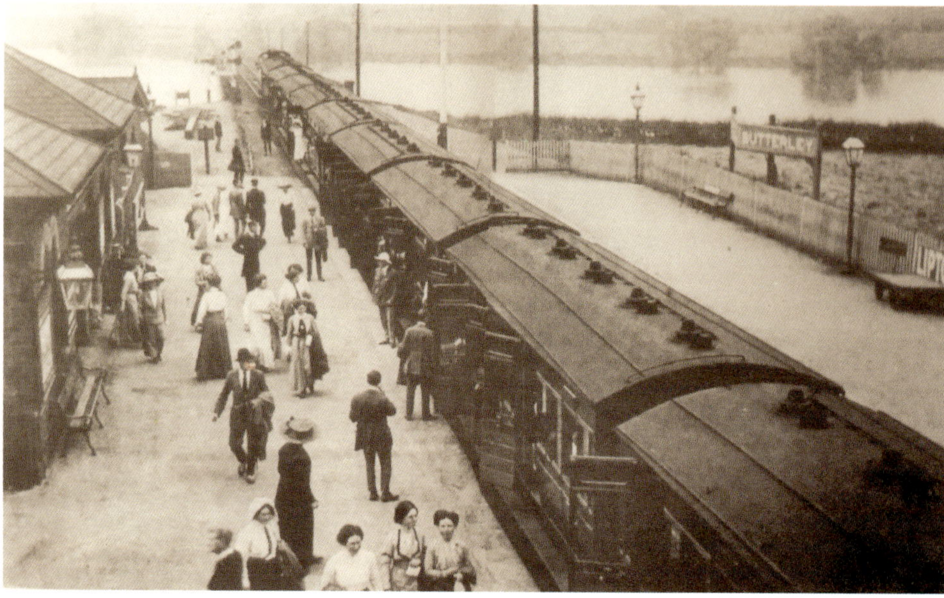

Butterley Railway Station

The vast number of conference visitors came by train, arriving at Butterley station on the Midland Railway's Pye Bridge to Ambergate line. Our photograph from around 1920 shows a busy platform at Butterley station. From here it was necessary for visitors to walk to the centre while the company collected their luggage by pony and trap. In 1935, the people of Swanwick asked the LMS to change the name of Butterley station to Swanwick, but this was declined. They did, however, change the sign to read 'Butterley for Swanwick'. Butterley station is no longer connected to the main line, but is still in operation at the Midland Railway Centre. The postcard shows five views of The Hayes as an early conference centre.

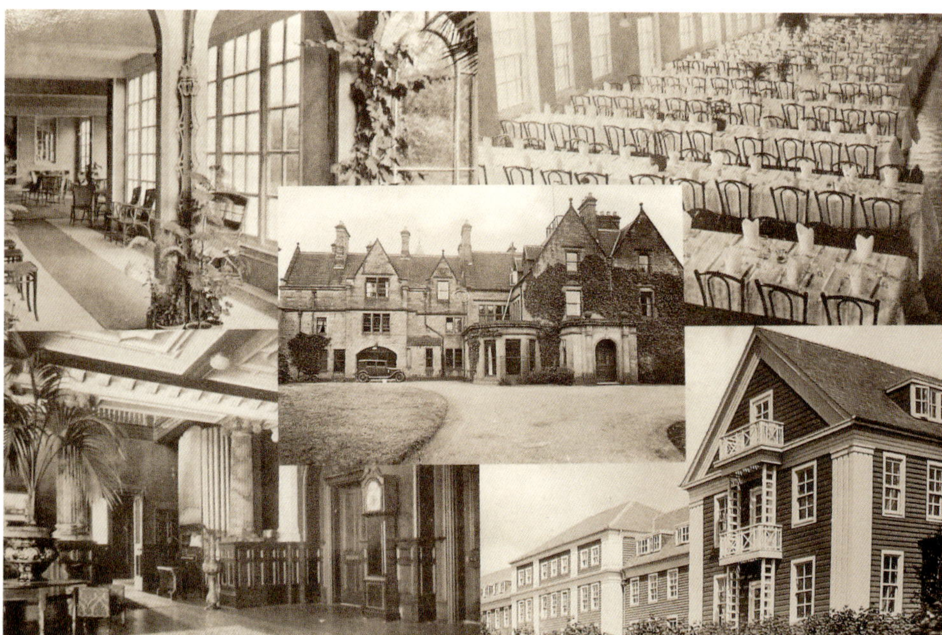

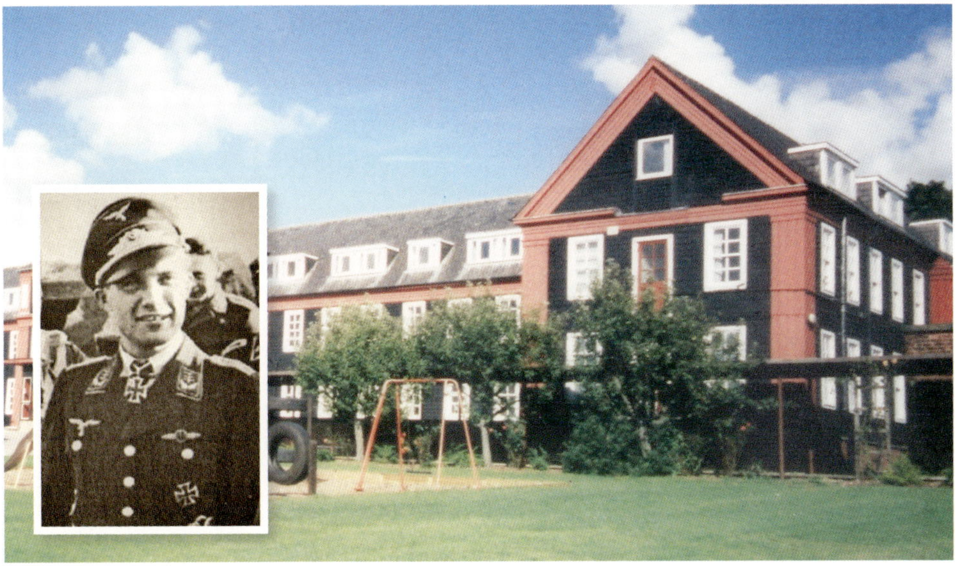

The One That Got Away

In 1939, The Hayes was taken over as a prisoner of war camp. Among the officers was a German fighter pilot named Franz von Werra, and he instigated an escape. Tunnelling under the Garden House on 20 December 1940, five prisoners escaped, but for four of them, their freedom was short. Franz von Werra, posing as a Dutch air force officer made his way to Codnor Park railway station, where a suspicious ticket collector called the police. They interviewed Franz von Werra who obviously fooled them completely, as they took him to the nearest RAF base at Hucknall. There, he attempted to take a prototype Hurricane bomber, was arrested in the cockpit and sent back to Swanwick. He was sent to Canada, where he escaped and returned to Germany as a hero. He died seven months later when his aircraft disappeared over the North Sea. In 1956, Kendal Burt and James Leasor wrote the book *The One that Got Away,* chronicling the true exploits of Oberleutnant Franz von Werra, and the following year it was made into a film of the same name. The Garden House, as shown in the photograph, and the tunnel have now been demolished.

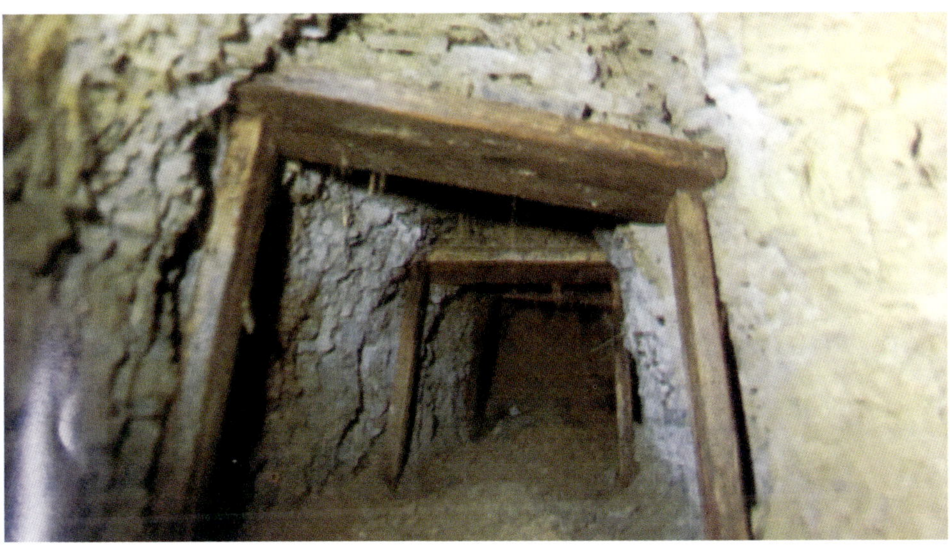

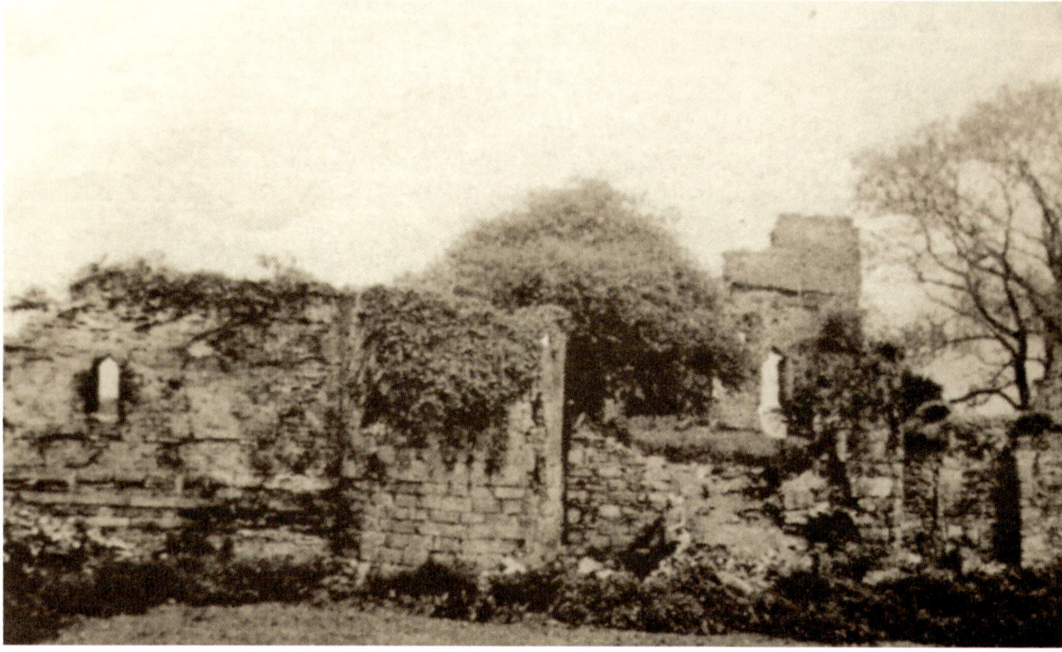

Cadnor Castle and Park

From Butterley, the canal tunnel runs under Butterley Park and on to Codnor Park, which, as the name implies, was the park of the Grey's, followed by the Zouch family of Codnor Castle, one of the great feudal castles of the Middle Ages. The castle is now in a ruinous state. The 1,130 acres were divided into ten farms, with the nearby Knowts Hall Farm and cottage, dating from 1665, built from some of the castle's stone.

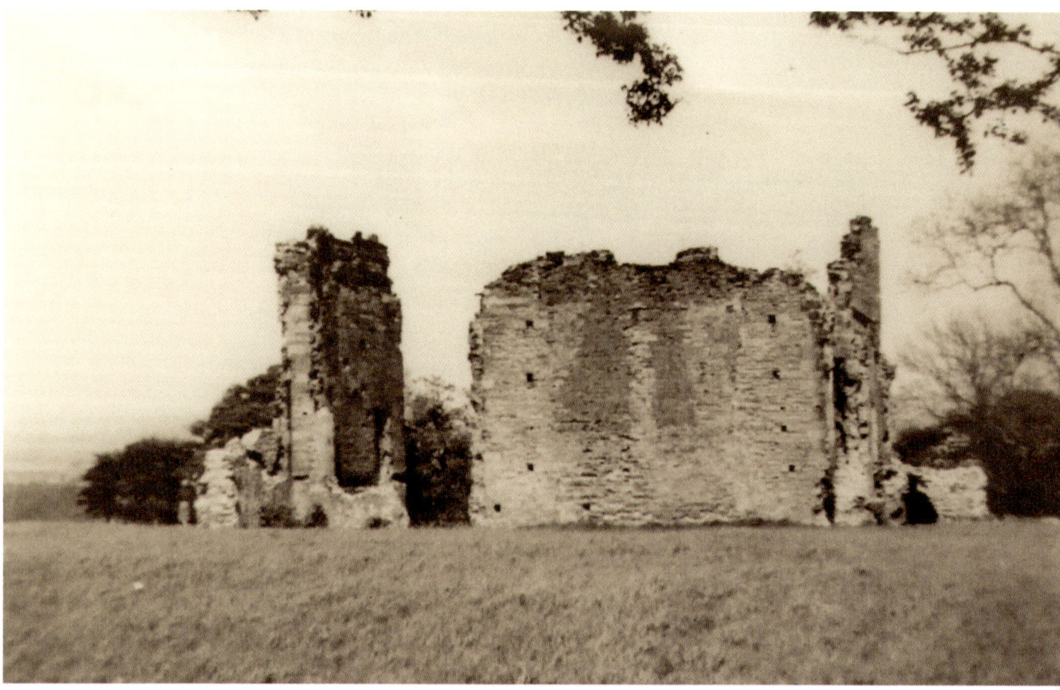

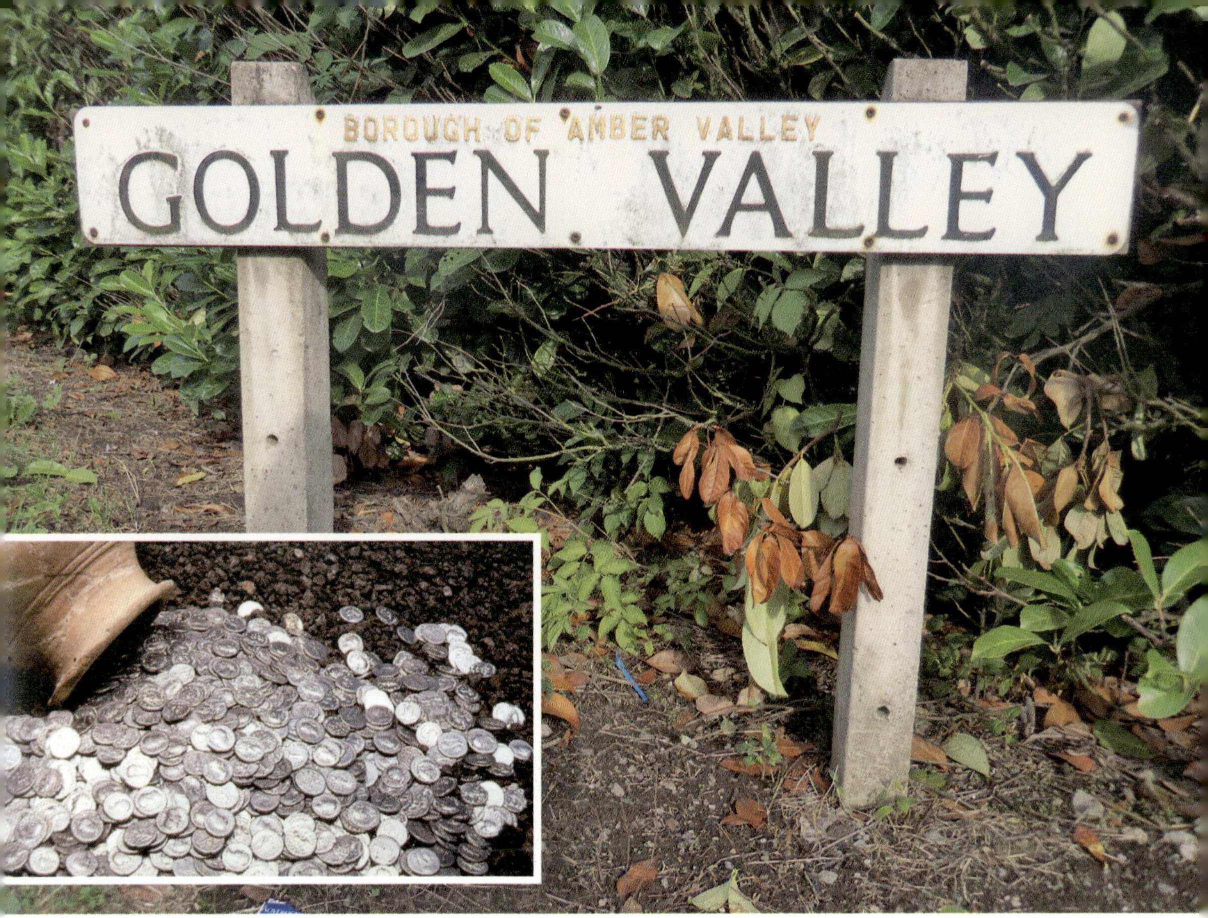

Newlands and the Roman Hoard

The tunnel portal at its eastern end emerges at an area known as Newlands, which in a charter dated 1200 is described as 'the grove of Alfreton'. It was primeval woodland with a sinister reputation and the expressive name Wormstall. In medieval terms, Wormstall was the abode of a dragon or serpent and, in folklore, dragons guard buried treasure. The woodland was cleared and enclosed by Zouch of Codnor when he conveyed the 200-acre New Lands, with all the minerals and tithes, to William Harris of Oakerthorpe in 1617. Then in 1740, they found that fabled buried treasure. An urn filled with Roman denarii was dug up in a hedge bottom in Greenhaigh Lane (Greenhill Lane). Eight years later, on 20 September 1748, two labourers digging a drain on Newlands Farm found 1,500–1,600 silver denarii in an urn. A report by Reginald Johnson from the time states:

> It was agreed among a farmer and his work men ye Roe [Samuel Roe the tenant farmer] should sell and when sold ye money to be divided into three shares amongst them ... Roe took some of it to Nottingham and some to Mansfield, to see if it was silver or not ... all ye while keeping it a profound secret, lest ye Chief Lord should claim it as Treasure Trouve, and so was willing to sell it, at any price, where secrecy could be had ... Mr Dakeyne allowed them ten shilling [50p] ye ounce, for ye same ... Danl Elliot and his partner disclosed the matter 30th November 1748.

A third find of silver coins was made on 18 October 1754, giving more evidence that the Romans frequented this area.

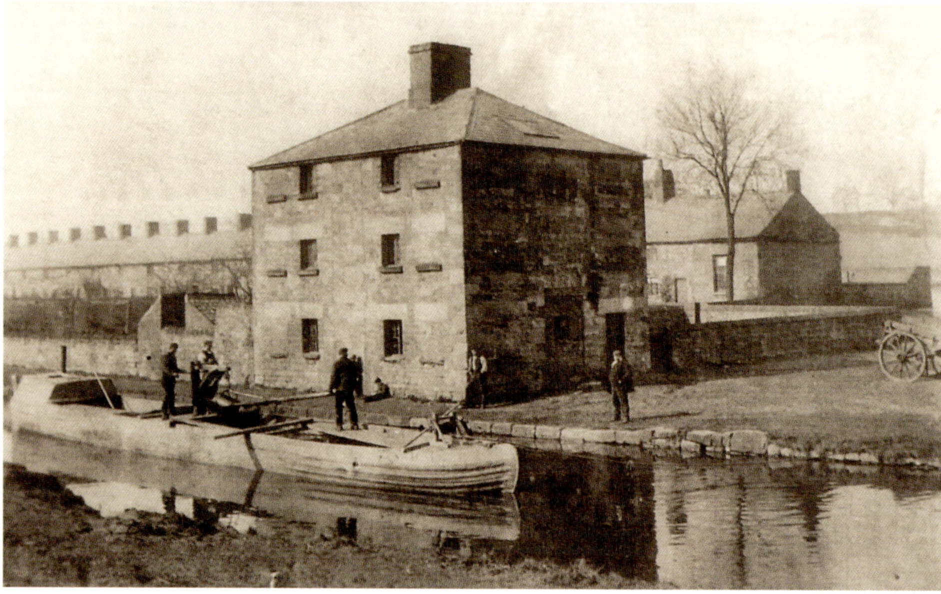

The Golden Valley

While digging the canal and tunnel, valuable seams of coal and 30-foot-thick ironstone beds were discovered, prompting the Butterley Company to open a second works at Codnor Park in 1801. The lower portion of the Newlands estate was given the name the Golden Valley. Although its name could now be associated with the gold of broom or dandelions, buttercups or corn, it was the great mineral wealth that was accrued from this industrial passage that created the Golden Valley. The photograph above shows a warehouse beside the canal, which may afterwards have served as a church and living accommodation before it was demolished in the early 1900s. Behind it is Stone Row, the first twenty houses to be built specifically for the workers in the Golden Valley in 1795.

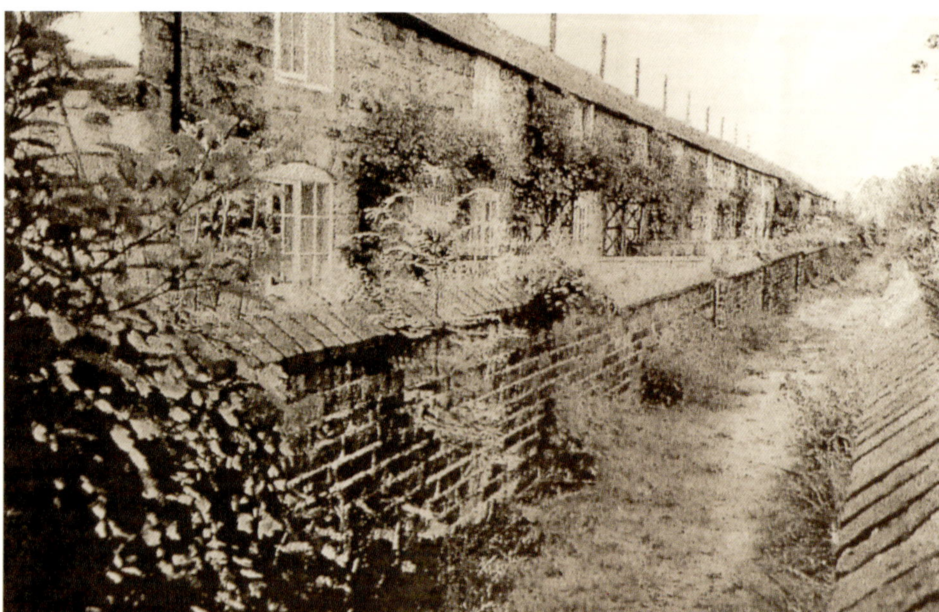

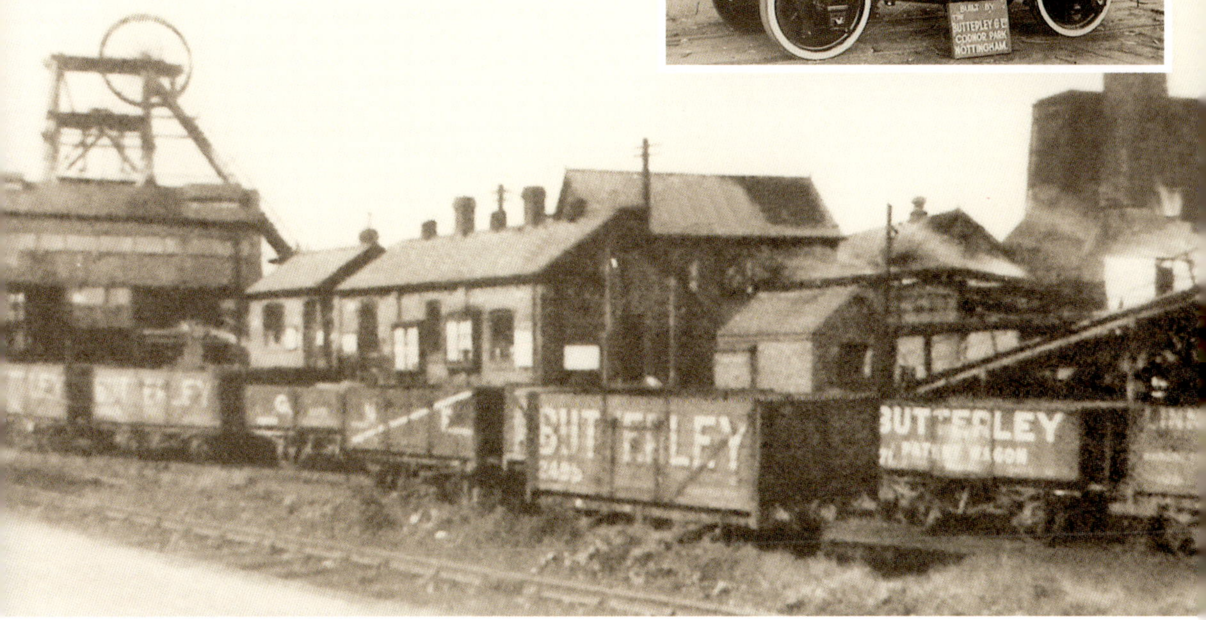

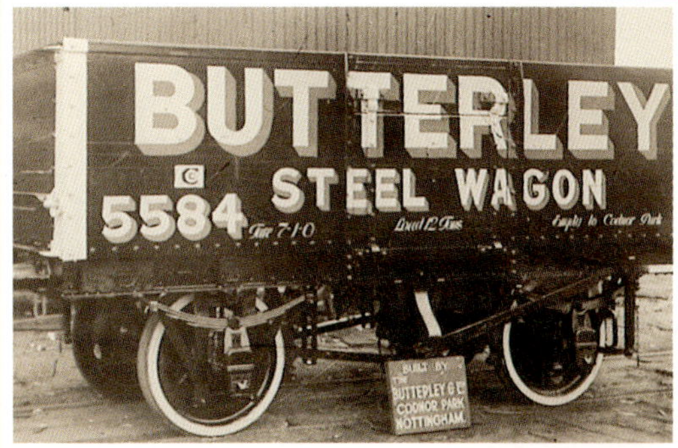

The Cordnor Park and Butterley Works

At Codnor Park, the Butterley Company erected two stone furnaces and an iron forge, followed by a third furnace in 1825. In 1829, 29 tons of iron were being produced per furnace per week. In 1835, this figure had increased to 49 tons per furnace per week. In *Black's Tourist Guide to Derbyshire* (1882) it says,

> The Codnor Park Works and those at Butterley are connected by a private railway on which the locomotives dragging immense trains are constantly steaming to and fro, whilst in every direction rise up tall chimneys from almost innumerable steam engines attached to coal and ironstone pits, plying their endless work of fury, and continually tearing up the bowls of the earth, whilst intermixed with them are the more homely gins worked by horses and doing their labour in a more quiet and primitive manner. All around are tramways and canals and railroads intersecting each other in every possible direction.

The photographs show a Butterley display wagon and a series of wagons at work.

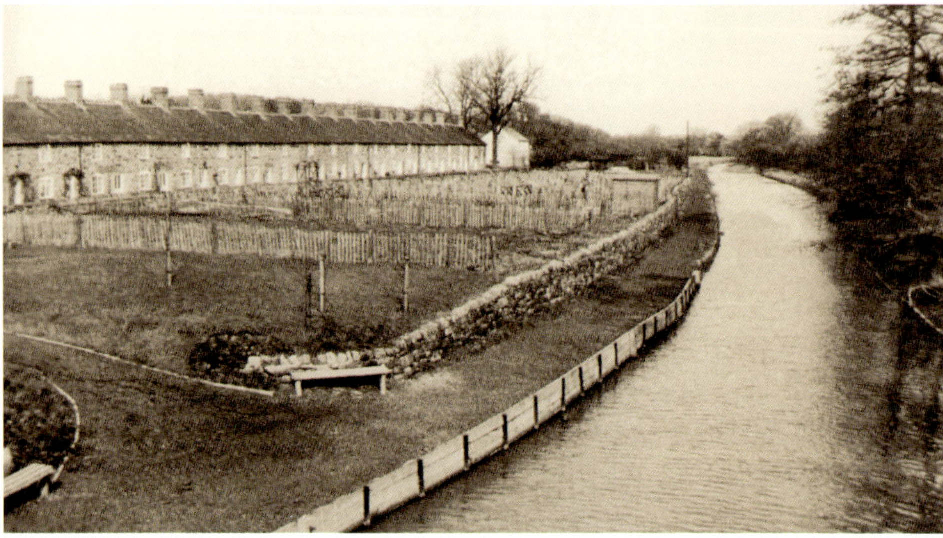

The Golden Valley Company Housing

These new industries needed manpower, so a company house and free fuel did much to encourage men to leave farming and enter the more dangerous occupations of mining, quarrying and foundry work. Housing varied considerably. Butterley Company houses generally had living space of around 530 square feet, comprising of two living rooms downstairs with two bedrooms over. In the 1800s, several rows of brick houses were built with gardens at the front or back, a small backyard with a coalhouse, a privy (called locally 'the bucket and chuck it'), and walled ash pits, where cold ashes and household rubbish was emptied. The streets were lit with gas, and a lamplighter walked along with a pole, lighting the gas lights every evening and extinguishing them each morning. It was also customary for the lamplighter to knock on the bedroom windows of the men who needed waking for the early shift.

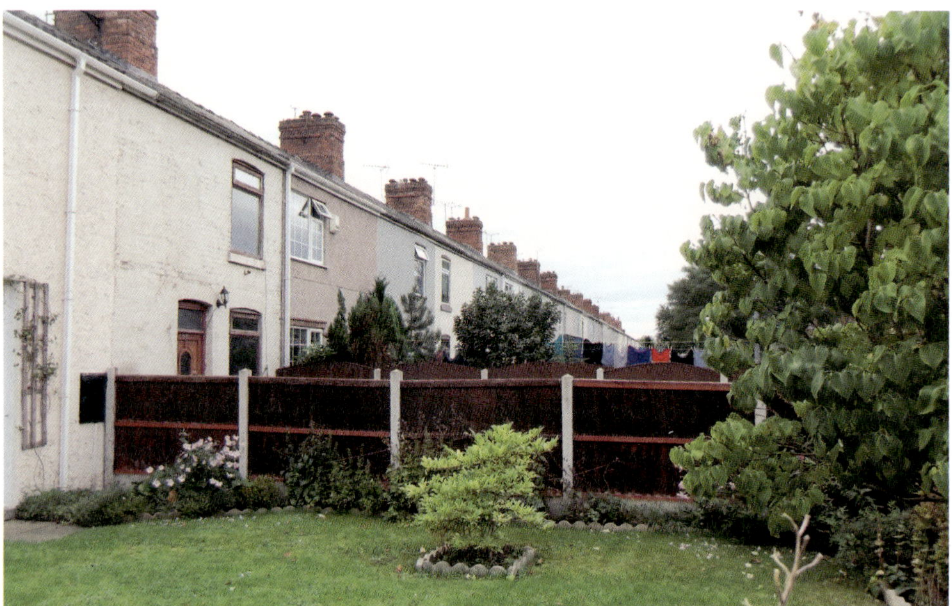

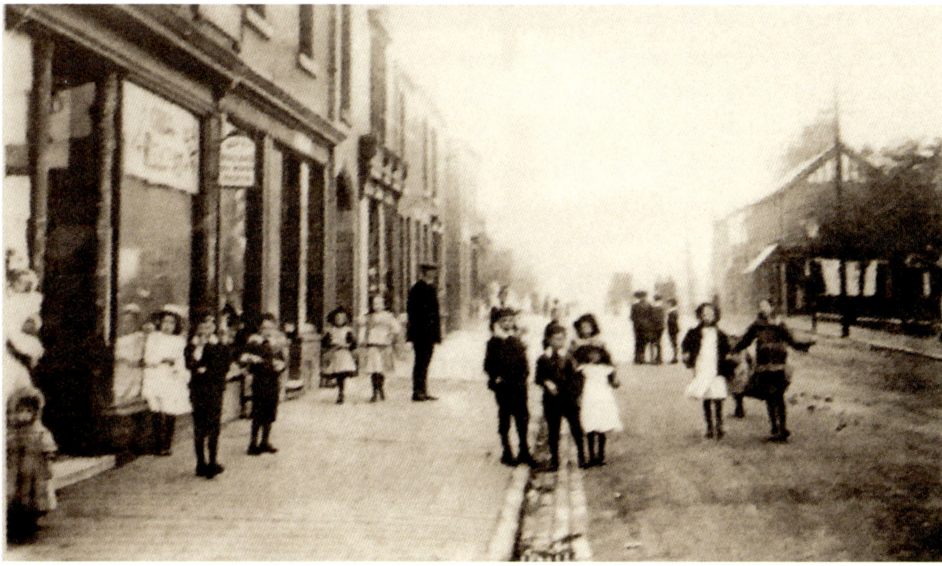

Attracting Workers

The Butterley Company didn't have a monopoly in the Golden Valley. There was strong competition from the Morewoods of Alfreton, the Turners of Swanwick and the Oakes of Riddings, plus many smaller industrialists who owned mines and factories in the area. This was a time of tremendous change when the mineral resources of the area were being exploited, bringing great prosperity for owners, plenty of work for labourers and a rapid population explosion. The new industries needed more manpower than the district could supply, and the continuous flow of immigrants all needed accommodation. The demand for housing was met by the owners because the nearer they could put labour to the workplace, the better the investment. This was the ultimate weapon against poor performance. Men would not be late for work, and if the standard of work was below par, they would not only lose the job, but their families would also lose their homes.

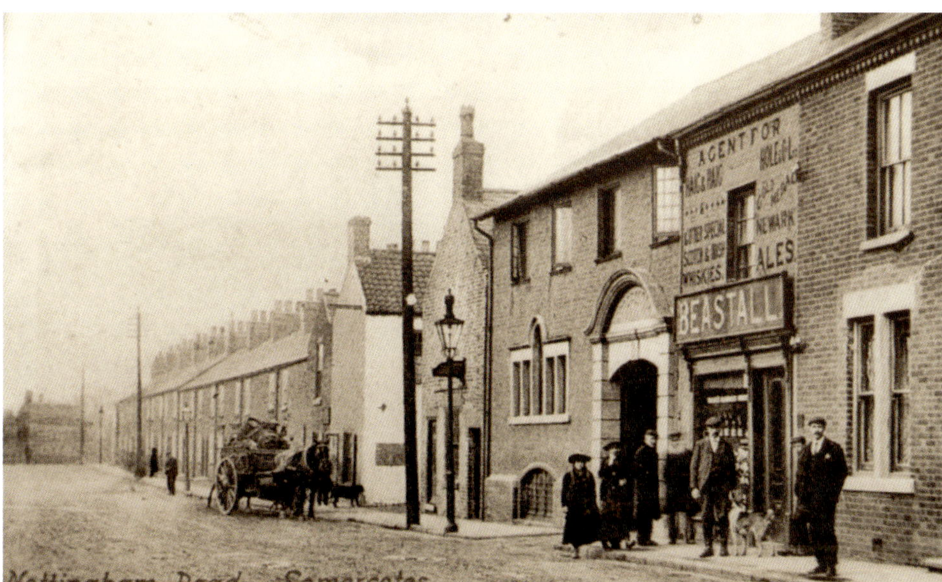

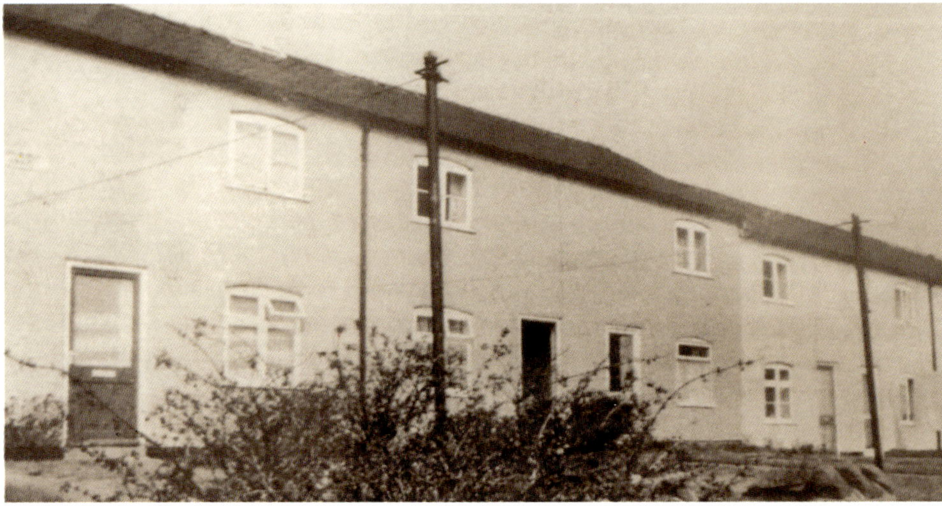

Ironville, the Model Village

John Wright and William Jessop purchased an unpopulated district of Riddings from Lancelot Rolleston of Watnall in 1809 to build a model village for their workers. Prior to the building of the canal, it had been farmland with no roads, but by 1823 there were thirty-two houses, built as Furnace Row and Foundry Row. The names were apt and left no doubt why the village was built, so it seemed obvious to call the place the iron village, or Ironville. Further housing following the basic pattern were built with bricks from the company's brickworks at a cost of £40 each. The entire parish was the creation of the Butterley Company who owned the church, the school, institutes, reading rooms, the library, baths, and the gas and water works. By 1851, there was a population of 1,541, and the planned village gained much praise. The rural setting and spacious layout formed a refreshing contrast to the contemporary back-to-back houses built to house many workers in the north's industrial towns. With rent at just 1*s*/6*d* per week, it did much to attract more workers to the area. Unfortunately, most of this model village has gone since the old Butterley Company folded, and the then local authority took over the village and redeveloped the site. They saw no point in preserving the gas lights, the original shop fronts in uniform green, the humpbacked canal bridge and the original cast-iron street signs, which all combined to give a period feel to what was undoubtedly one of the best examples of a nineteenth-century industrial village.

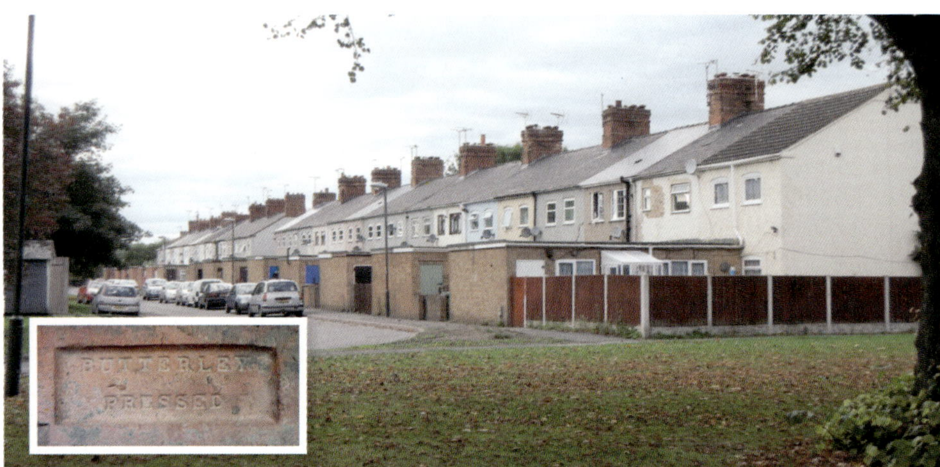

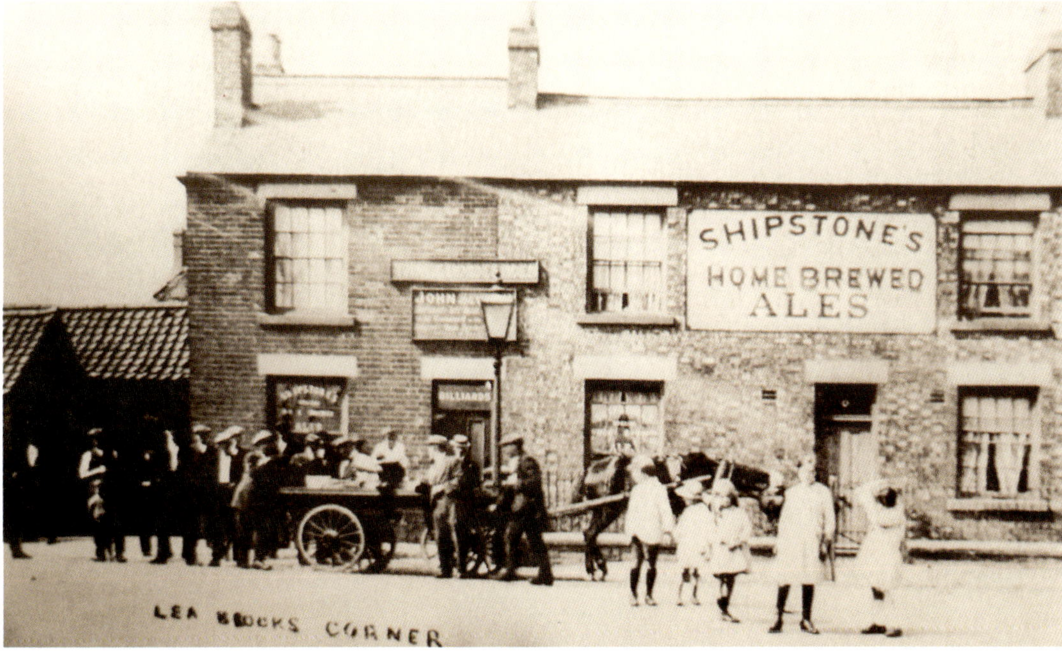

Greenhill Lane, Leabrooks, Riddings and Somercotes

The hamlet of Greenhill Lane merged into the Swanwick Hayes estate on its western side, and the ancient track still known as Greenhill Lane on its eastern boundary. It was mined by the Palmer Morewoods of Alfreton Hall, but now the only reference to coal mining is Slack Lane running down to the Golden Valley. The rapid industrial expansion that took place in the area required new houses, trades and services, and by 1857, Greenhill Lane had merged Leabrooks, Somercotes and Riddings.

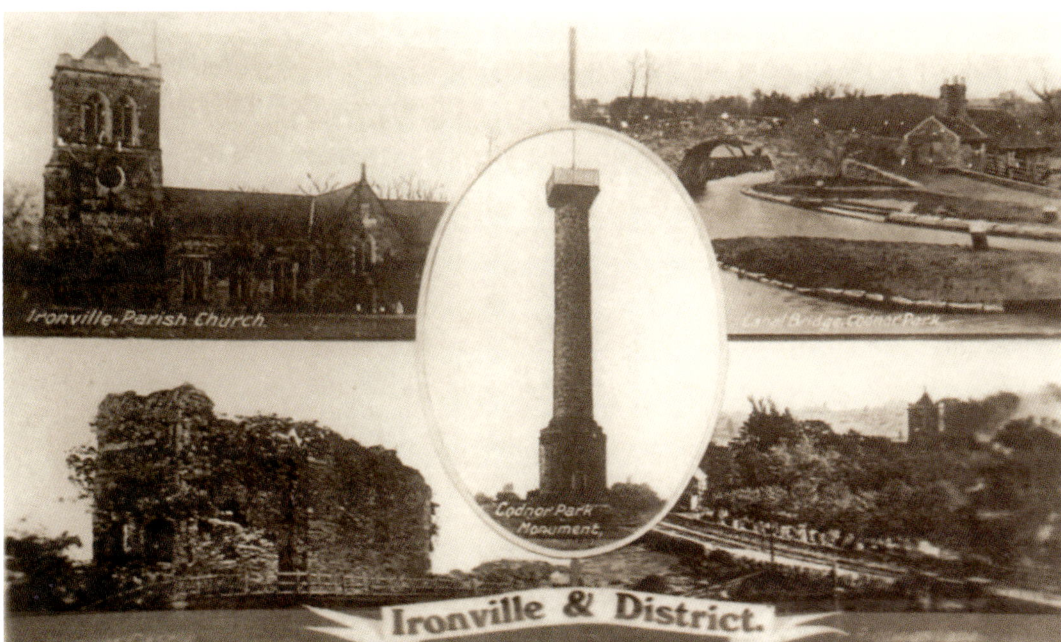

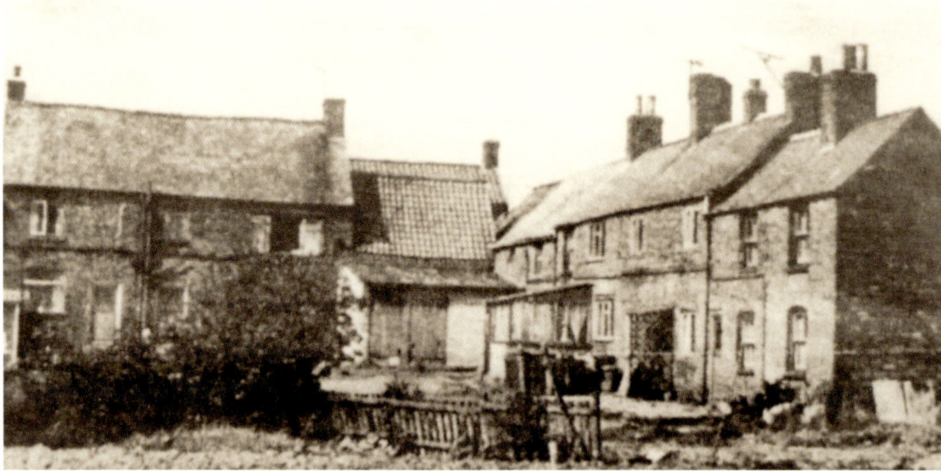

Somercotes

In early centuries during the summer months, this area was devoted to the grazing of cattle. Herdsmen lived in summer cotes (crude shelters made of branches, osiers and turf) while tending the large herds, and from this comes the name Somercotes. Thomas Chaworth, Lord of Alfreton granted 'The Cotes' and Birchwood to Beauchief Abbey, who owned the land and collected the tithes until 1525. Until demolition in the 1970s, there was a tiny hamlet of five houses, as shown in the above photograph, named Pennytown situated about 300 yards down Pennytown Lane. The name apparently comes from those early tenants of Pennytown who paid rent of one silver penny to Beauchief Abbey. Somercotes Common was enclosed in 1823, and with the invasion of new industries, a village of considerable size grew on the hilltop. It now forms part of the ecclesiastical parish of Riddings, but the old industries have gone. In March 2001, the Somercotes Parish Council erected this striking memorial, the old pit wheel, and on the plaque it says 'In Commemoration of the Mining Community of the Parish of Somercotes'.

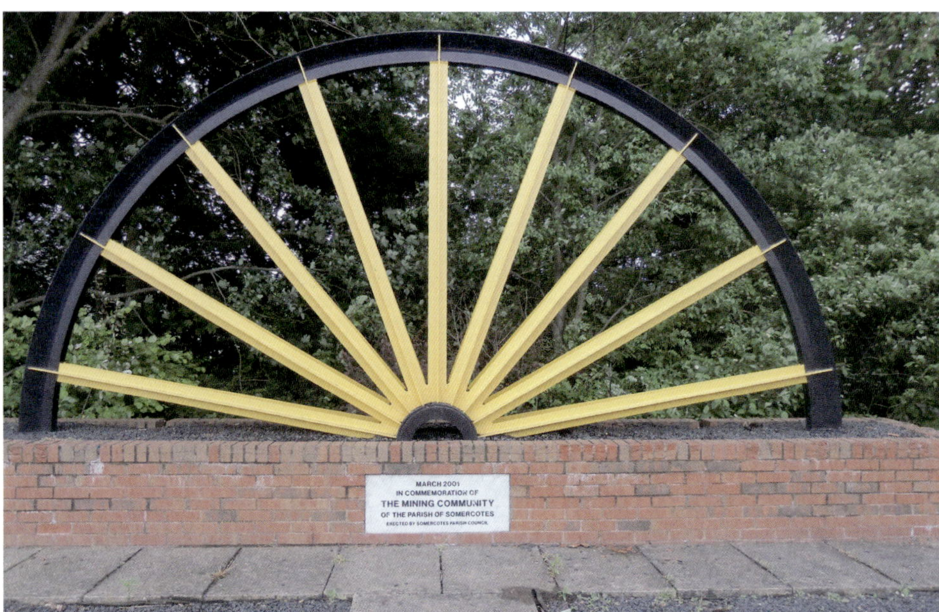

Twin Windmills

The summit of Greenhill Lane had been the site of a windmill since ancient times. There's record of a post mill and adjacent land that was sold in 1826. Twin windmills were built by James Oakes in 1877, and named James and Sarah after Mr Oakes and his wife. They were used to mill flour for the Oakes family and tenantry, and as feeding stuff for livestock on the estate farms and the horses employed in the Riddings Collieries. The mills ceased to be economical when new milling processes dispensed with expensive and capricious windmills. They were converted to factory use, but in January 1963, one of the mills was gutted by fire. Later that year, both windmills were demolished, the site cleared and new industry introduced.

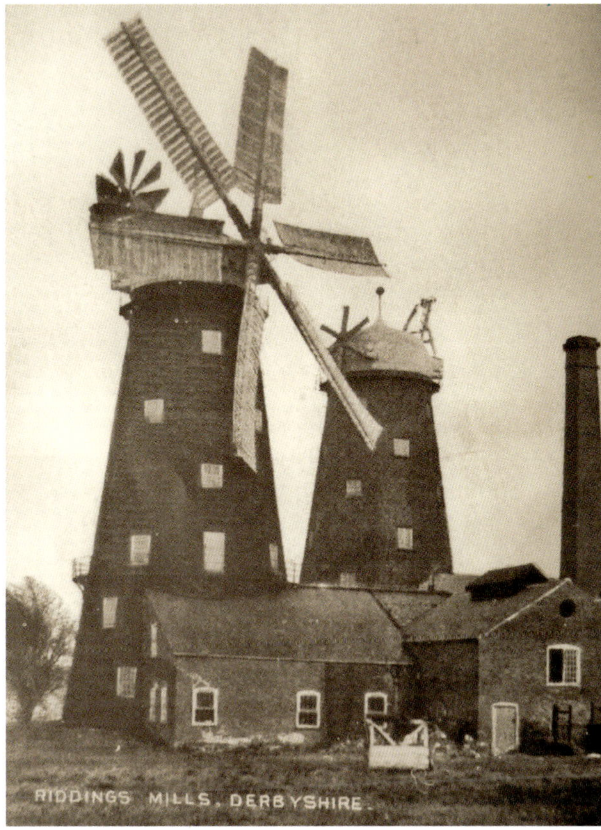

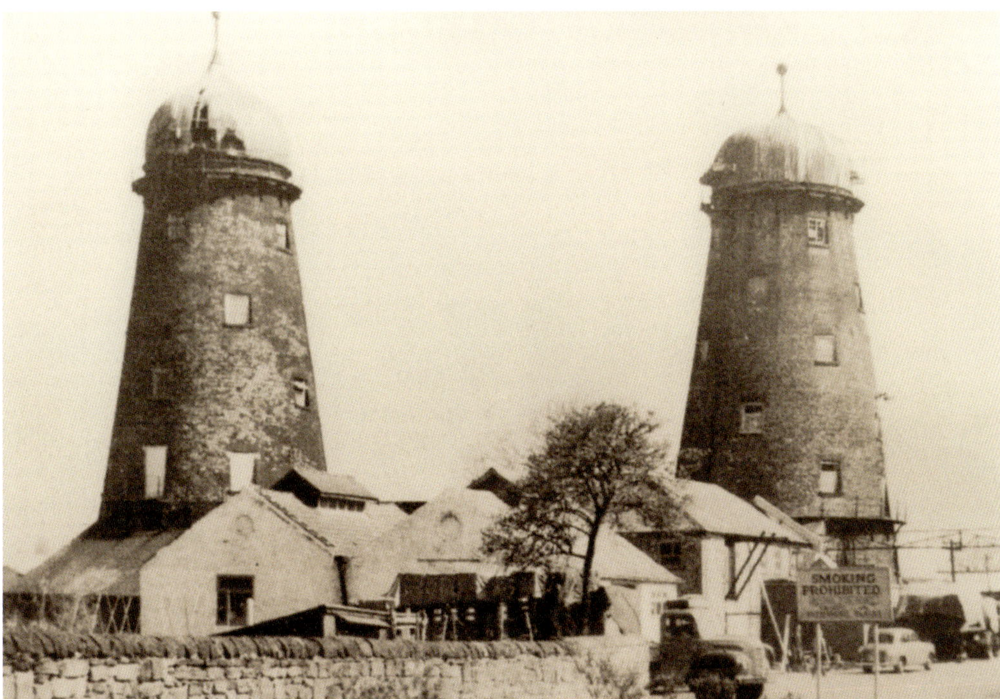

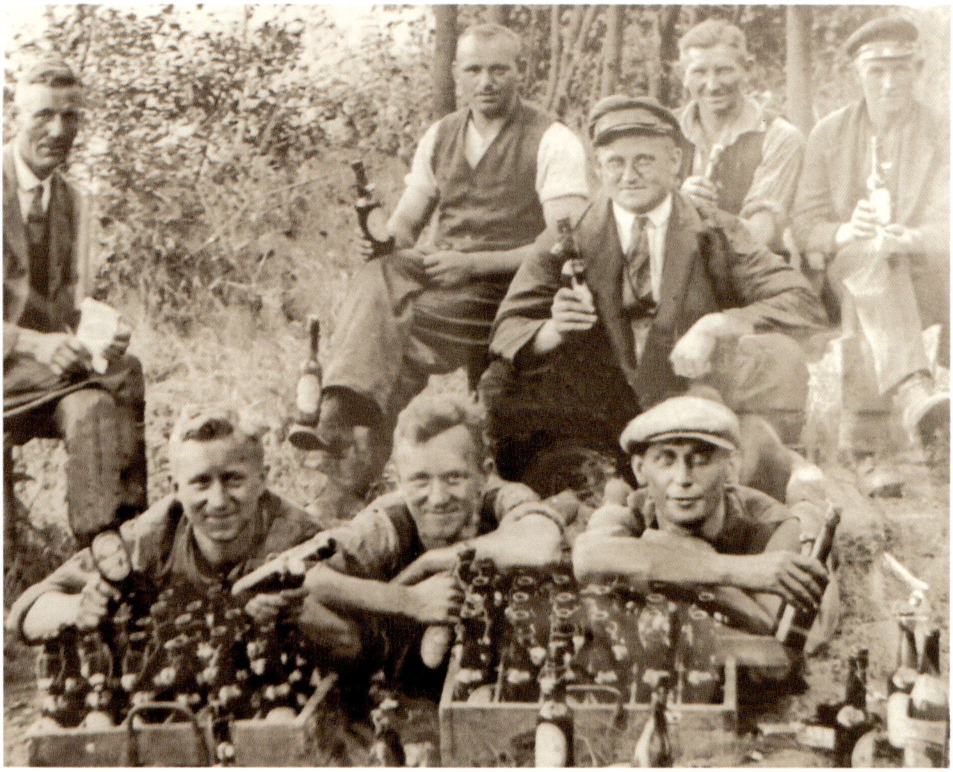

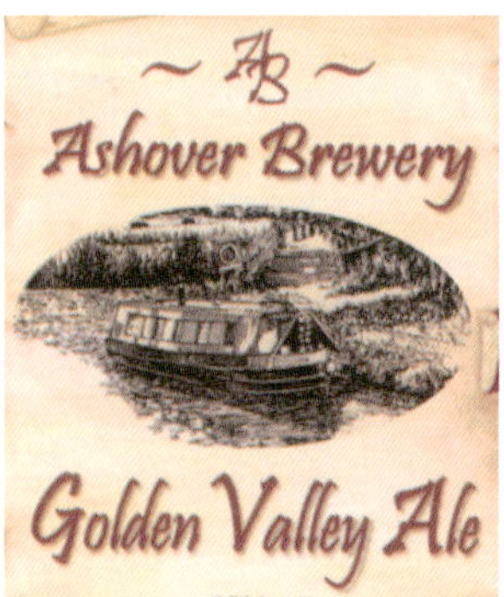

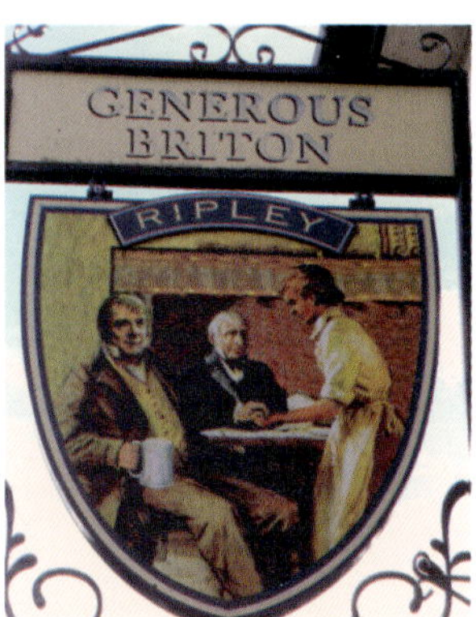

A Surprising Discovery

Riddings is an ancient name derived from Ryddynges, which would signify a clearing where a settlement grew. Coal and iron have been mined here since at least Tudor times, but in 1808, the mining company was taken over by James Oakes, whose family dominated Riddings for the next 100 years. They owned the Riddings Ironworks, several local collieries, and founded companies to manufacture coal derivatives such as tar and sulphuric acid. In 1844, James Oakes & Co. invited the German chemist W. R. Bunsen, who gave his name to the laboratory Bunsen burner, to Riddings, to analyse the chemical behaviour of coke-fired blast furnaces. At the same time, the company was sinking the New Deep pit to mine the Kilburn seam and struck a salt water spring. The water was run into the nearby canal. The Codnor Park Brewery then complained that the water they drew from the canal to use in brewing gave their ale an odd taste. The workers in our photograph seem to be enjoying the local brew, and Golden Valley Ale is now produced by the Ashover Brewery, guaranteed not to taste odd.

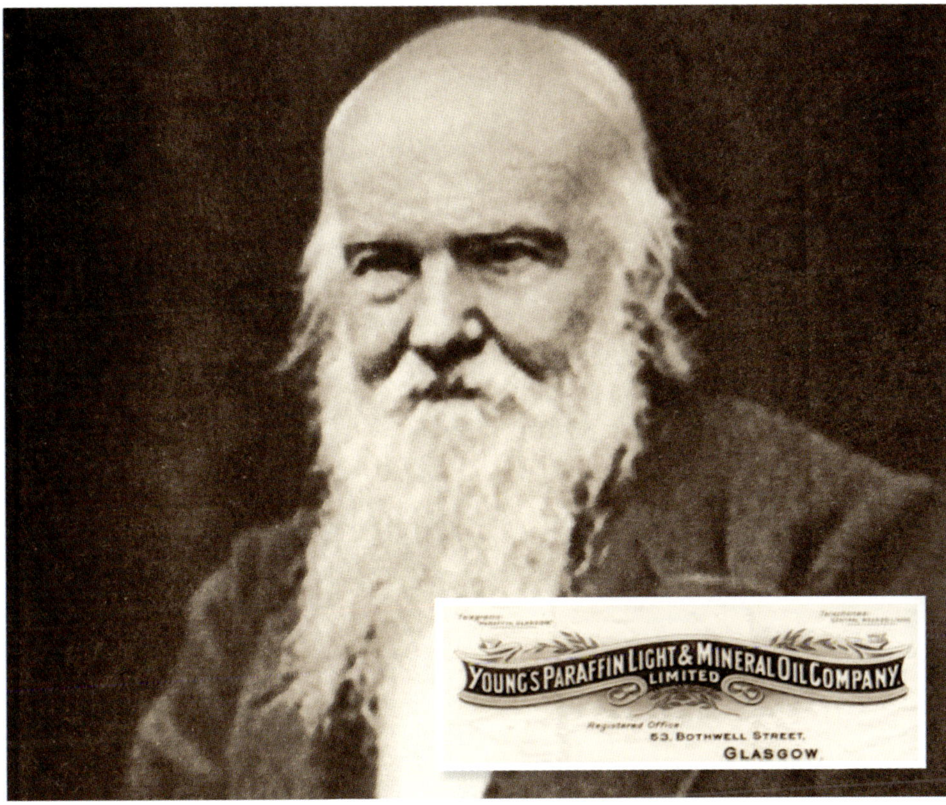

Striking Oil

It wasn't just the taste that was strange. Gradually a skim of oil began to form on the surface of the water, and when a housewife threw hot cinders into the canal it caught fire. This was an unheard of phenomenon. Water did not catch fire. Nothing like this had ever been seen in Britain. James Oakes' brother-in-law, a Scottish professor called Lyon Playfair, later Baron Playfair, made preliminary investigations into the nature of this newly discovered mineral/liquid, which was about the same consistency as thin treacle, and realised that it was mineral 'naptha', which we now call petrol. This was the first known spring to occur in Britain. He enlisted the help of a pioneering fellow scientist named James Young, who was then engaged in the experimental stages of coal-shale distillation in Bathgate, Scotland. James Young learnt carpentry skills from his father, and before his friend David Livingstone went as a missionary to Africa, James taught him how to use carpentry tool. James Young became contracted to Oakes & Co. to develop the paraffin oil industry, develop its distillation and refine the crude oil. Although he returned to Scotland where he distilled the oil, in 1848 the Riddings' site was producing 30 tons per month. Young patented his methods in 1850, and became popularly known as Paraffin Young. It was through his initiative and perseverance that the world's first oil refinery got started. He made a considerable fortune, and when Dr Livingstone returned to England to seek further financial backing for his missionary work in Africa, Young made a handsome donation towards a steam boat for Livingstone's use on the River Zambezi. For half a century the industry prospered, then competition from directly extracted crude oil from the more profitable wells that spring up in the USA and Persian Gulf wiped out the industry. The New Deep pit closed in 1885, and despite further drilling operations in Riddings in the hope of tapping a reservoir of petroleum, the results have been negative. In 1920, the Stanton Coal & Iron Company purchased the Riddings Ironworks, ending the Oakes 120-year association with Riddings. In 1969, the British Steel Corporation closed the Riddings works.

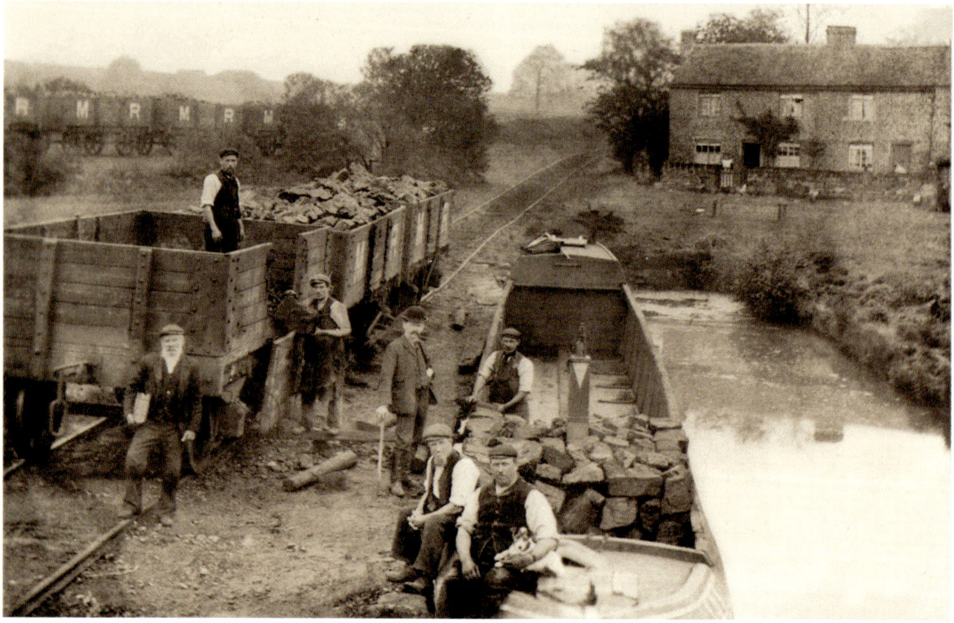

Transporting from Canal to Rail

To meet an ever increasing demand for coal, the Ripley district was sending 867,000 tons of coal, carried by the Cromford Canal, which linked with other canal and river ports around the country. Our photograph shows a barge on a spur of the canal being loaded from coal wagons at Hartshay wharf. The charge was 11*s* 1*d* per ton over the 200-mile distance from Ripley to Paddington, London, and took 10–14 days. The increasingly prohibitive canal charges were hampering expansion of trade, so a meeting of the coal owners was called in 1832 to determine what could be done. This resulted in the Derby to Ripley Midland Counties Railway, which afterwards became the Midland Railway Company, constructing a route from Derby to Ripley, initially for mineral traffic only.

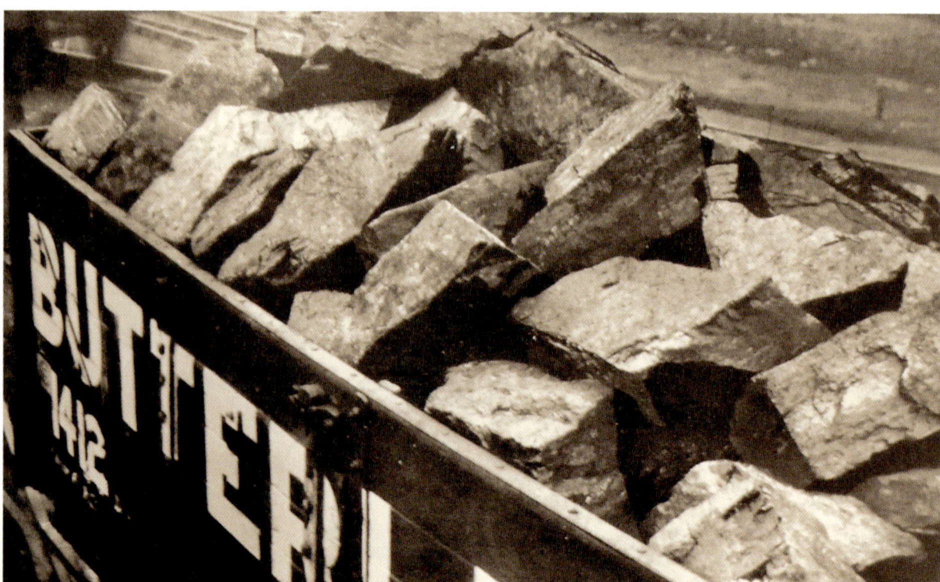

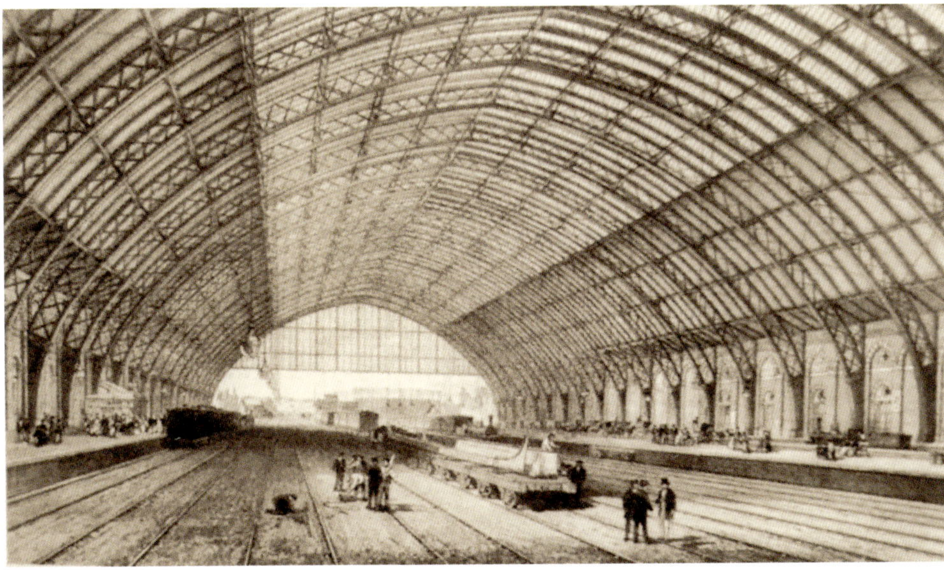

Butterley's Greatest Work

The inventions of the eighteenth century brought rapid development to Ripley and the Butterley Company, who by the early 1800s was providing 1,000 tons of pig iron annually, plus cast products and general forgings, wrought iron and plate. Contracts were won to build steam pumping engines for pulling wagons, and draining mines and fen lands. They made canons for the Napoleonic wars, and undertook rail, dockyard and naval projects. In 1863, Butterley was rolling the largest iron beams and joists yet made, a technique that made possible such decorative structures as the cast-iron colonnades for the front of London Opera House. One of its most ambitious projects was the roof of St Pancras Railway Station, London. At the time of its erection in 1867, with a free span of 240 feet (72m), 6,894 tons of ironwork and covering an area of 4½ acres, this thing of beauty and wonder was the largest and most impressive structure in the world. It still looks very impressive, as our recent photograph shows.

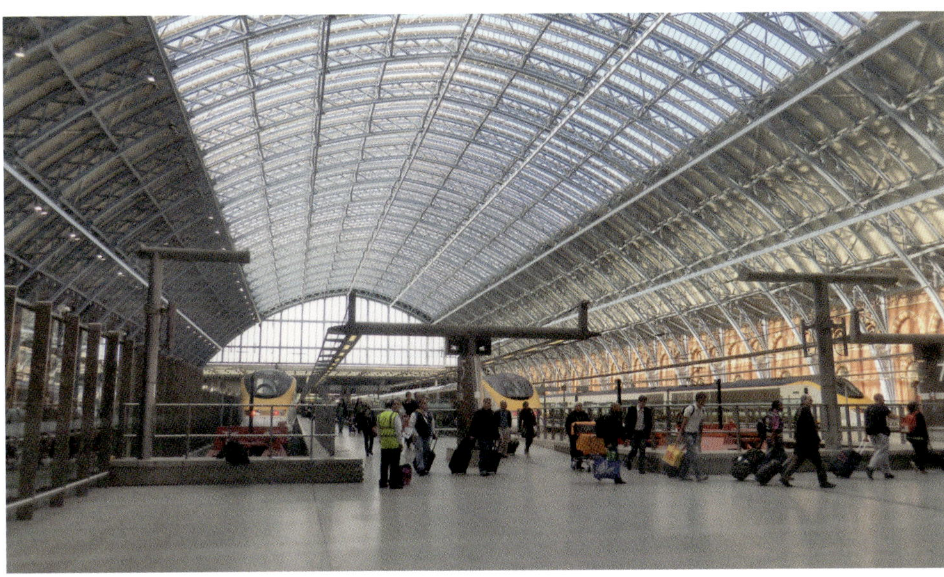

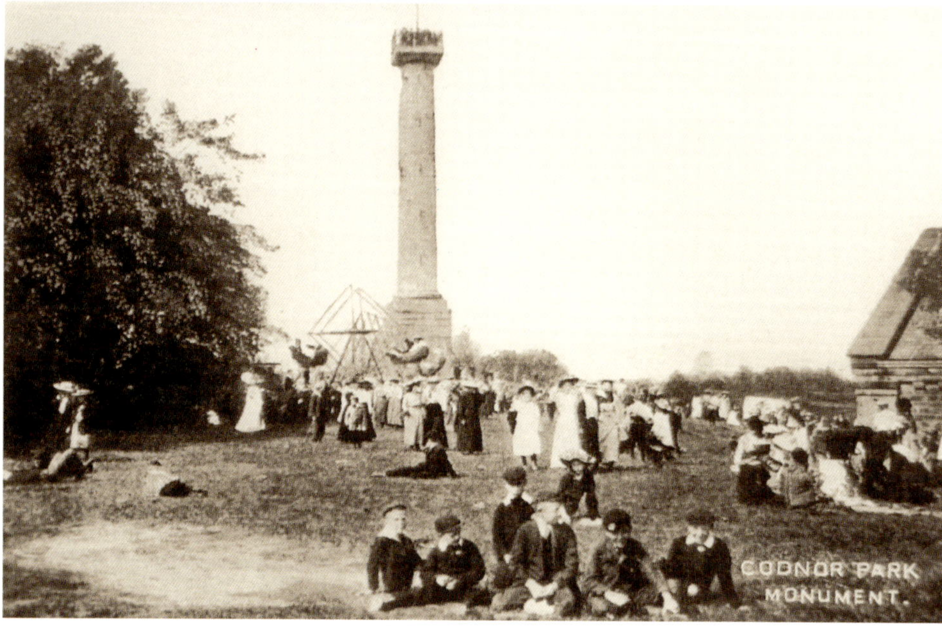

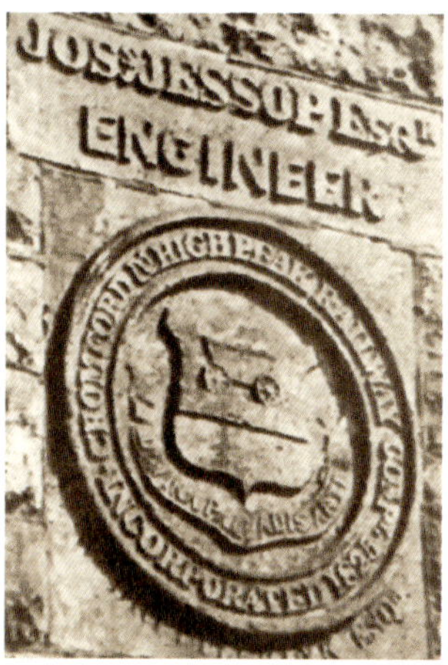

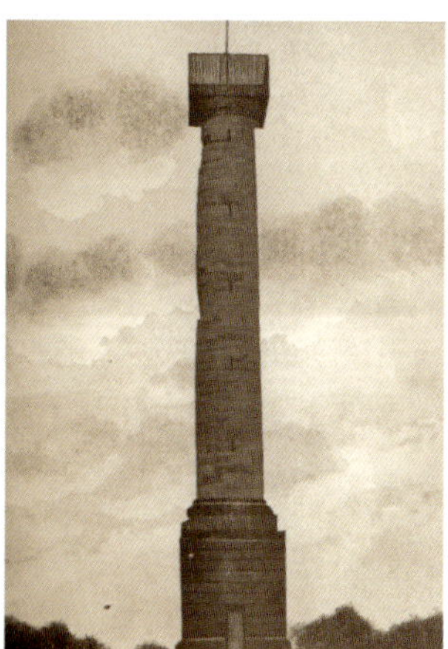

Codnor Park and the Jessop Memorial

Codnor Park works suffered a period of depression after the First World War when there was a considerable decline in trade. The antiquated furnaces were no longer economically viable, yet the Butterley Company rejected the idea of closing the works, knowing the distress that would ensue in the district. The works made a full contribution during the Second World War. The buildings were given a coat of camouflage paint as they were intended to look like houses when viewed from above by enemy aircraft. They continued producing steelwork until their closure.

A proportion of the ancient park was given as a recreational park, and here the Jessop Memorial was erected to the memory of William Jessop who died in 1814. William Jessop is best known locally for his involvement in the building of the Cromford canal and the Butterley Company, but he was employed as the surveyor or chief engineer on at least twenty-five navigational and canal projects. From 1784 to 1805, Jessop lived in Newark, Nottinghamshire, where he twice served as town mayor, but he became increasingly inflicted with a form of paralysis and died on 18 November 1814 at his home, Butterley Hall. He is buried in Pentrich churchyard. The 70-foot (21m) Doric column is a familiar landmark, and used to be a popular place for Whitsuntide rallies and summer outings. With its lightning scars, it is no longer safe to climb and can't be accessed by the public, partially due to its unsafe condition.

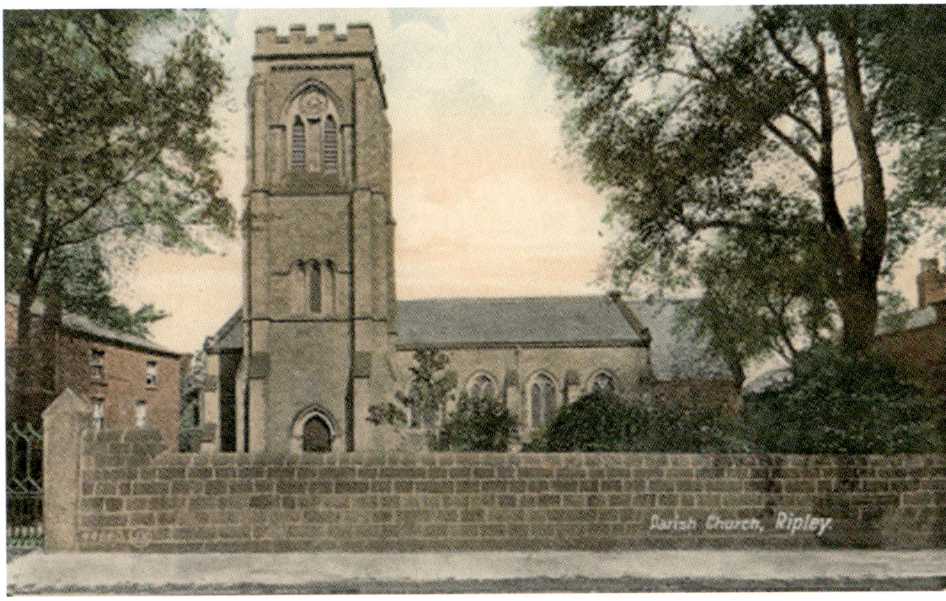

All Saints Church, Ripley

A meeting of the inhabitants of Ripley was held on 13 July 1818 to consider the pros and cons of erecting a parish church to cater for the rapidly growing population. The foundation stone was laid in 1820, and the completed building was dedicated on 27 July 1821 by the Bishop of Chester, acting for and on behalf of the Bishop of Lichfield. This period postcard can be dated prior to 1923 when the Ripley war memorial, which now stands in the church grounds, was unveiled and dedicated to the servicemen of Ripley killed in action during and since the First World War.

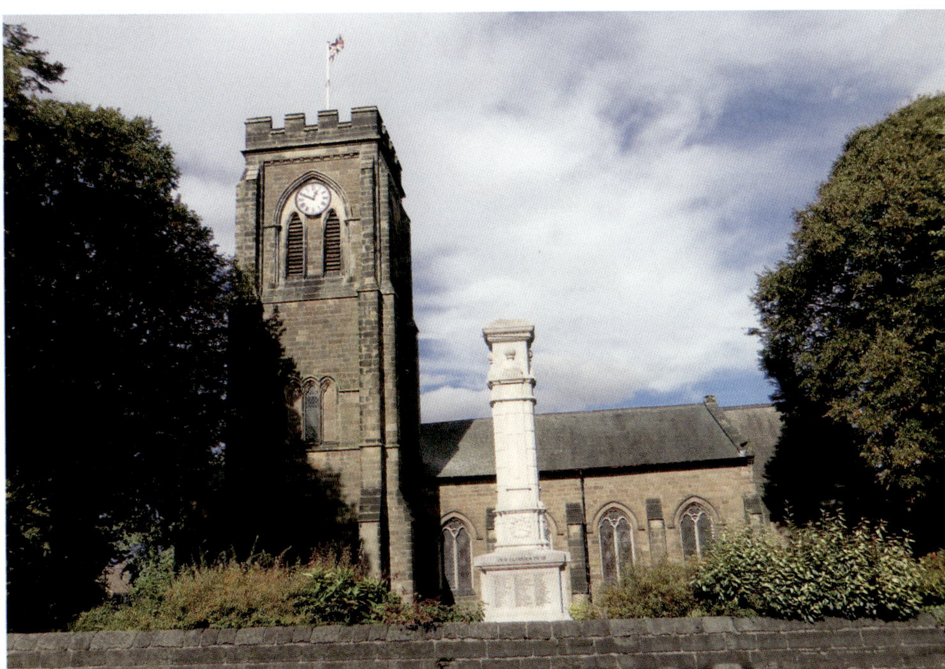

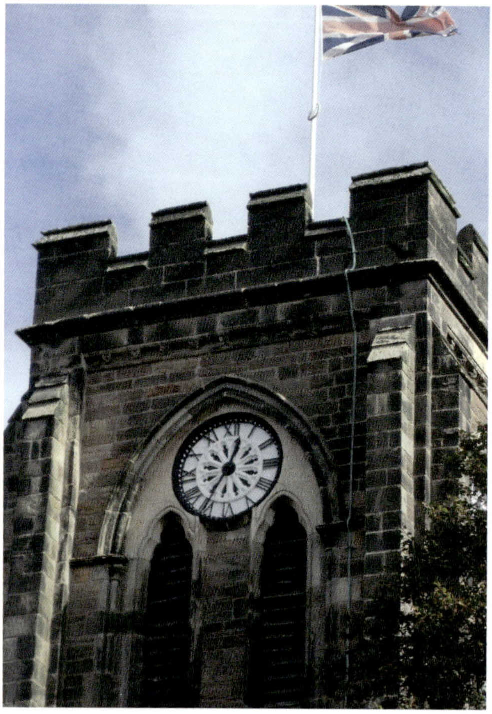

The Input of Sir John Alleyne

A report dated 1834 states that the church interior was 44 feet 11 inches by 39 feet 11 inches, with seating for 600, of which 400 were free. Sir John Alleyne joined the Butterley Company in 1852, and served as manager and chief engineer of the ironworks for twenty-eight years. His inventions made possible the production of large plates and sections in wrought iron, and his input was used when the church was enlarged and altered in 1861. Could that be why there are no pillars, arches or other forms of support across the whole roof span? Sir John was also responsible for designing and donating the church clock with its two characteristic faces. Further alterations to the church were made in 1921 and 1951, and more recently, the interior has been redesigned and all the pews removed to make the space more versatile.

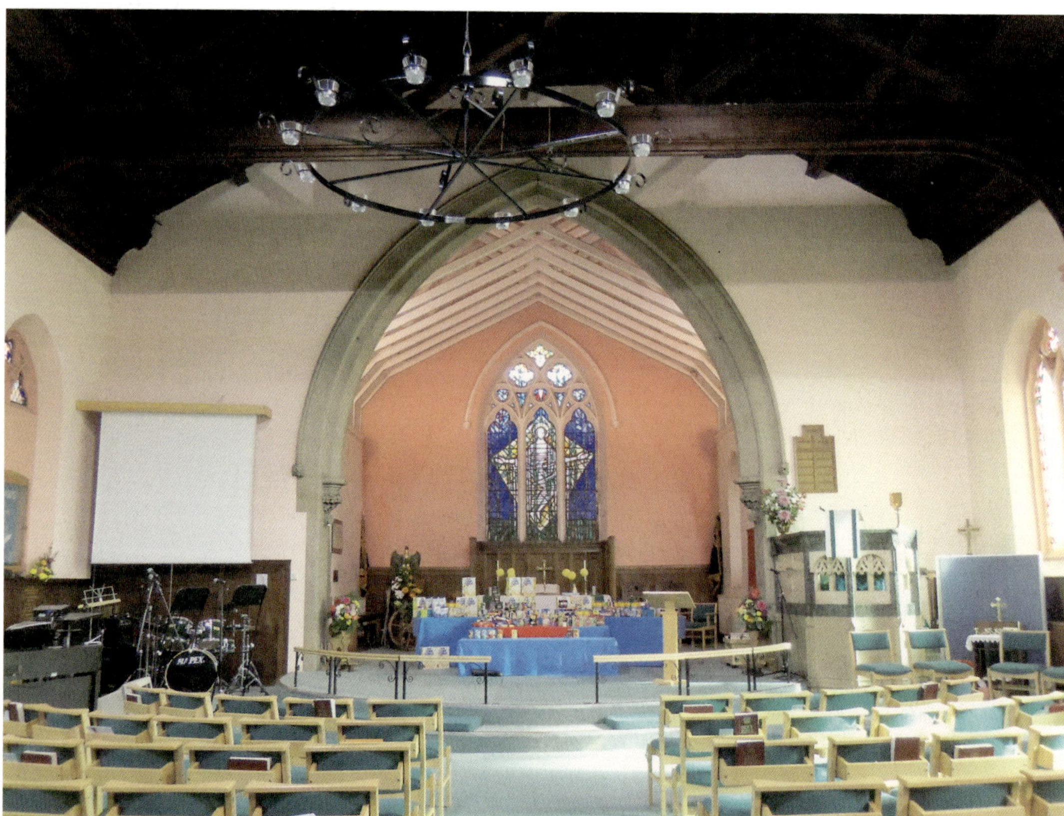

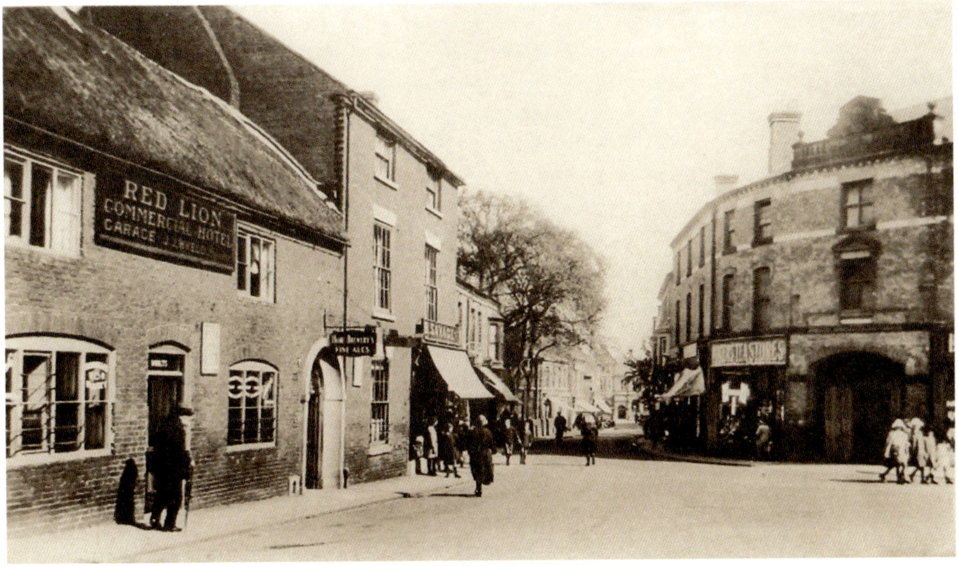

The Town of Ripley Develops

A map of Ripley from 1821, the year the church was built, shows a very small village still centred around the village green, with thatched cottages made of local stone. Four roads radiated out – Derby Road then called Wood Lane, Lowes Lane, Hartshay Lane and Nottingham Road. Situated at the heart of a rapidly developing industrial region, the population of 1,000 in 1800 had increased to 3,071 by 1851. Streets were laid out and shops, houses, schools and places of worship were built. Mining had provided an abundance of clay for brickmaking, which replaced the earlier stone. The Red Lion, White Lion and Thorn Tree inns were all flourishing coaching inns, and our 1920s photograph shows the old Red Lion on the end of Church Street is still thatched. The building was damaged by a lorry in a road accident in 1956, and subsequently demolished. A new Red Lion was built, and there's no mistaking the new build and its impressive red lion. Although the left side of the road at this end of Church Street has changed and allows us to see the church, the right side remains largely unchanged.

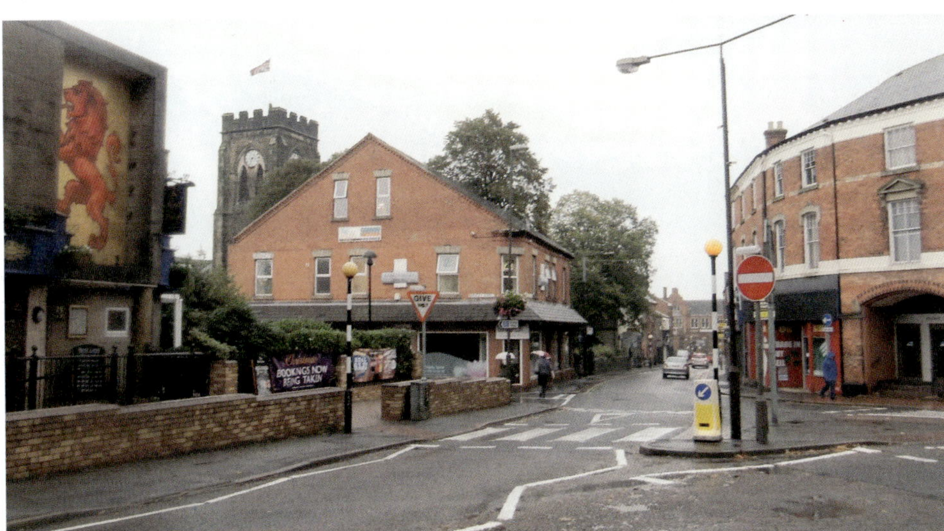

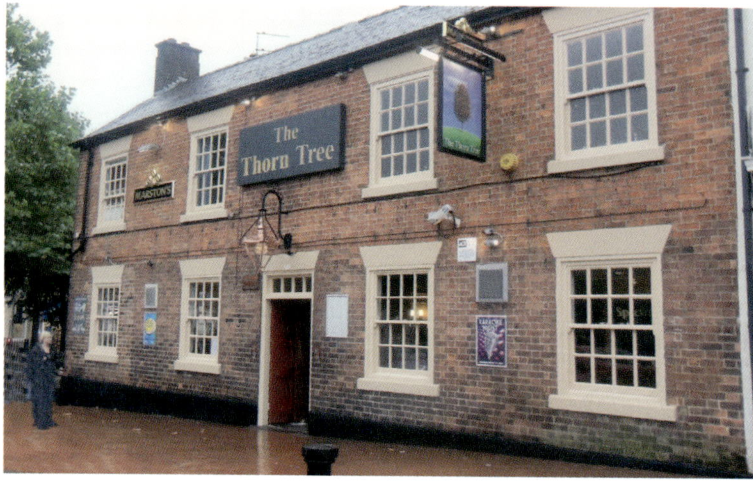

The Old Thorn Tree

On the village green stood an old thorn tree – although many called it an elm tree – that was reputed to be over 300 years old. On 14 June 1742, John Wesley visited Ripley and preached on the village green under this old tree. The occasion gets a scant mention in his journal: 'I left Sheffield, and after preaching at Ripley on the way, hastened on to Donington Park.' When it was chopped down in 1910, the trunk was taken for display at John Marshall's zoo, where this notice was attached. The tree gave its name to the nearby Thorn Tree Inn and the Thorn Tree Well, which was found during recent modernisation of the market place.

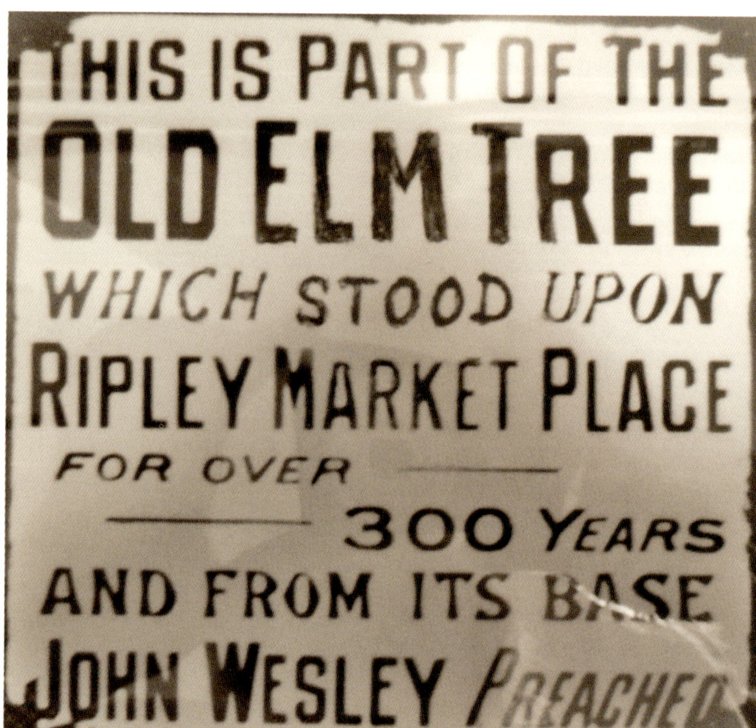

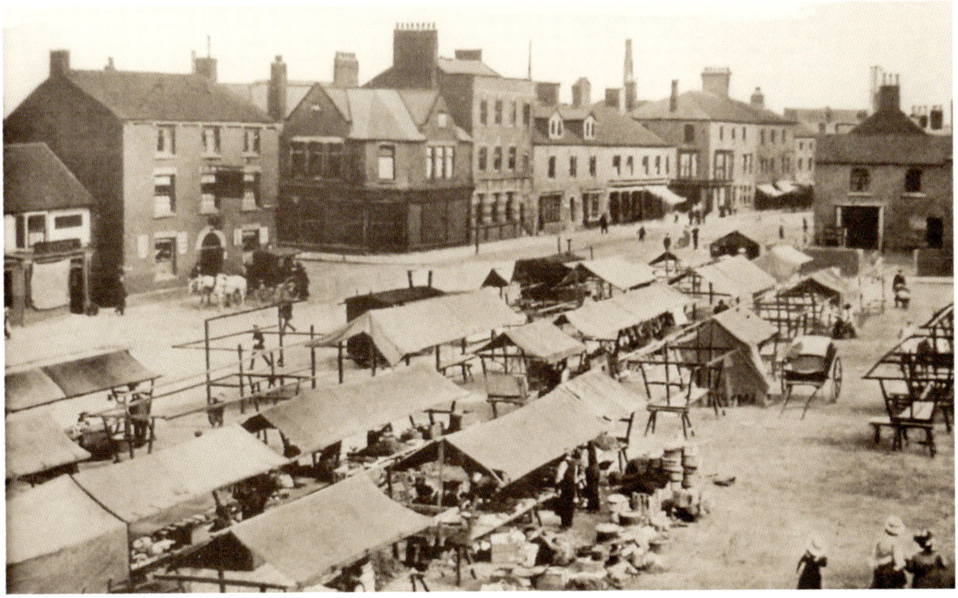

Market Place

The last of the whitewashed stone cottages around the green were demolished during the wars, and Ripley Green ceased to be green and became a market place, with market day changing to Saturday. With stalls lit by paraffin flares, the market would continue until midnight, with shoppers waiting to buy in order to get a bargain as prices dropped. This photograph of around 1900 was taken from an upper floor of the town hall looking towards the High Street. The three-storey building on the left with the white horses and carriage outside is the White Lion Inn. On the right is a section of the Thorn Tree Inn. The recent photograph is looking from the town hall steps over the same area now used for car parking and softened by trees, which have changed the scene considerably. Directly ahead is the much altered Thorn Tree Inn.

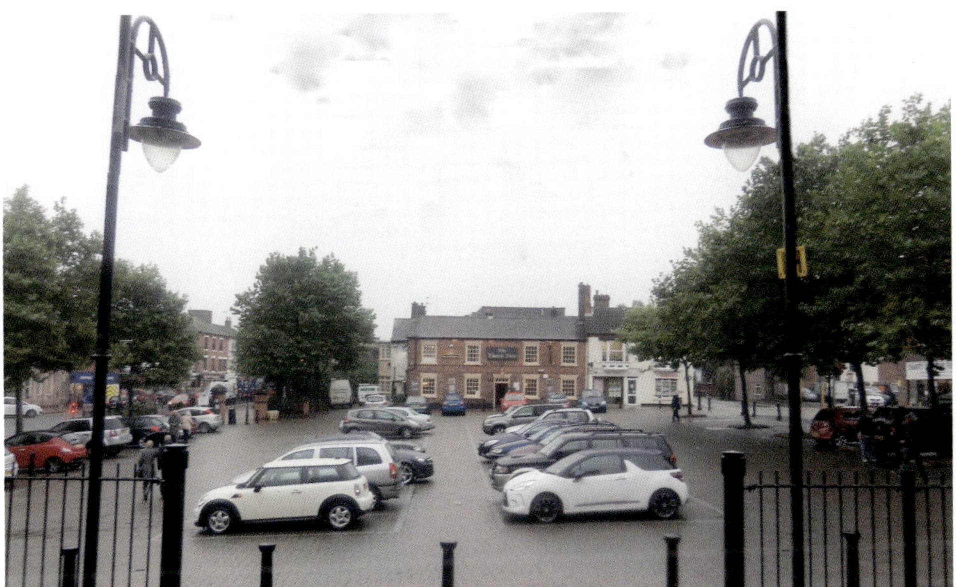

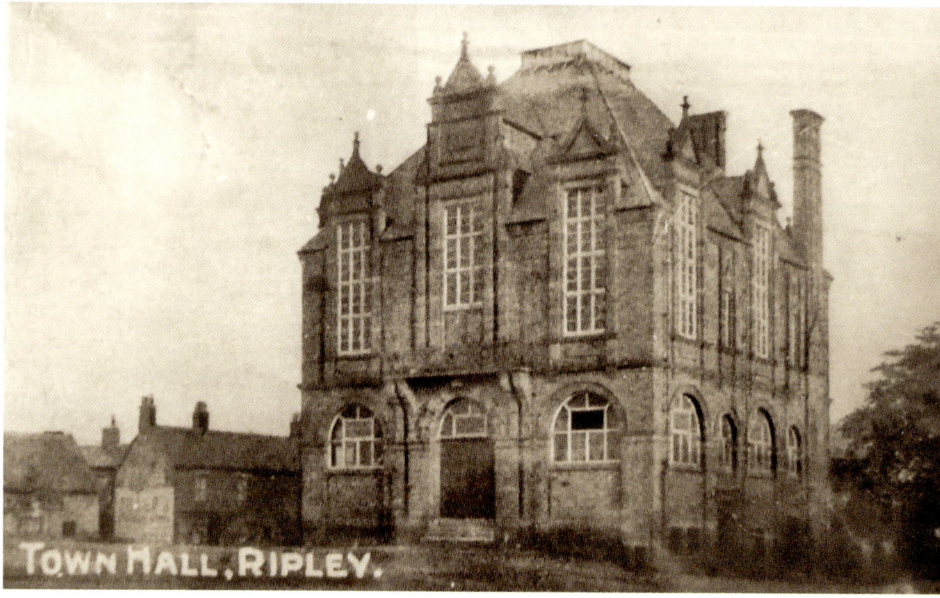

Ripley's Magnificent Town Hall

Ripley's impressive town hall, built in 1880, stands at the top of the market place. Officially opened on 2 March 1881, it had a large meeting room on the first floor for public use, council chambers on the ground floor, and the cellars had a public weighbridge and were used for market storage. The old thatched cottage on the left of the photograph of around 1900 was replaced by the memorial gardens, which were demolished in 1992 to make way for the new Amber Valley Headquarters. In March 2011, Amber Valley Borough Council announced plans to sell off or let the town hall building, which was valued at between £5 million and £7 million. There were many protests and Ripley Town Council made an offer of one penny for the premises.

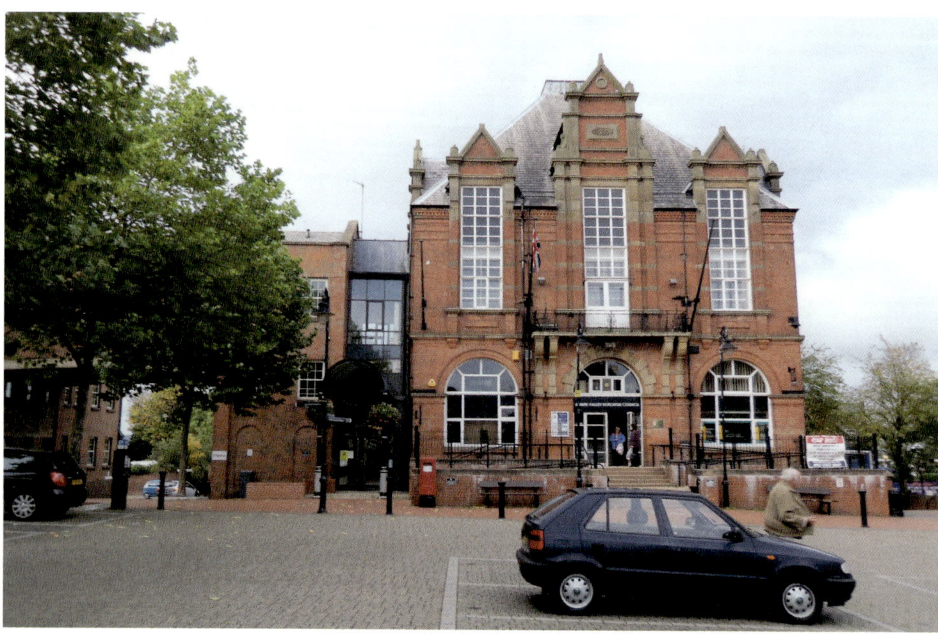

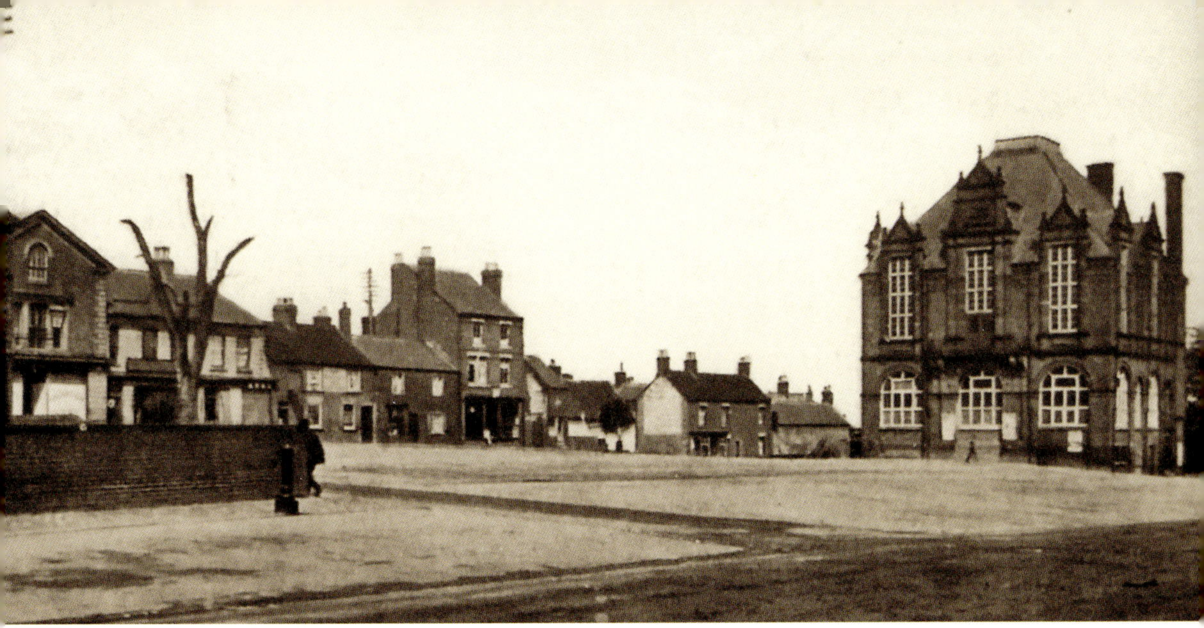

Market Place

Our period photograph makes the market place look deserted, but it was a popular meeting place until the traffic got too heavy. This early photograph shows the bare branches of the thorn tree on the left, presumably the only tree there. Recent planting has ensured that the market place is now well supplied with trees.

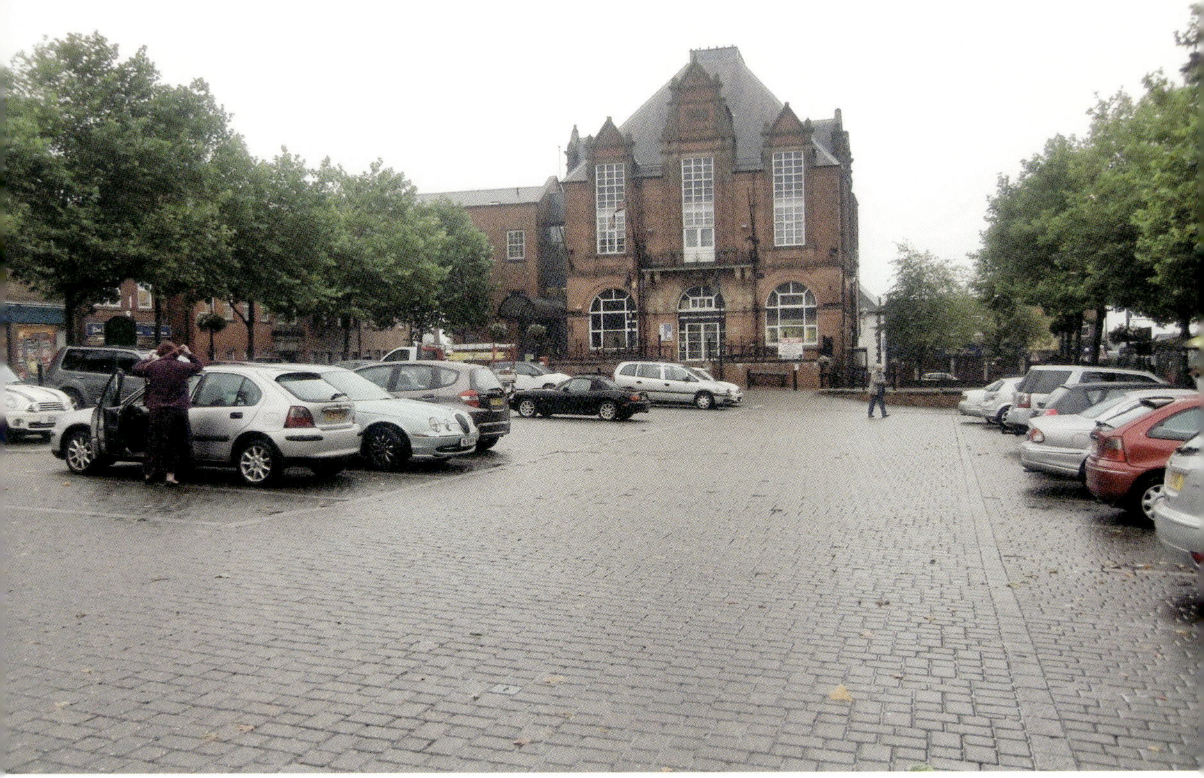

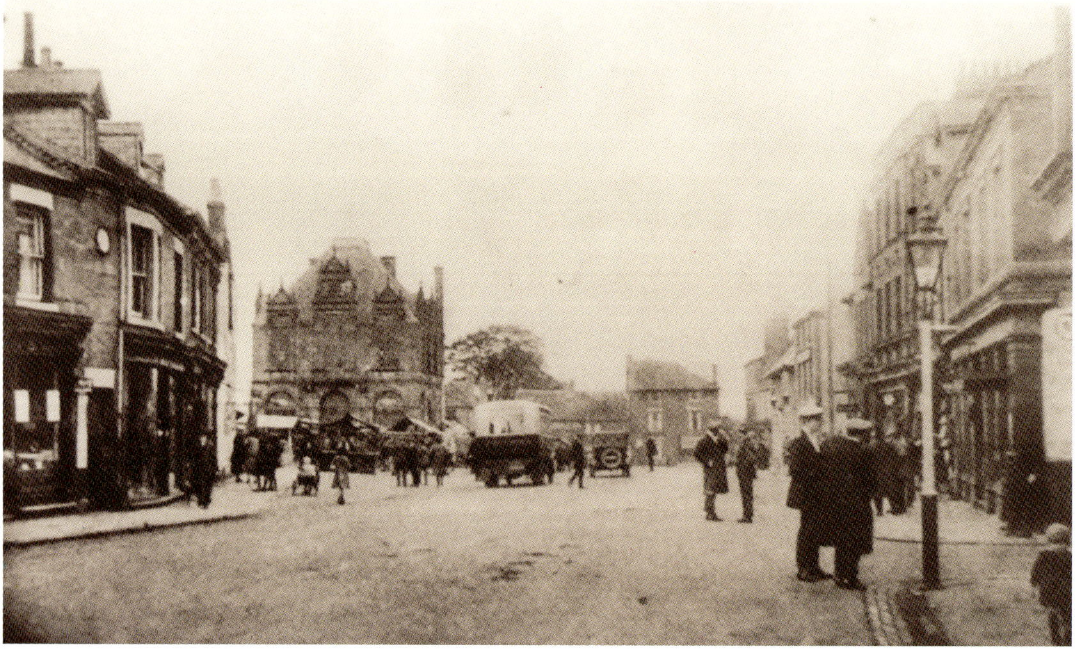

High Street

This early 1920s view of the High Street is looking north towards the market hall. The circular clock on the wall on the left was on the post office, which opened in 1857. The marks are still there but the clock, like the post office, has gone. The town hall can just be seen between the trees.

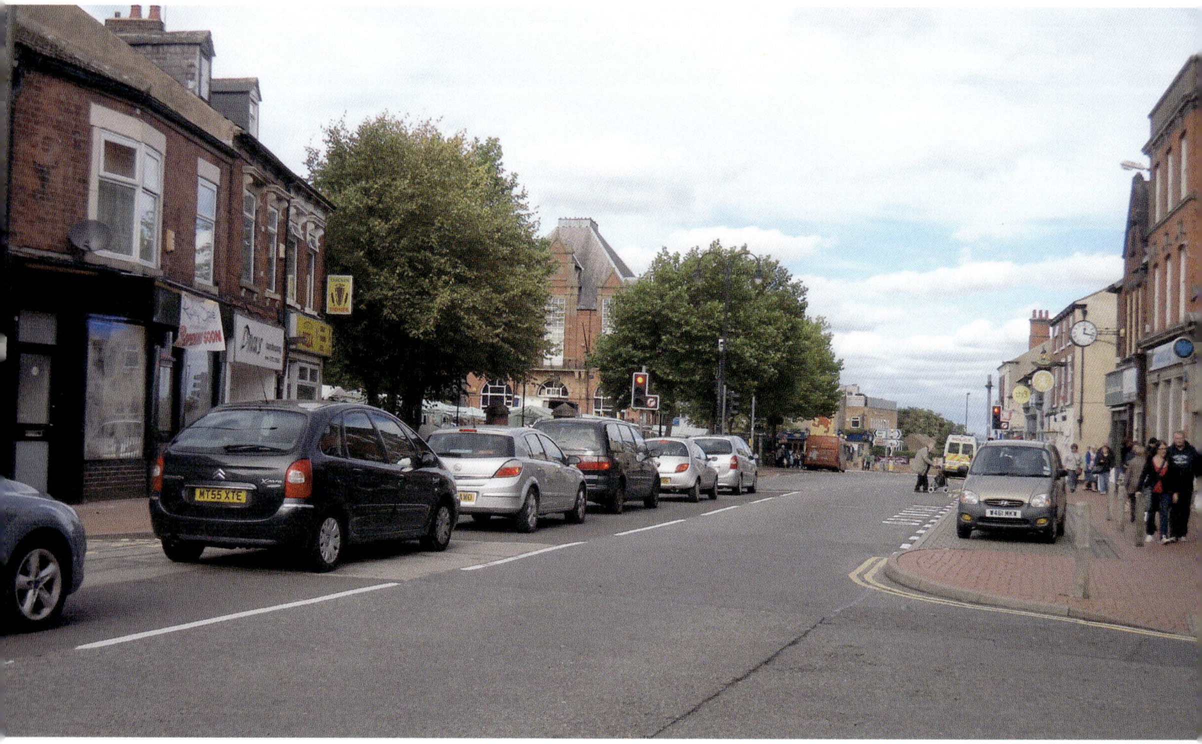

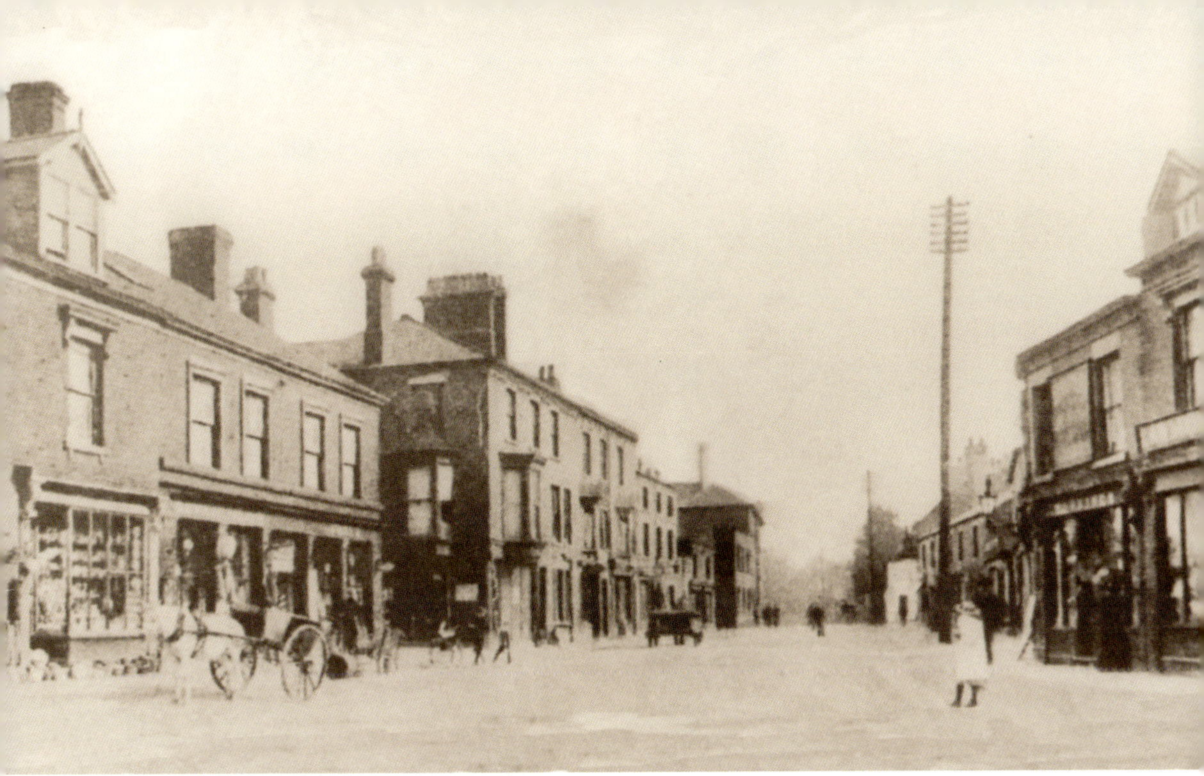

High Street

The High Street, pictured here around 1908, looks south down Derby Road from the market place.

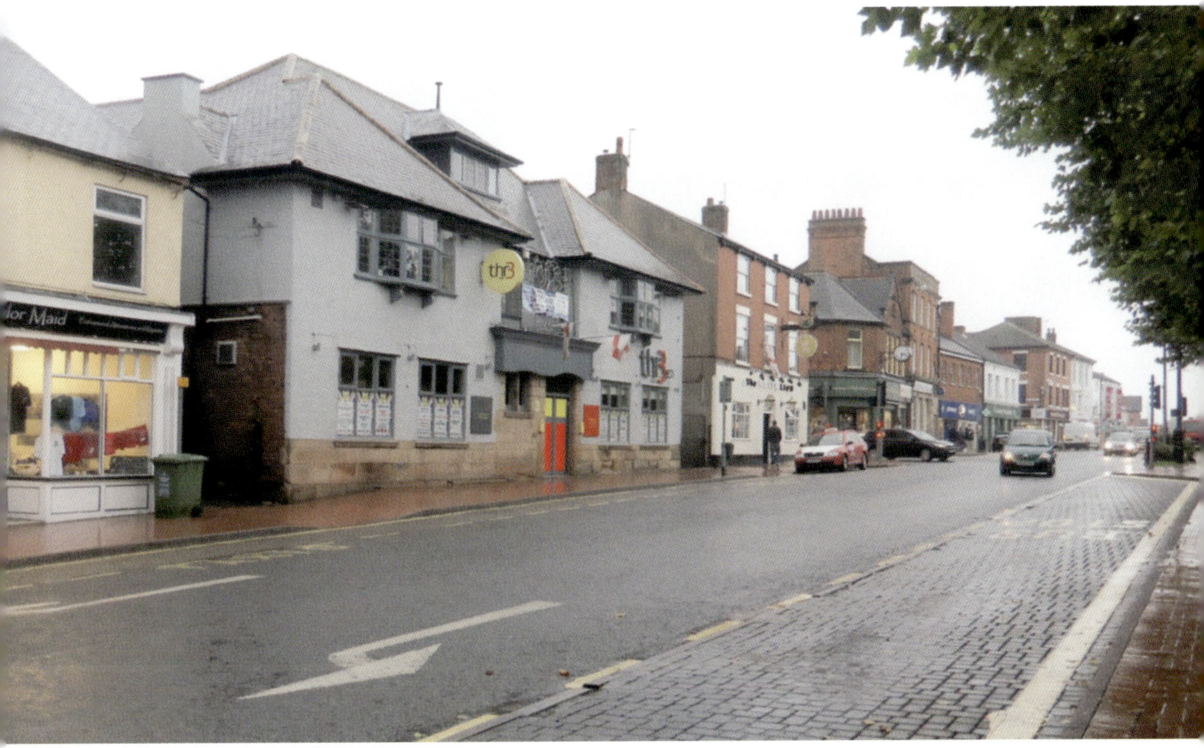

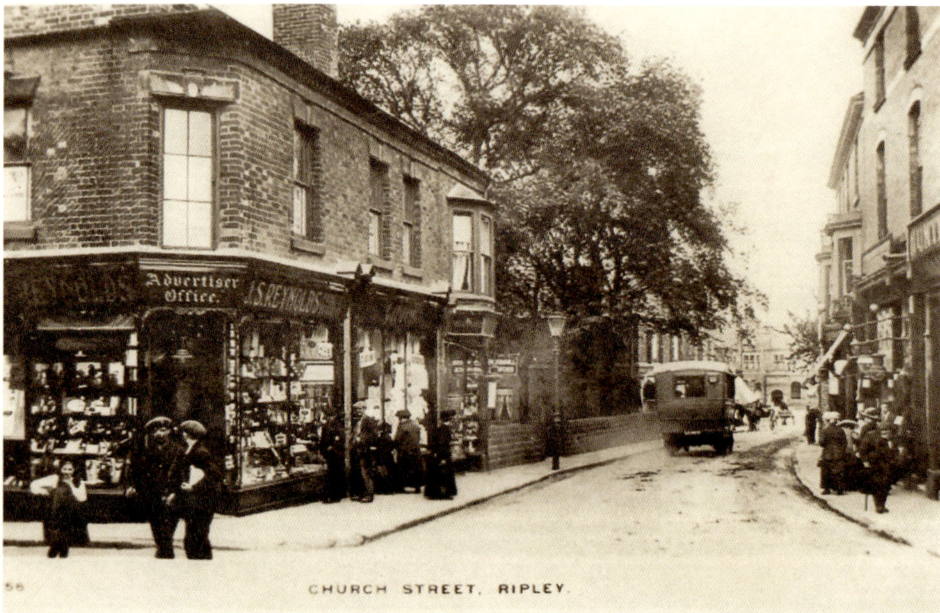

Church Street

Our photographs are looking east down Church Street, with Moseley Street going off to the left. The church is amongst the trees after the block of shops on the left. Note the black faces of the guys in the early photograph. They would have worked at a local pit. Pithead baths were not introduced until the 1930/40s, but even then many colliers refused to use them and continued to travel home in their pit dirt.

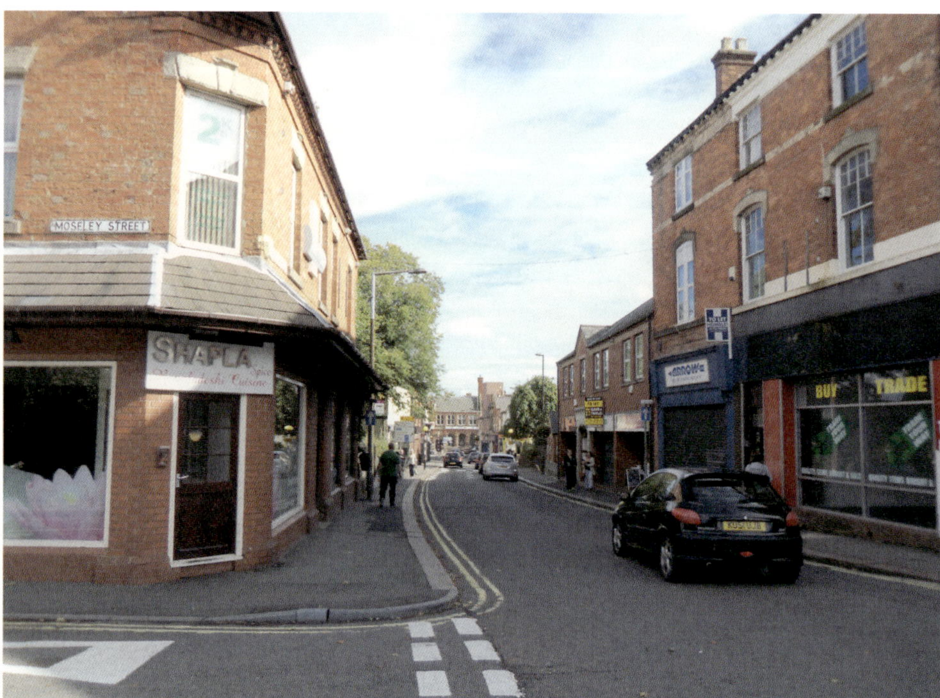

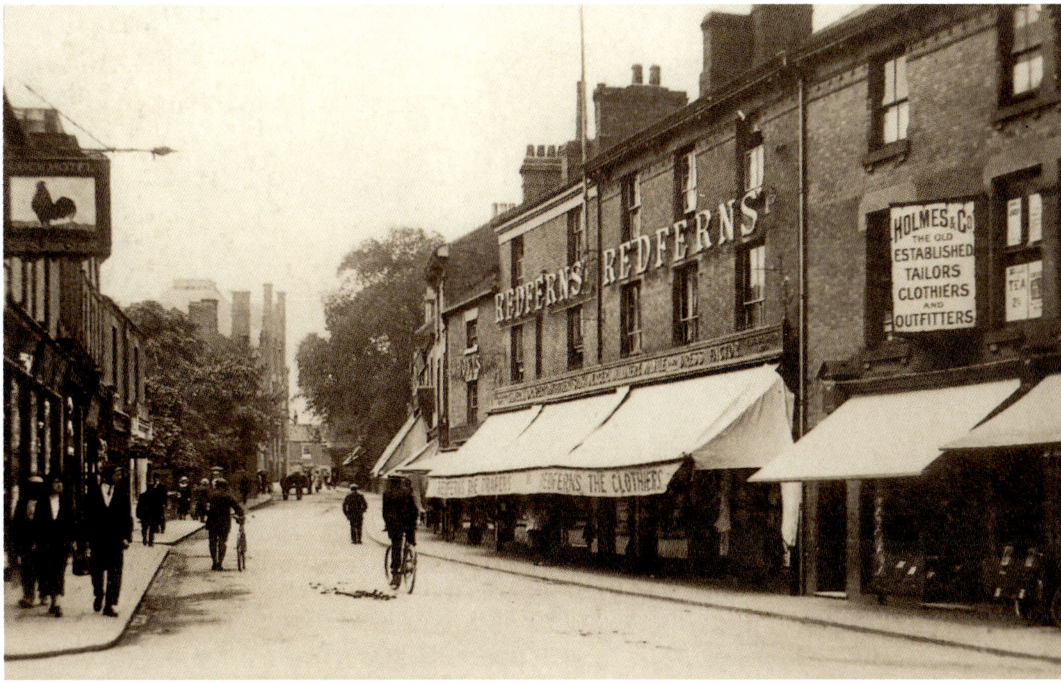

Church Street

Our photographs are looking west along Church Street, which is now part of the one-way traffic system. In the distance is the town hall and although the sign for the Cock Inn in the mid-1920s photograph is obvious, the inn is still there in the modern view, but the signage has changed. On the right, Redferns clothiers is next to Holmes & Co., tailor, clothier and outfitter, but by the 1970s, these shop premises had been taken over by Woolworths. They are now Amber Value.

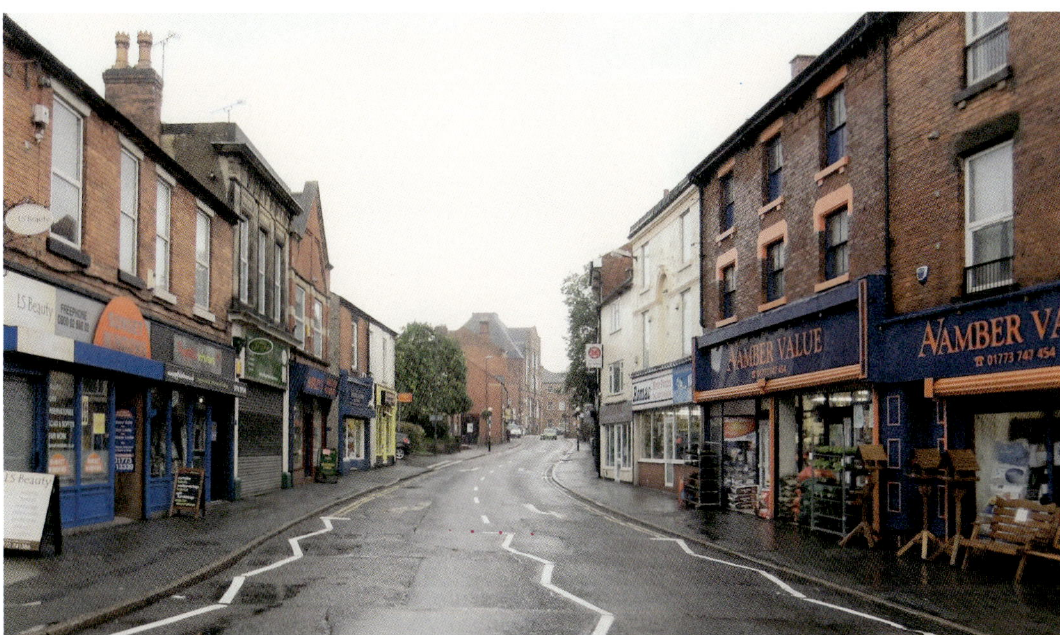

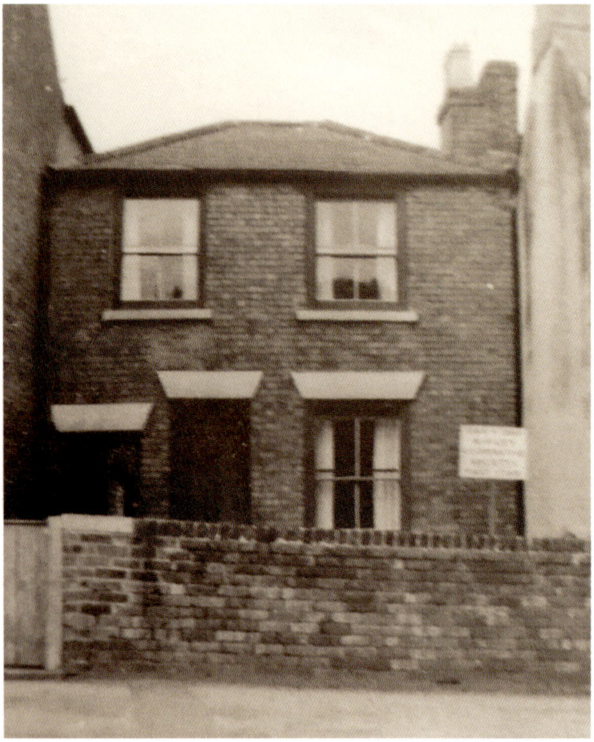

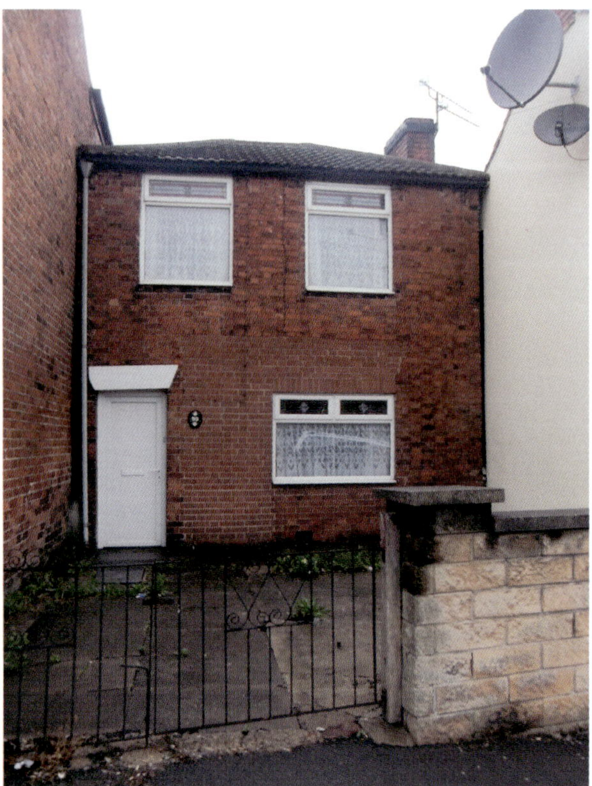

The Butterley Co-operative Society

In 1860, George Atkin, a workman at the Butterley Company, broached the subject of starting a store with his colleagues. Thirty were enthusiastic, and in March 1860, they met at the home of Patrick Parkin, No. 99 Butterley Hill, to discuss opening a store with profits shared between the members in the form of vouchers to be exchanged for goods. They collected 5*s* in subscriptions, drew up rules and called themselves the Butterley Co-operative Society. By August, they had £14 and the use of the two front rooms of Patrick Parkin's house for the shop. It was open for business from 8 p.m. to 11 p.m. every Friday and Saturday night, with the members running the store, weighing out food and serving behind the counter. Like any business, they experienced difficulties, but by 1862 they were making a profit and membership had risen to fifty-five. The following year, they moved to their first purpose-built shop on Lowes Hill, next door to the Blue Bell Inn.

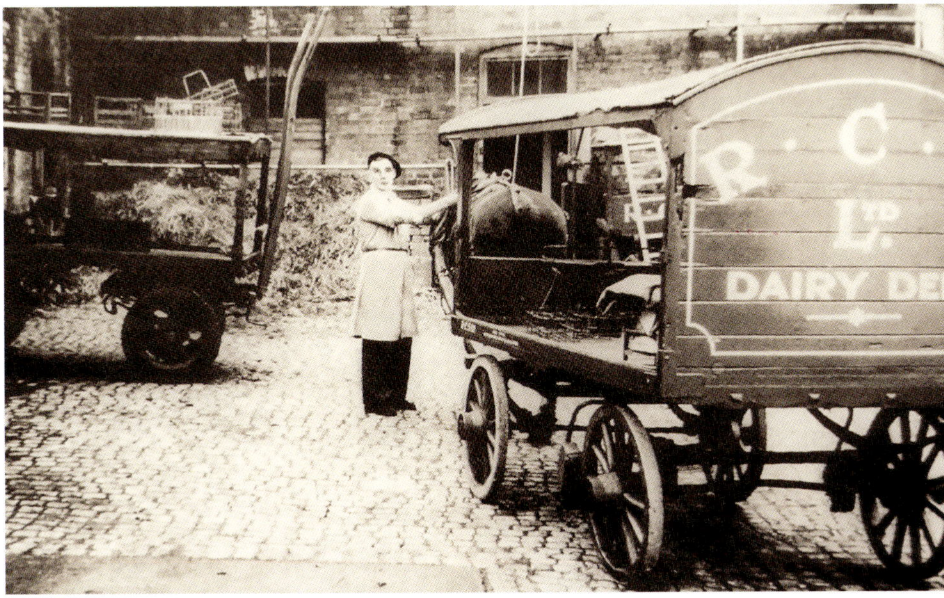

A Change to the Ripley Provident Industrial & Co-operative Society Ltd

On 11 December 1872, the society was re-registered as The Ripley Provident Industrial & Co-operative Society Ltd, with its registered office at Park Corner, Ripley. Branches were opened in the surrounding villages, and by 1885 sales had reached £1,000 per week and there were 2,000 members. Sales of foodstuff was supplemented by butchery, drapery, footwear and tailoring. Our photographs show the early delivery vehicles. The Ripley Co-op horse-drawn milk floats were retained until the 1960s. In 1888, vouchers were abolished and dividends were paid in cash. A penny bank was opened to encourage thrift, and in 1889, a scheme was inaugurated to assist members in purchasing their own dwellings. The co-operative moved into a succession of premises that grew larger with the committee's ambitions.

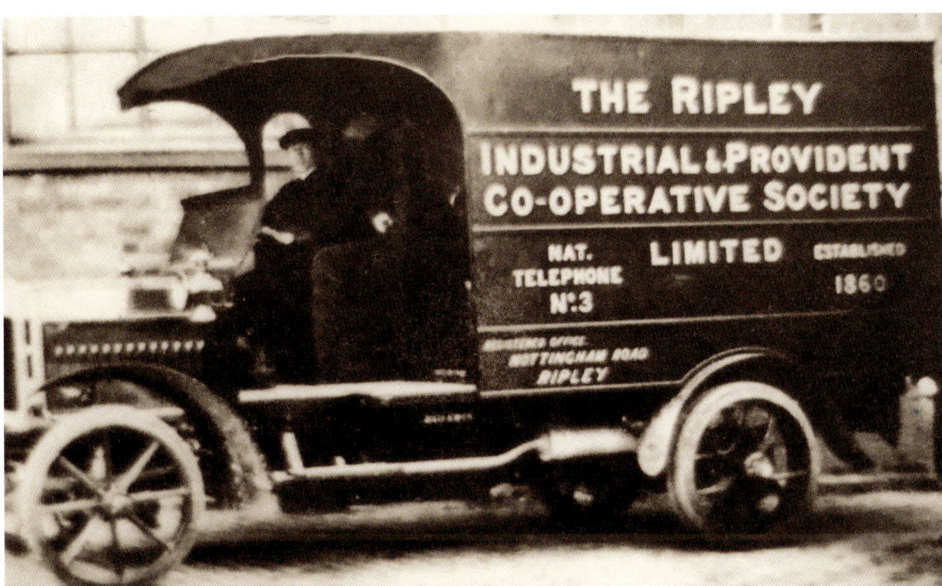

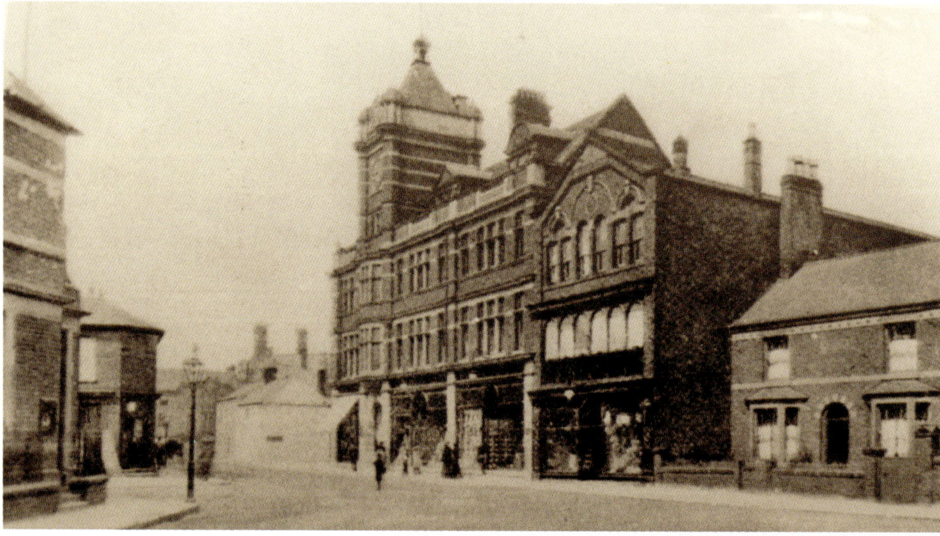

Co-op Square

By 1900, membership of Ripley Co-operative was 7,359, with twenty-three branches. In 1902, sales topped £250,000 pounds, and the following year the society moved into the newly built Nottingham Road Central premises. The site became known as Co-op Square. Topped by its 82 foot-high clock tower, it was the finest shopping centre for miles around. The Co-op saw steady expansion, despite rationing during the war years and the depression of the 1920s. When the society celebrated its 75th anniversary in 1935, Mr William Bradshaw, a director of the Co-operative Wholesale Society (he became president in 1936), addressed a public meeting with the words, 'there is no movement in this country that is so capable of helping, or is so effectively helping the mass of people to a better life'. Ripley's largest building closed as a Co-op in 1980 and is now looking for a new identity.

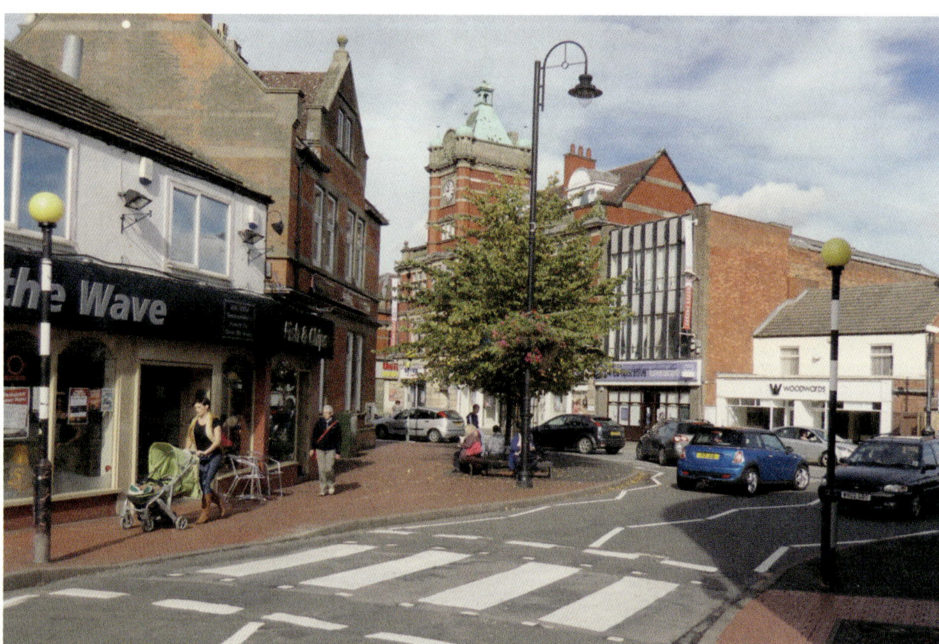

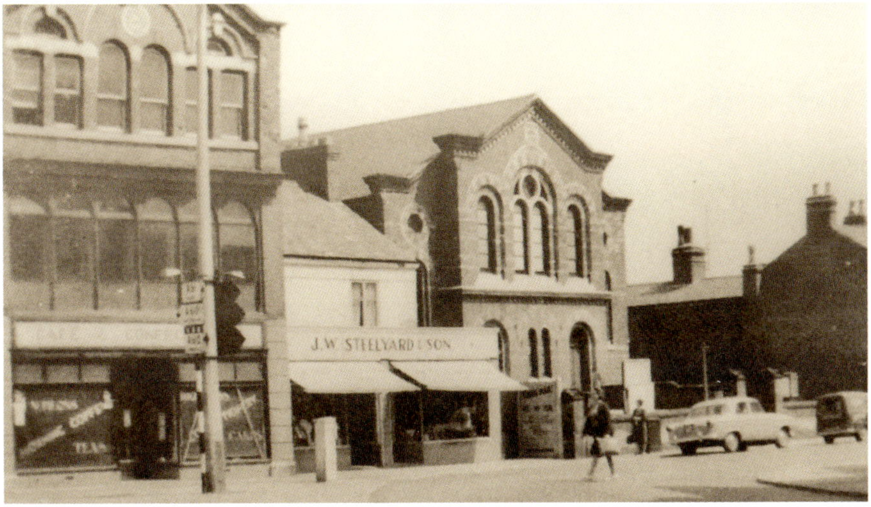

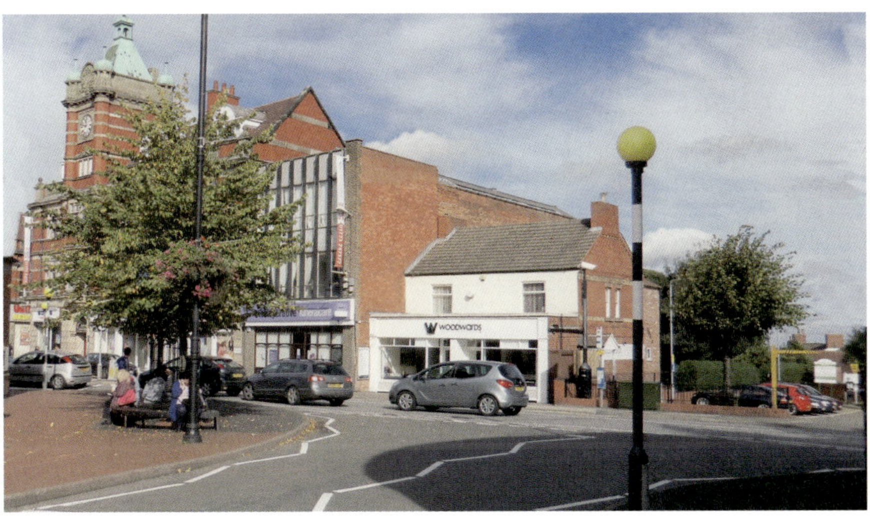

The Ebenezer Chapel and Manse

The early photograph is a continuation of the previous ones. The building with the pointed apex was the Co-op café and confectioners, and is now a funeral directors. Seemingly squashed between the Co-op buildings and the Ebenezer United Free chapel is the chapel manse. In this photograph it has been painted white and is Steelyard & Son, gentleman's outfitters. It is now an independent financial advisers. Next to the manse was the Ebenezer chapel, built by the Primitive Methodists in 1860 on a previous quarry site, which they purchased for £180. The cost of the building, which could accommodate 600 people, was £1,700. As well as providing a place of worship, the chapel also had schoolrooms and a large room for concerts and meetings. It closed as a church in 1962/63 when it was purchased by the Co-op. For twenty-five years, it housed the county library before they moved to the purpose-built building on Grosvenor Road. The small bore heating system that had been installed in the chapel when it was built in 1860 was one of the oldest systems still in working order, with the original pump still in use. When the building was demolished in 1974, the land was flattened to form a car park, but the heating system was taken to the Science Museum in London.

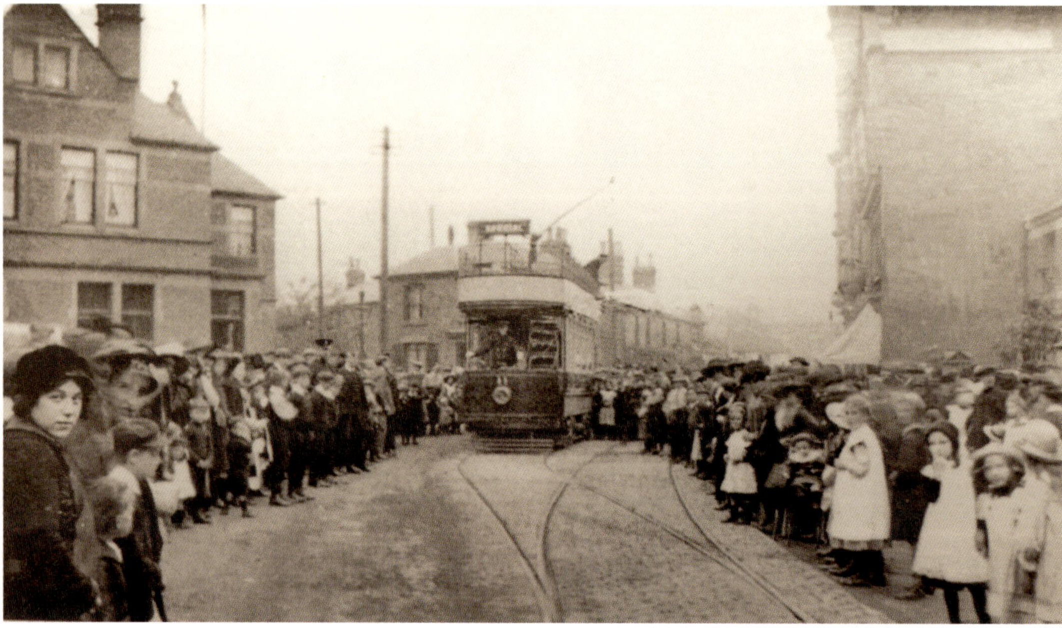

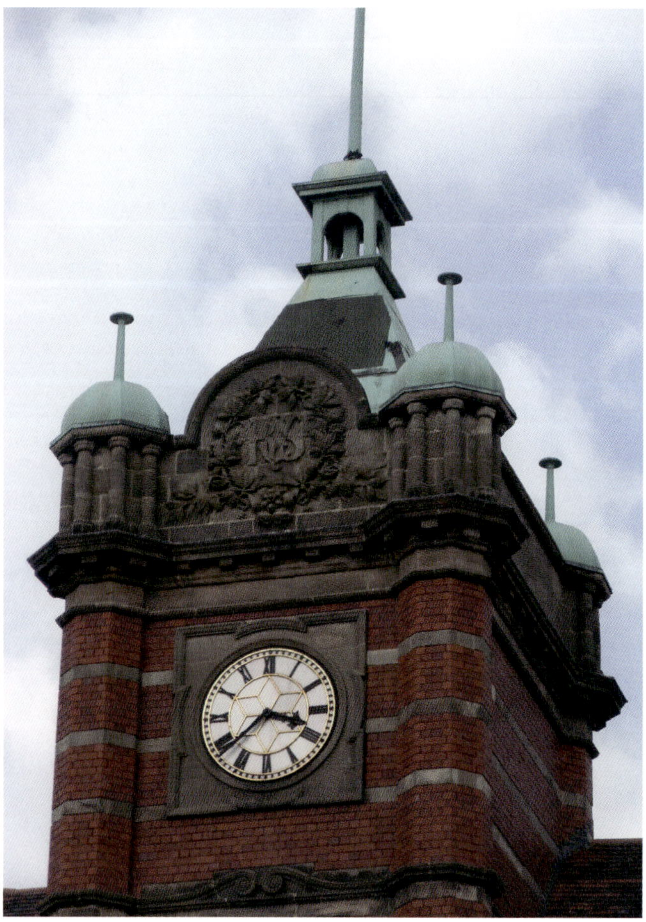

The Ripley Rattler

Co-op Square with its lofty 82 foot-high clock tower became the terminus of the Nottinghamshire and Derbyshire Tramway Company, which opened on 1 January 1914, and ran from here to Upper Parliament Street, Nottingham. Crowds turned out to witness the event, as our first photograph viewed from Nottingham Road shows. The route was 11 miles long, which made it the longest tramway in the world, and although it was intended to continue through to Alfreton, it never did. The rails were laid on granite sets, a source of considerable vibration and noise, gaining the tram the name of the Ripley Rattler. Around 1922, the manager decided the 13-ton rattlers were too noisy and ordered that the axel boxes be stuffed with sawdust. This was effective for a short time, until the material spontaneously combusted and the idea was abandoned.

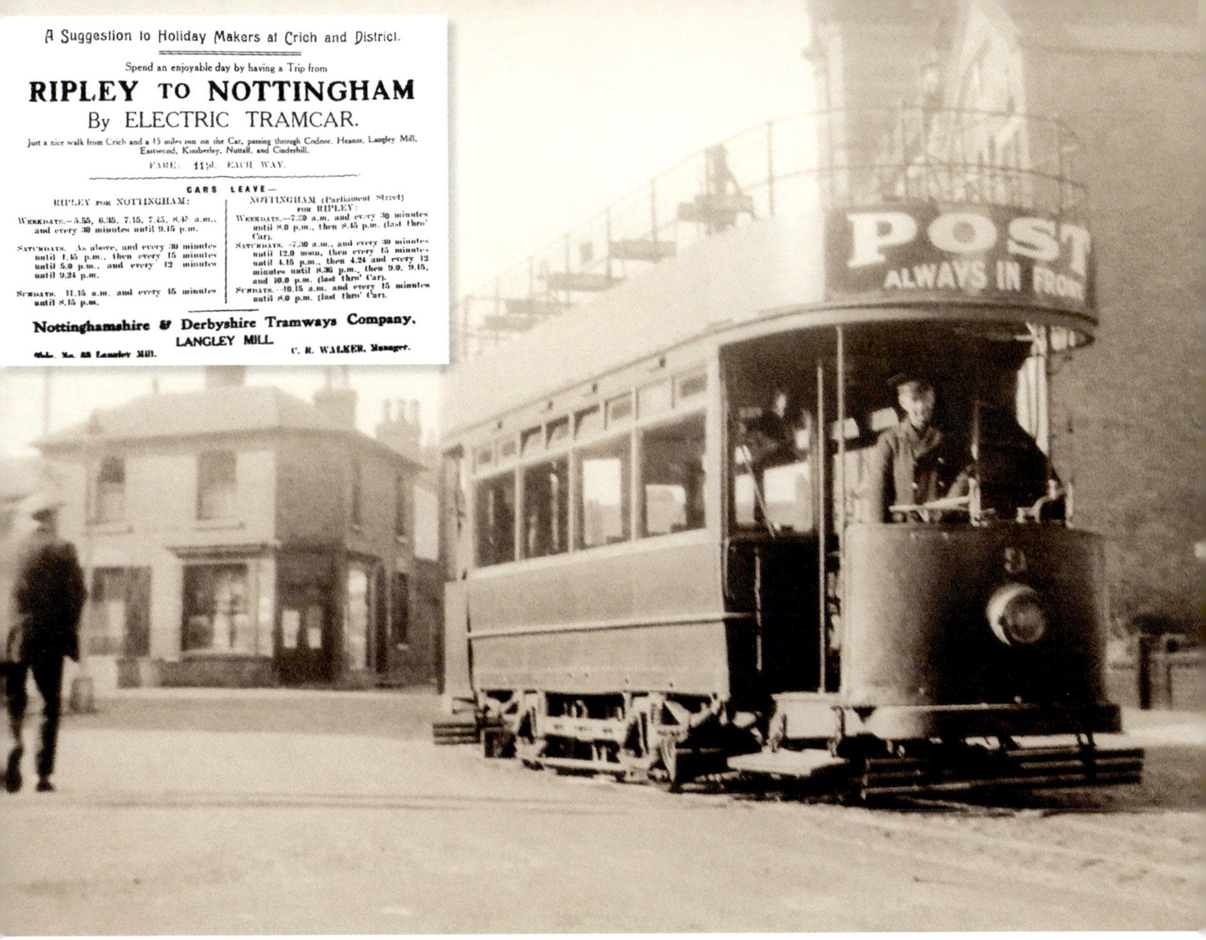

A Suggestion to Holiday Makers at Crich and District.

Spend an enjoyable day by having a Trip from

RIPLEY TO NOTTINGHAM

By ELECTRIC TRAMCAR.

Just a nice walk from Crich and a 15 miles run on the Car, passing through Codnor, Heanor, Langley Mill, Eastwood, Kimberley, Nuttall, and Cinderhill.

FARE: 11½d. EACH WAY.

CARS LEAVE—

RIPLEY FOR NOTTINGHAM:

WEEKDAYS.—5.55, 6.35, 7.15, 7.45, 8.45 a.m., and every 30 minutes until 9.15 p.m.

SATURDAYS. As above, and every 30 minutes until 1.45 p.m., then every 15 minutes until 5.0 p.m., and every 12 minutes until 9.24 p.m.

SUNDAYS. 11.15 a.m. and every 15 minutes until 8.15 p.m.

NOTTINGHAM (Parliament Street) FOR RIPLEY:

WEEKDAYS.—7.30 a.m. and every 30 minutes until 8.0 p.m., then 8.45 p.m. (last thro' Car).

SATURDAYS. –7.30 a.m., and every 30 minutes until 12.0 noon, then every 15 minutes until 4.15 p.m., then 4.24 and every 12 minutes until 8.36 p.m., then 9.0, 9.15, and 10.0 p.m. (last thro' Car).

SUNDAYS.–10.15 a.m. and every 15 minutes until 8.0 p.m. (last thro' Car).

Nottinghamshire & Derbyshire Tramways Company,

LANGLEY MILL.

Tele. No. 88 Langley Mill. C. R. WALKER, Manager.

Tickets Please!

This is just one reason why it was considered the most dangerous tramway in Britain. Over most of the route, the single-track tramway ran on the crown of the road, compelling other road users to keep to the kerb. Accidents were regular. Trams came off tracks, and got wedged under bridges. A woman was killed saving a child from being run over, and a man called Harry Parkin was honoured for bringing a runaway tram to a halt. With 316 passing places all on the left of the main track, passengers had to endure a succession of swinging movements, which were more violent the faster it travelled. One double-decker tram crashed into the church wall, throwing the passengers travelling on the top deck into the graveyard. The tram was so notorious that D. H. Lawrence, who lived near the line and regularly used it to visit relatives in Ripley, wrote an amusing short story entitled *Tickets, Please*. He also described Ripley as the dreariest place on a dreary tram route. The tram ran from 1913 to 1932, and our photograph of around 1931 shows the tram outside the Ebenezer chapel, Nottingham Road. The route was converted to trolleybuses, which began running on 5 October 1933 and continued for twenty years, until 1953.

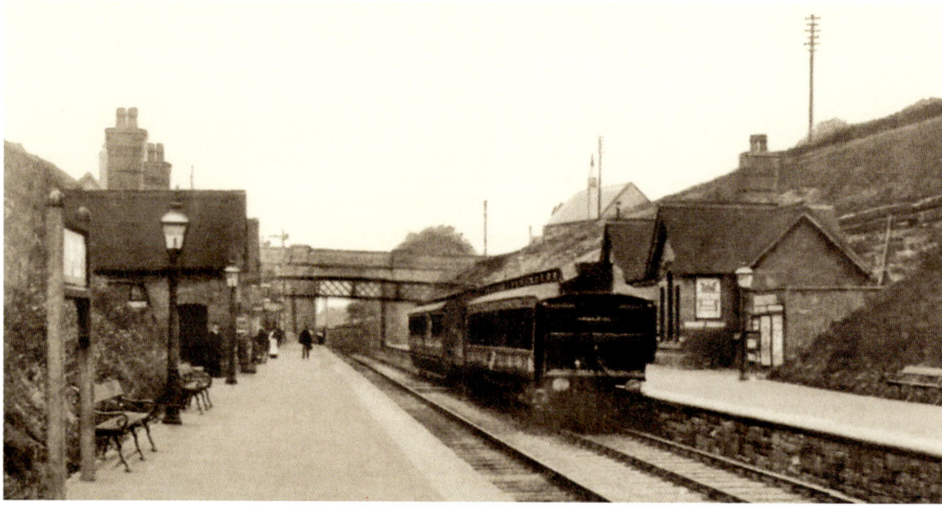

Ripley Railway Station

On 1 September 1856, the Midland Railway Company opened a passenger line with Ripley station in a deep cutting just a short walk from the busy shopping centre. The railway was faced with fierce competition when a reliable bus service began operating between Ripley and Derby, a route that ran alongside the A61 within sight of all the stations on the line. Towards the end of the 1920s, competition from the Trent bus service was too intense and passenger services were withdrawn from June 1930. The station saw occasional crowded trains for the holiday excursions to popular seaside resorts like Skegness, Rhyl and Blackpool, which continued until the station closed on 1 April 1963. It was suggested that Ripley Urban District Council should buy the station buildings, but their response was: 'We have enough white elephants already!' Clowers used the building for storage for a while, but the abandoned railway station rapidly took on an air of neglect and fell into a sad state of disrepair until it was demolished in 1985.

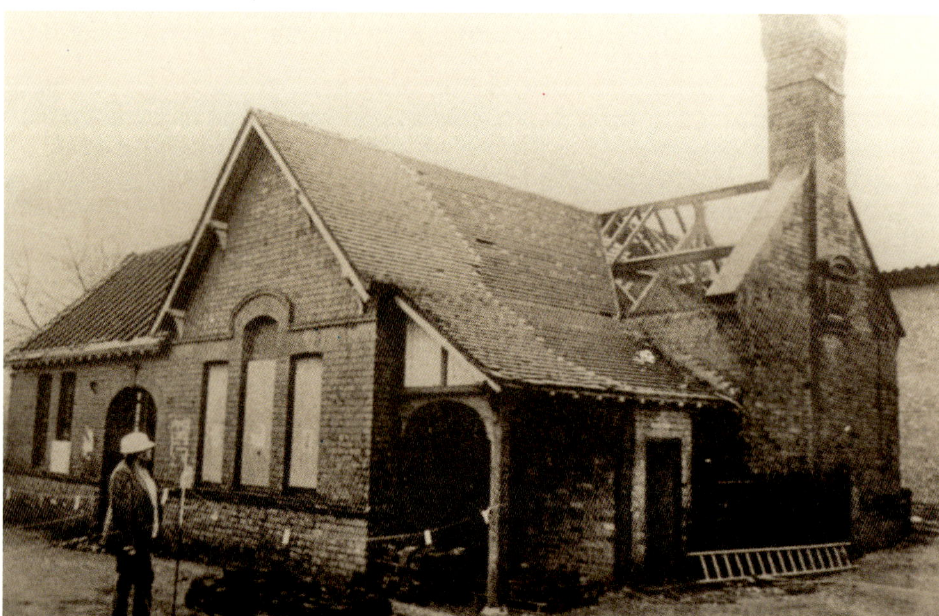

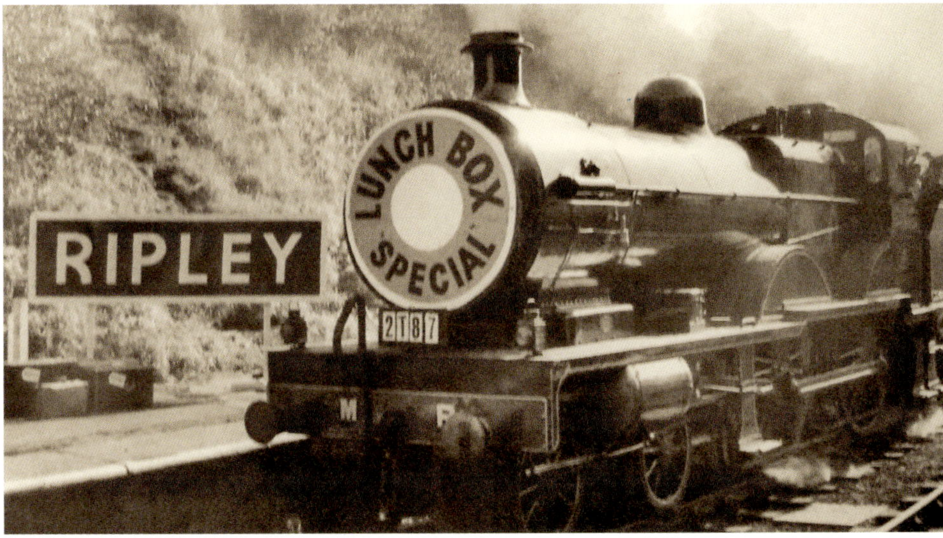

Lunchbox Special

In 12 October 1961, the ITV programme *Lunchbox* was filmed at Ripley. Five hundred people travelled on a special train from Derby to Ripley, where more spectators crammed the platforms, the bridges and vantage points on the embankment. The broadcast went out live from Ripley station. The format of *Lunchbox* pioneered daytime broadcasting, which was still in its infancy, and was the forerunner of many of the shows that followed. It was presented by Noele Gordon, who is credited to be the first woman to be seen on colour television in the 1940s, and the first woman to interview a prime minister – Harold Macmillan. *Lunchbox* ran from 1957 and came to an end in the summer of 1964 after 2,000 episodes. It was axed to make way for a new daily soap opera entitled *Crossroads,* in which Noele Gordon took the role of motel owner Meg Richardson. Ironically, Jane Rossington, who played her screen daughter Jill, was born a few miles away in Derby in 1943. There's now no sign of the railway or station, there is just a walkway that runs straight through the town in a cutting known as Greenway.

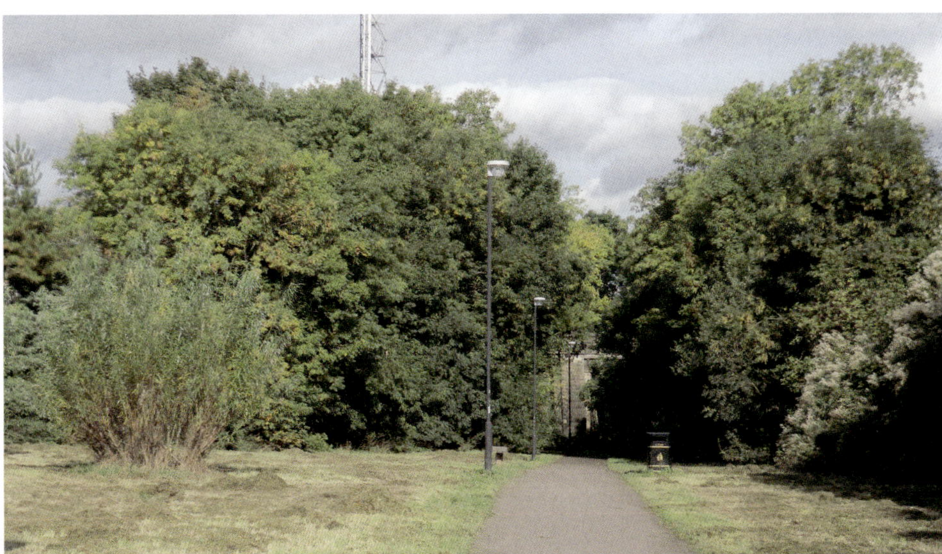

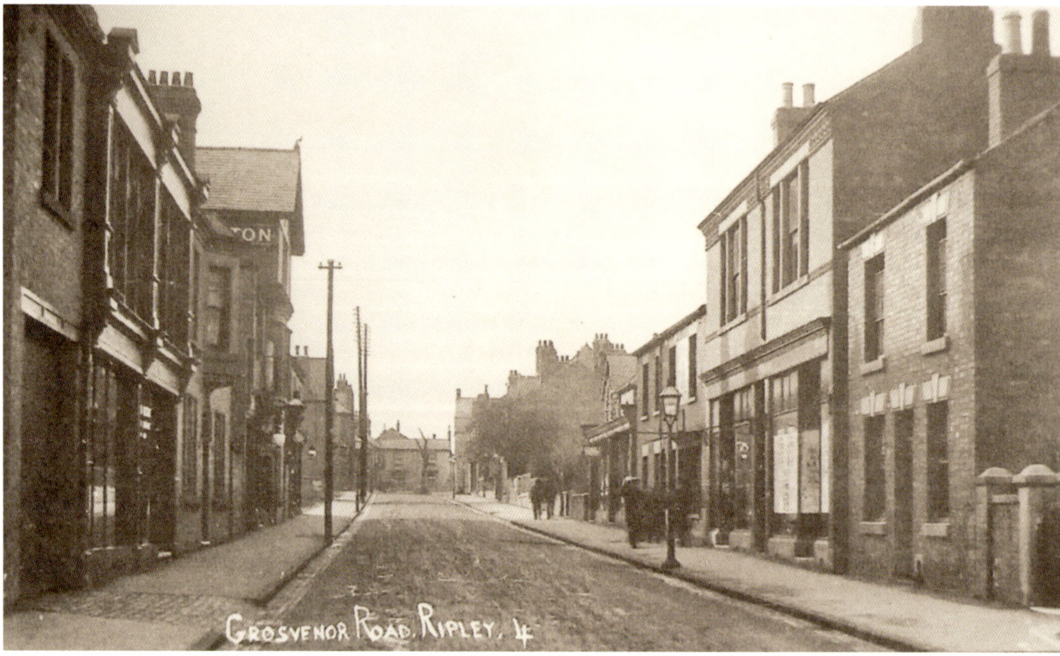

Grosvenor Road

These photographs show Grosvenor Road looking west towards the market place from Co-op Square. The first, taken around 1922, shows Cope's house on the right, which was at one time one of the numerous chapels in the area. Further along is the library, which replaced what was a maternity home. The street is now part of the busy one-way system.

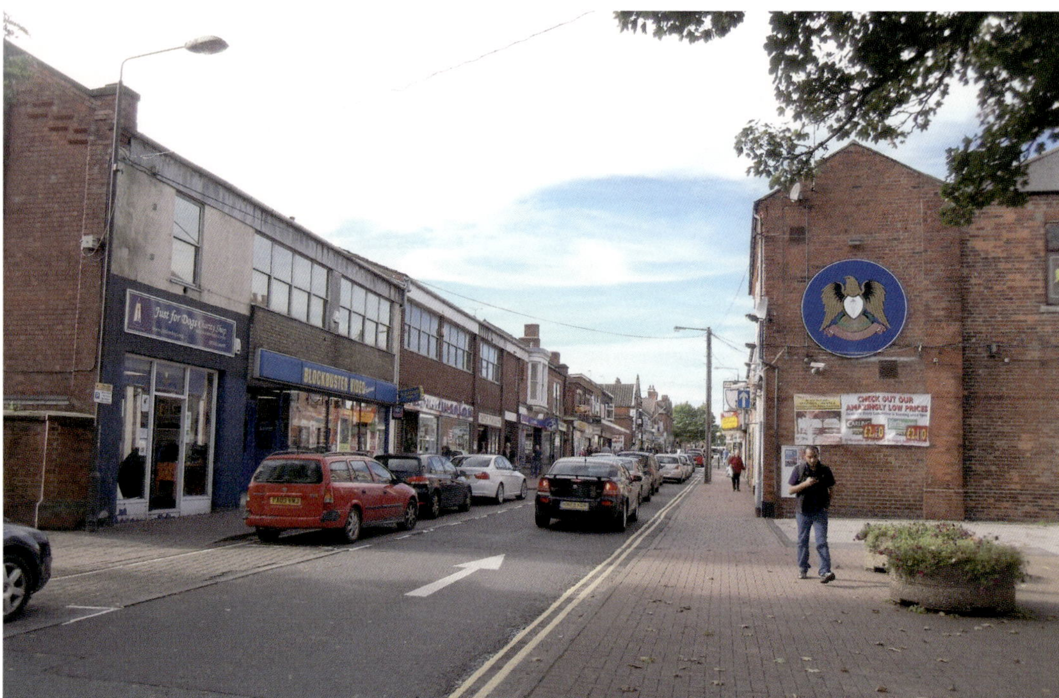

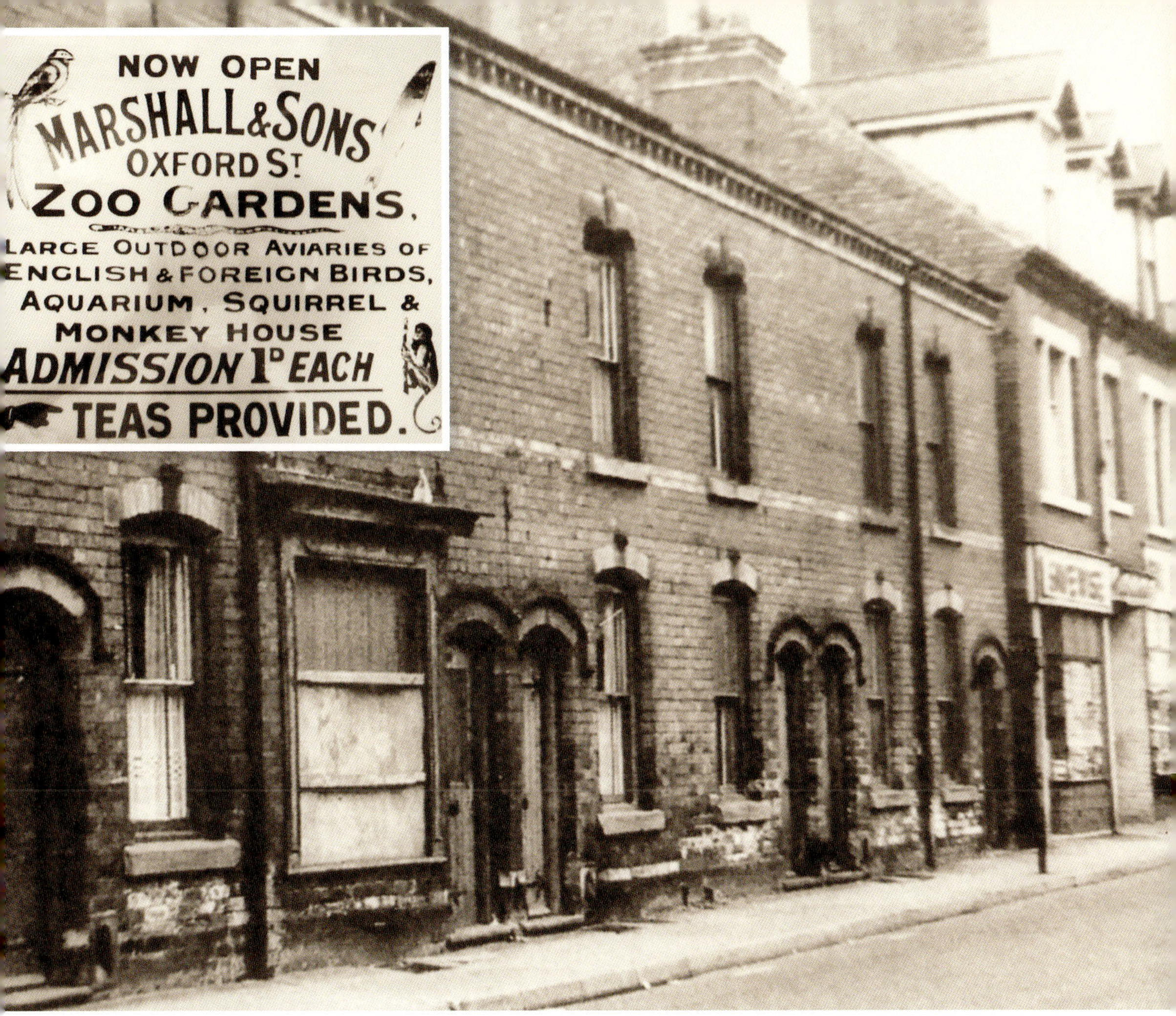

The Enterprising John Marshall

This row of houses at the bottom end of Oxford Street was demolished in 1977, but the converted house with its enlarged window was where entrepreneur John Marshall started his business. John Marshall arrived in Ripley in 1888 with a capital of £20 and opened his first shop, selling watches and jewellery. By 1900, he had moved further up Oxford Street and, alongside his Wedding Ring King shop, he opened a hardware store. Adjacent to the other two family shops, John Marshall's wife, Sarah, ran a confectionery shop and the combined backyard of these three shops was converted to a zoo in 1904. Entry was 1*d* via a passage between the shops. Alongside the children's roundabout, waxworks display, stuffed animals and refreshment room were aviaries, a reptile house, and squirrel and monkey houses. Roof gardens and platforms among the chimneys added more space and a view over Ripley's rooftops. The zoo closed due to a shortage of food for the animals during the First World War when its largest exhibit, a bear, was put down by the local pork butcher. It was skinned and the hide cured to make a rug for the Marshall home.

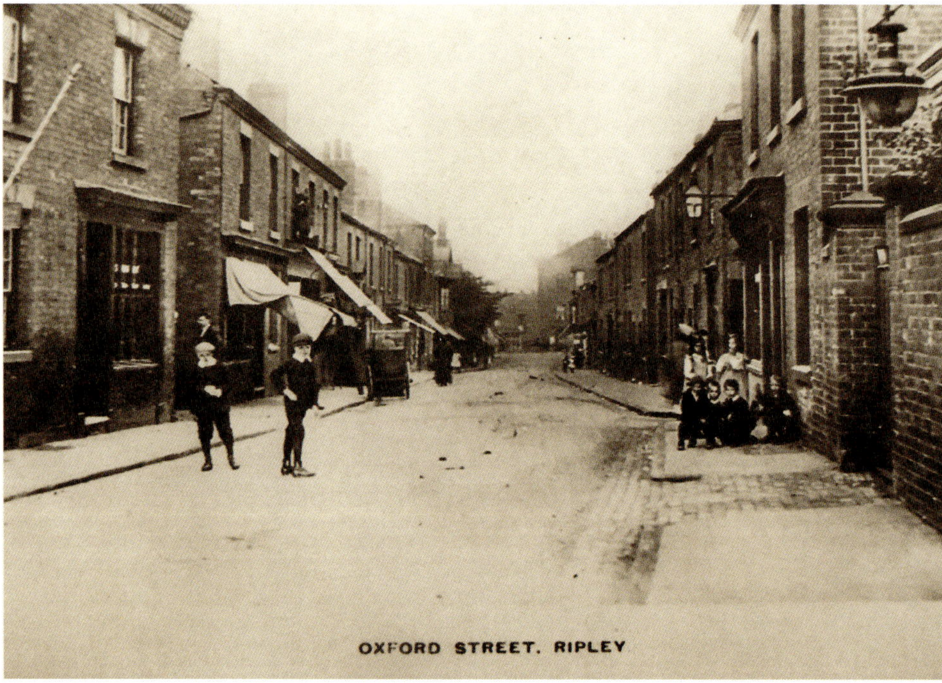

Oxford Street

Now pedestrianised, Oxford Street is a busy shopping street in the centre of Ripley, much changed from this early photograph. The only recognisable building is at the far end at the junction of Oxford Street and New Street. This distinctive building with the apex roof was the Co-operative Hall, built in 1879 and now Ripley Glass.

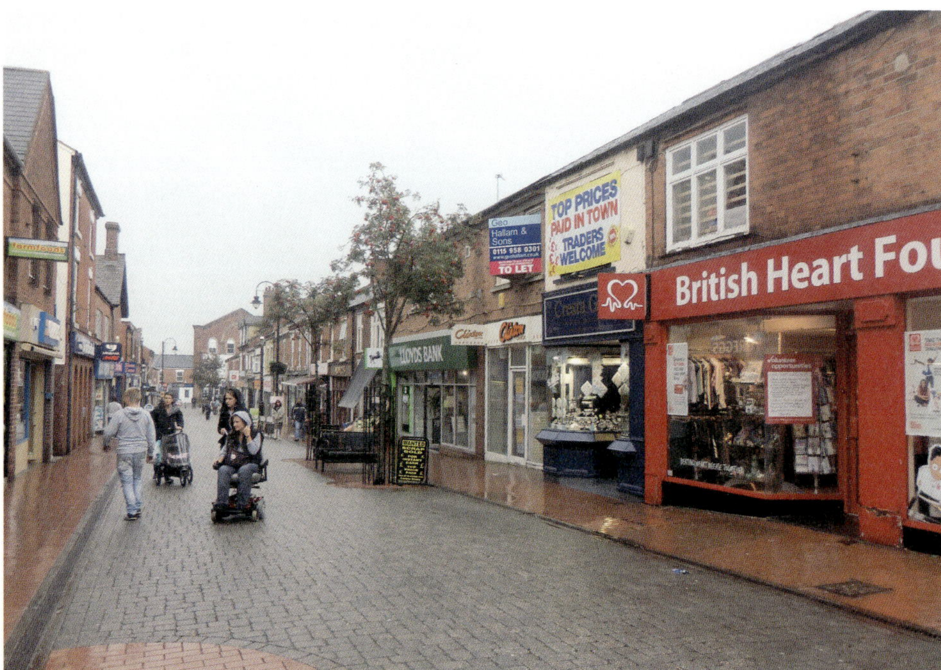

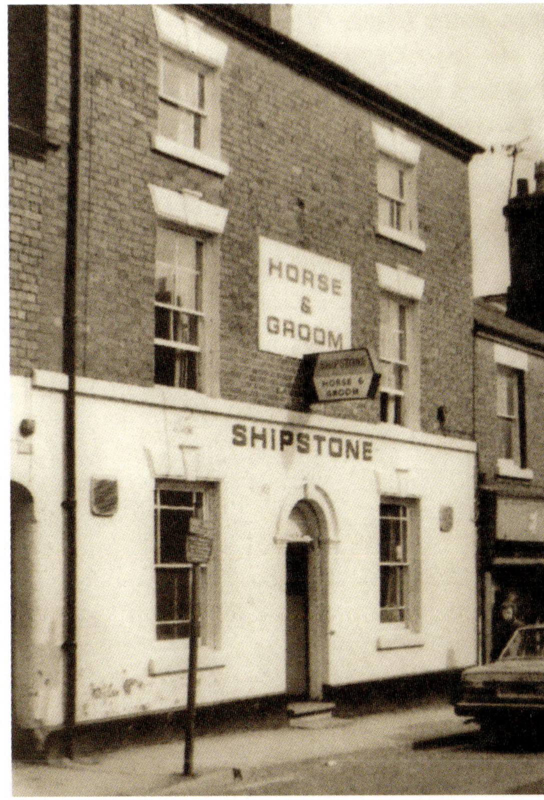

From Pub to Bank

Not all Oxford Street is unrecognisable. The dignified three-storey red-brick building halfway along was the Horse and Groom public house until it closed in 1980. After a complete revamp, it was converted to its current use as Yorkshire Bank premises.

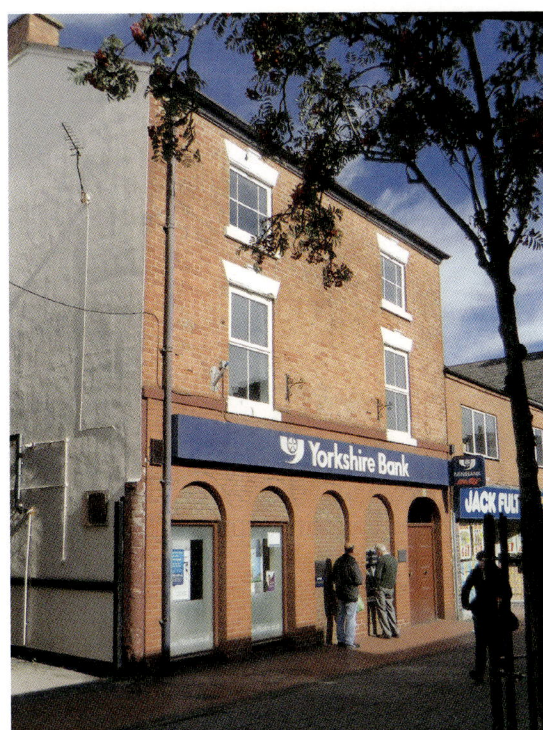

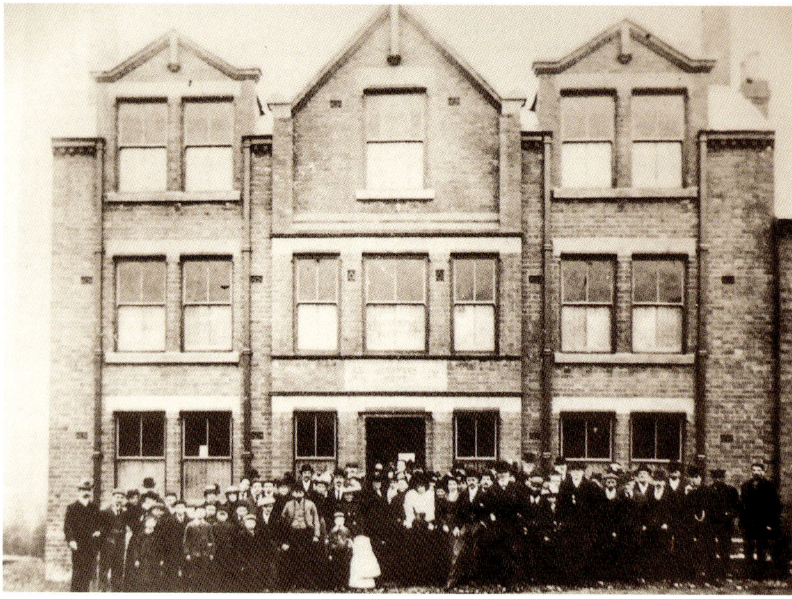

Workmen's House

Construction of the tramline of the Nottinghamshire and Derbyshire Tramway Company began in February 1913 and employed 1,000 labourers. Some 20,000 tons of earth were removed. They used 10,000 tons of cement and 12,000 tons of granite sets, on which 1,500 tons of rails were laid. New water mains and sewers were dug at the same time, and not only did this cause great inconvenience, it also caused an accommodation crisis for the navvies working on the projects. Their work was hard and they had a reputation as drunken, violent troublemakers. These men needed housing, and although this was usually temporary, the companies mining the area's rich mineral resources also needed a supply of labour. Ripley entrepreneur John Marshall saw the opportunity and built a Workman's Home on Booth Street in 1910. The building could sleep nearly 100 people. Shared rooms were 4*d* or 6*d* and a private cubicle was 8*d*. The building is now converted into flats, but the nameplate above the door still shows the date 1910 and the initials 'JM'.

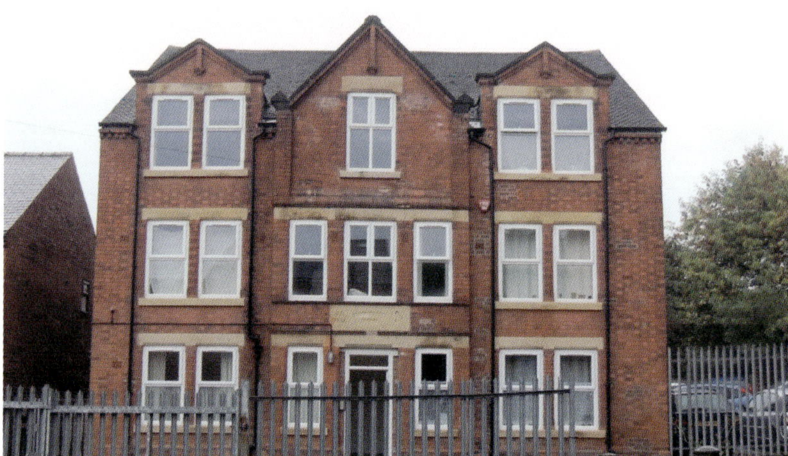

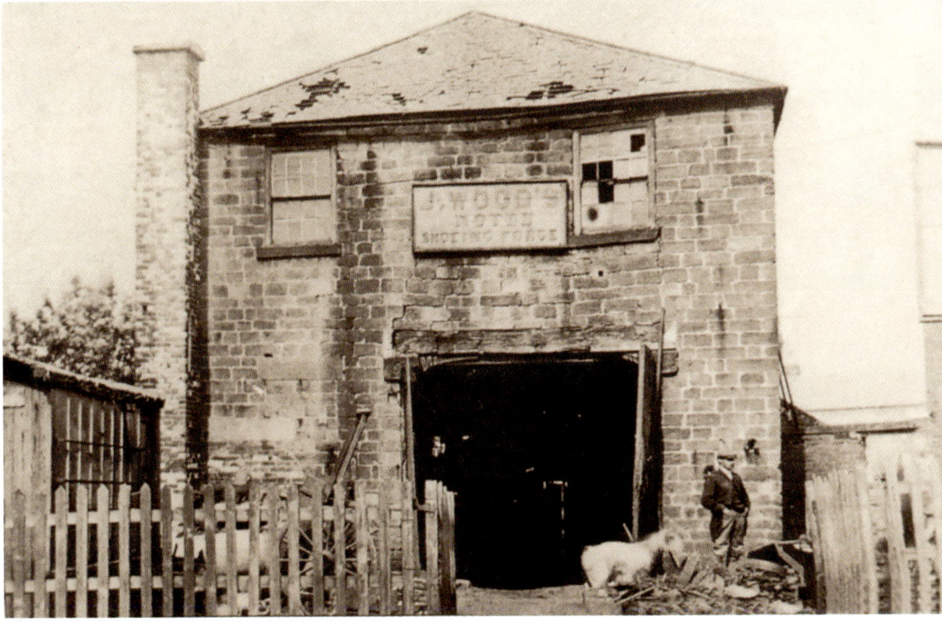

The Unitarian Chapel Becomes a Forge, Then the Electra Theatre

When the Unitarian chapel outgrew the building shown in the above photograph, it became a forge. John Wood, blacksmith, was the last occupant and when he moved into the Red Lion Yard, the building, seen here in its latter days, was demolished to build the Electra, Ripley's first purpose-built theatre.

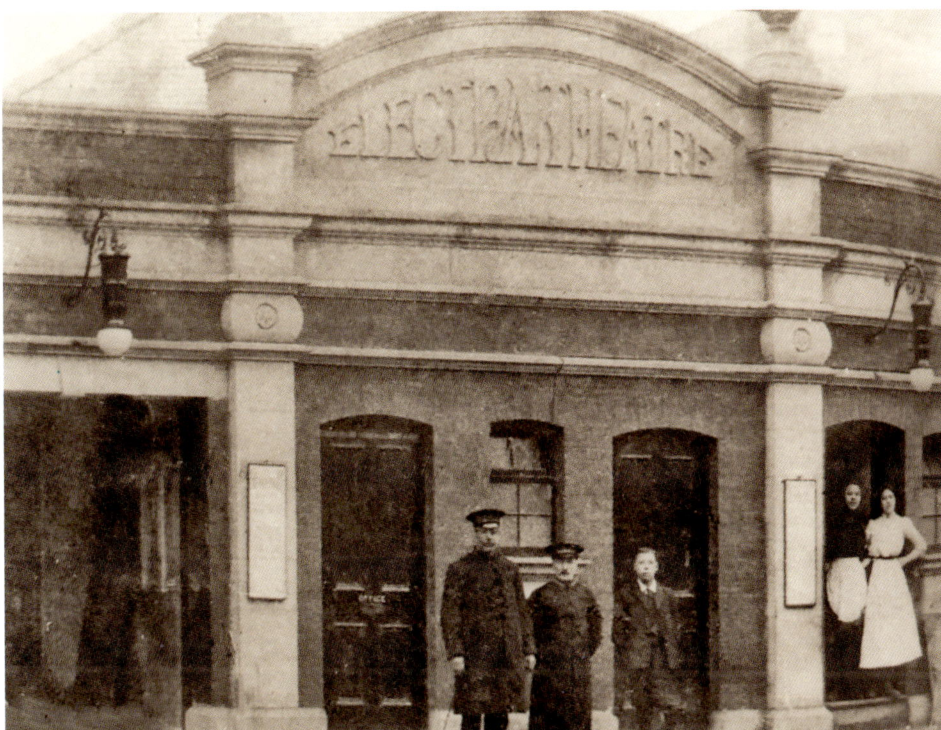

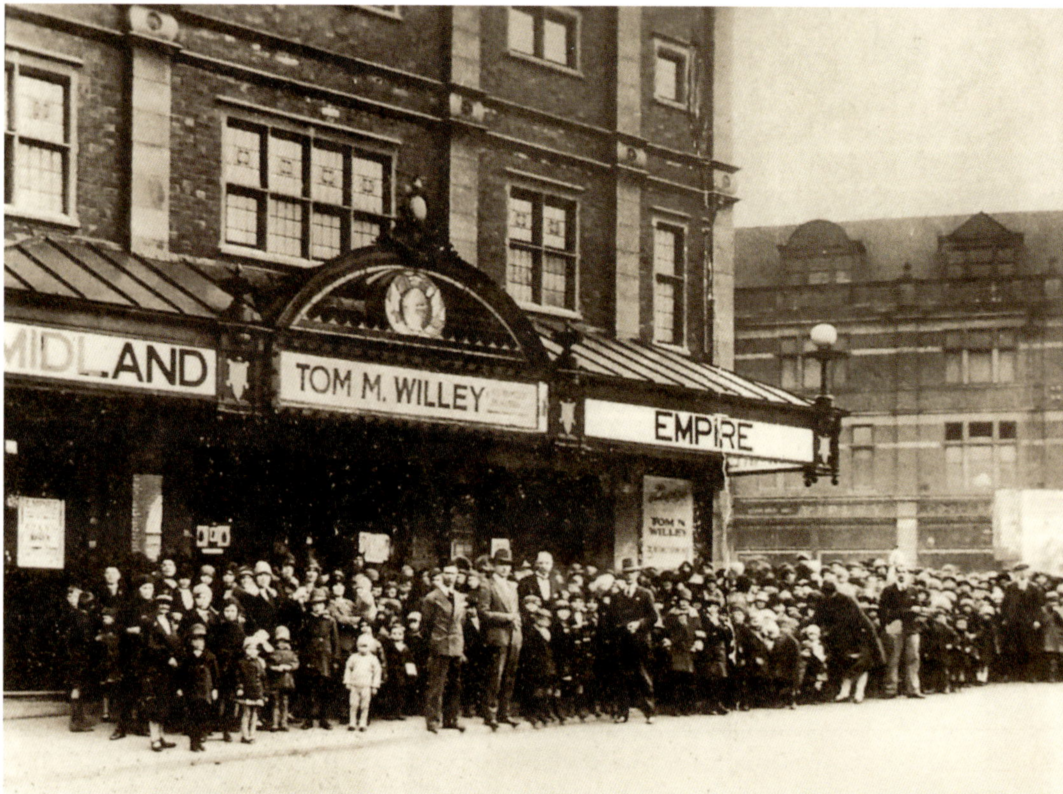

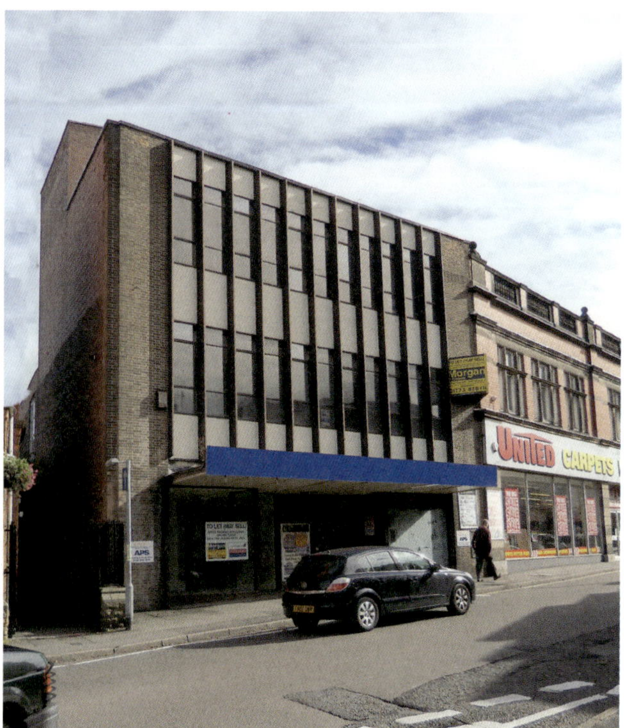

The Electra Becomes the Empire

By 1911, the Electra was considered too small to cater for the theatre-going audience. It was replaced by the larger and grander Empire, which closed in 1956. In 1931, the Co-op had built their central shops on the adjoining land, and in 1979, the site of the Empire was incorporated into the main Co-op buildings to become the Co-operative Food Hall. Later, it had other uses but is now looking for a new identity.

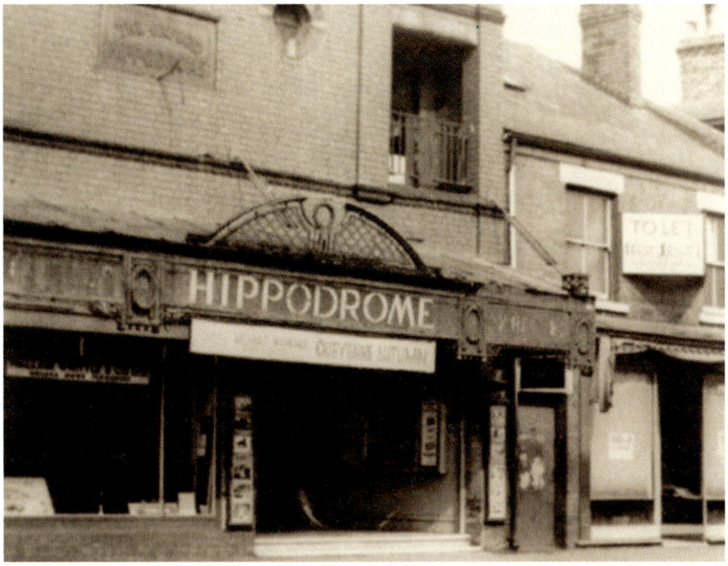

The Hippodrome

The Empire had stiff competition during the first half of the twentieth century. John Marshall had seen the need for a larger theatre and built one on the site of the White House, on the High Street near the market place. The Hippodrome, which could seat nearly 400 people, opened in 1913, with John's son-in-law, Jim Gration, as manager. Jim was killed in the war in 1917 after being awarded the DCM, and John's son Richard took over as manager. In 1921, the cinema was enlarged to seat over 900, with a new auditorium behind and at right angles to the earlier one. There were free concerts at the end of the war to celebrate victory, and during the General Strike of 1926, the Hippodrome provided free concerts for the striking miners. The Marshall family sold their interests in the Hippodrome in 1946, but it continued as a cinema until 1991, when it became a bingo hall and Tonker's nightclub. The building is just undergoing a complete internal overall, but the exterior upper floor remains the same with the plaque and side balcony.

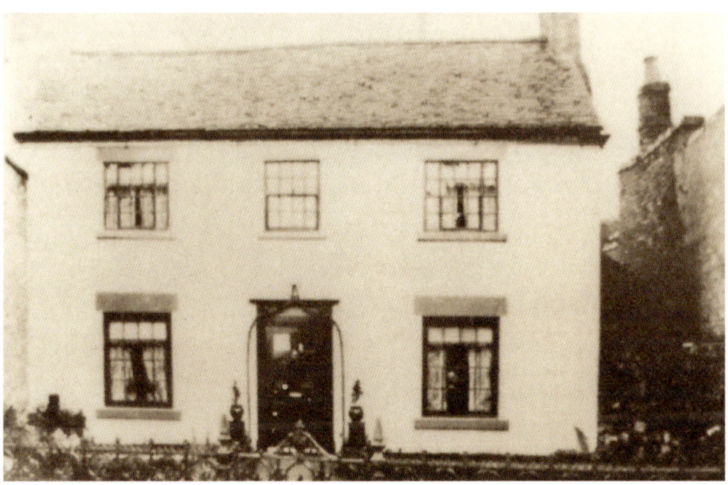

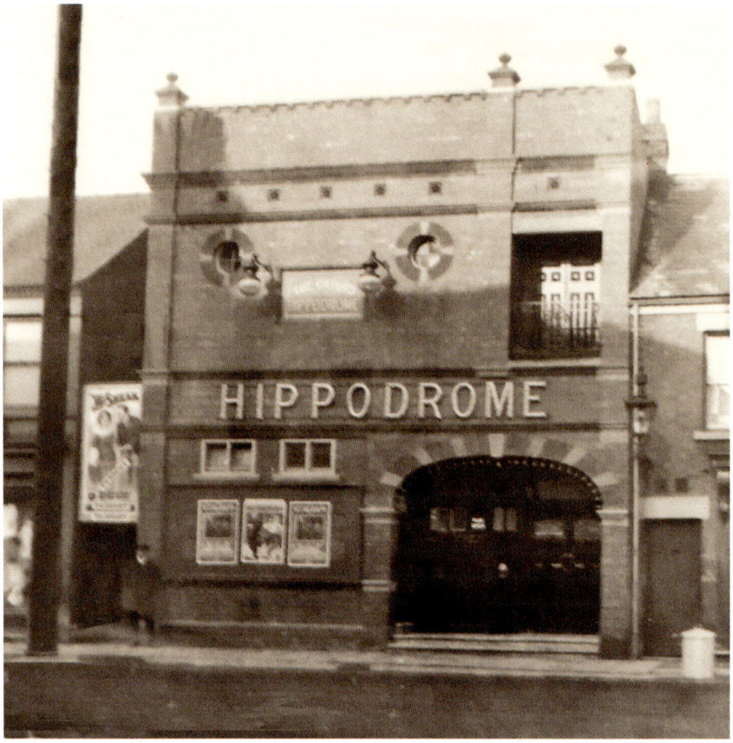

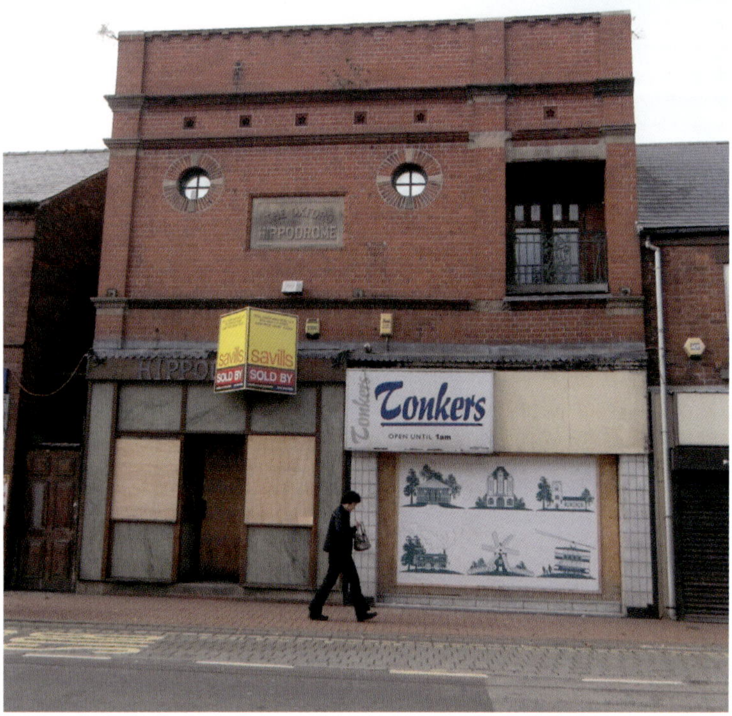

Ripley Archive Footage Found

It seems that John Marshall and his son Richard are still making news in and around Ripley long after their deaths. Both were keen amateur photographers, filming the people of the town and showing the footage to cinema-goers during evening screenings. On the BBC News of 9 June 2011, it was revealed by John Marshall's granddaughter, Valerie, that many of these old films have been stored in biscuit tins in a Derbyshire garage and, according to the tin label, the photographer was R. R Marshall, Hippodrome, Ripley. The events include a serious fire on 11 June 1923 causing more than £50,000 of damage at the Ripley Manufacturing Co. factory, and the unveiling of the war memorial at All Saints Church by the Duke of Devonshire. The film footage on nitrate film is highly flammable and can become solid and brittle with storage, but the Full Circle project hopes to preserve and make them available in modern media format. They are now in the possession of Media Archive for Central England.

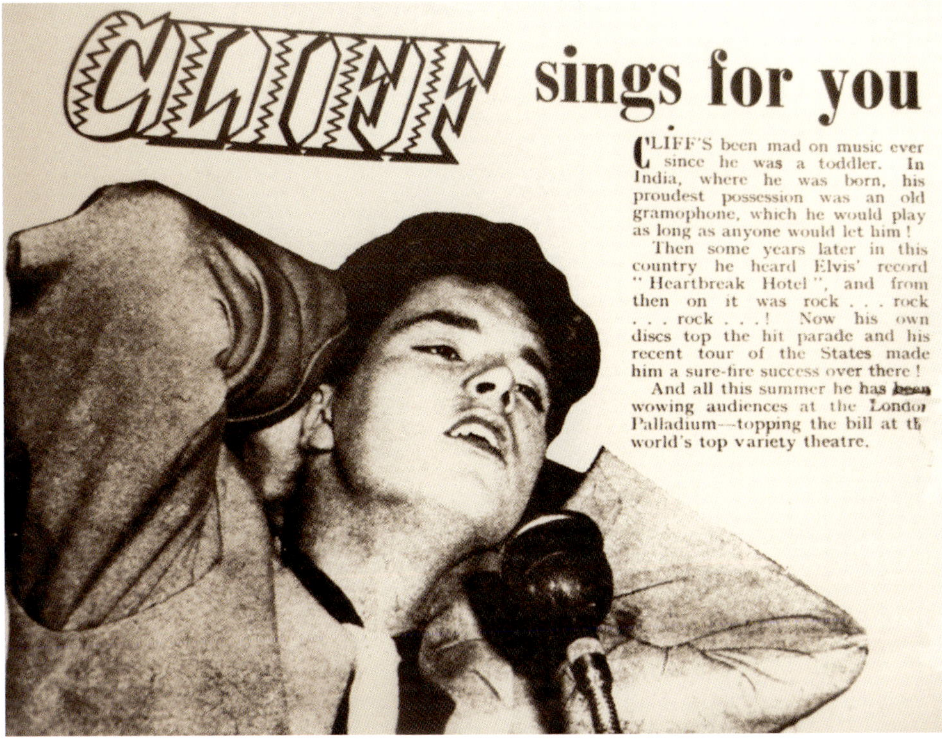

CLIFF sings for you

CLIFF'S been mad on music ever since he was a toddler. In India, where he was born, his proudest possession was an old gramophone, which he would play as long as anyone would let him!

Then some years later in this country he heard Elvis' record "Heartbreak Hotel", and from then on it was rock . . . rock . . . rock . . .! Now his own discs top the hit parade and his recent tour of the States made him a sure-fire success over there!

And all this summer he has been wowing audiences at the Londo Palladium—topping the bill at th world's top variety theatre.

The Regal Ballroom Launches the Career of Sir Cliff Richard

In 1956, Harry Greatorex bought the Temperance Billiard Hall on Nottingham Road, altered it and called it the Regal Ballroom. In May 1958, he offered to give a promising new group a chance to perform if the lead singer changed his name. He didn't want to bill them as Harry Webb, as Harry wasn't a particularly good name for a rock and roll singer. Harry had left school the year before and worked as a credit control clerk, but as The Quintones, he had performed with some school friends at the local Holy Trinity church youth club. After a brief spell with the Dick Teague skiffle group, Harry joined the Drifters with eighteen-year-old Teddy Boy John Foster, an employee at the local sewerage works, as manager. After initial suggestions of Cliff Russard and Russ Clifford, they came up with Cliff Richard. In return for a fiver plus travelling expenses, Cliff Richard and the Drifters (later changed to The Shadows) were given the chance to perform their first large-scale performance at the Regal Ballroom, Ripley.

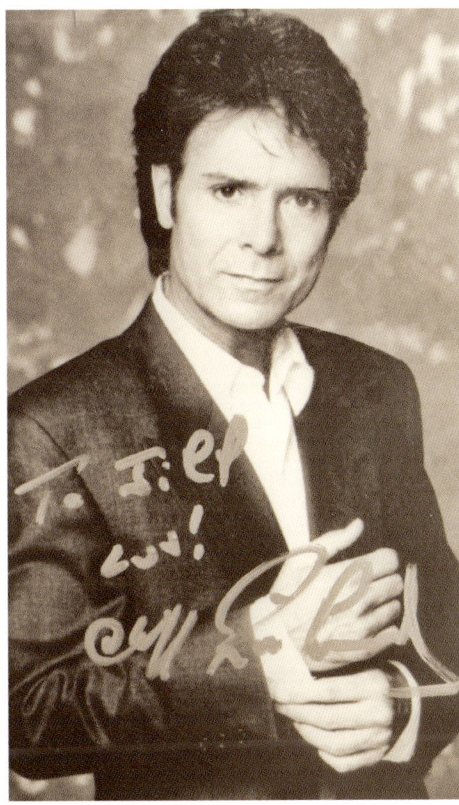

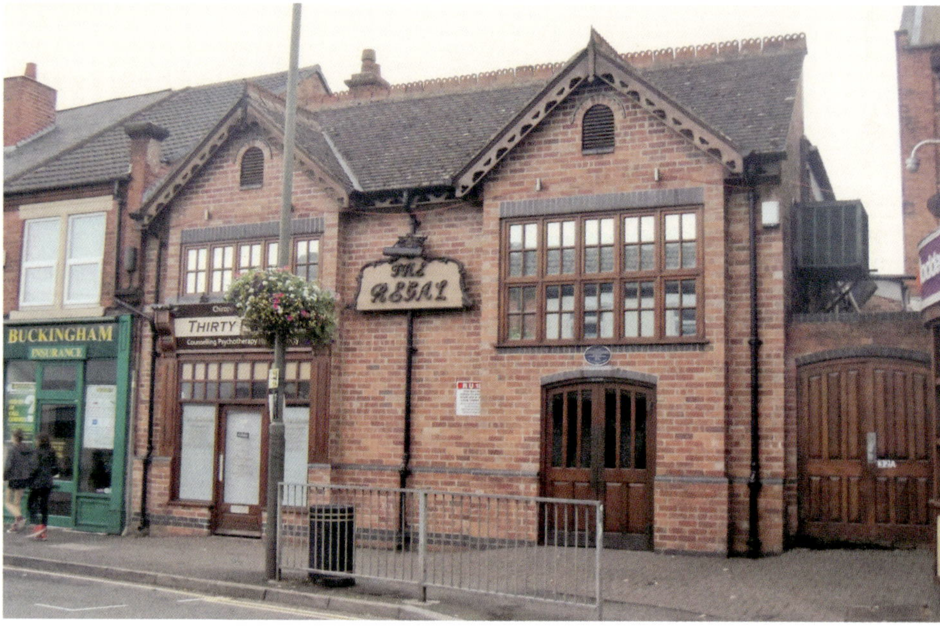

1958 and a Legend is Born

After their stage debut at Ripley, Cliff and the Drifters appeared at the famed 2i's club in London's Old Compton Street. They made a record that cost them £10, and had a nine-week summer stint at Butlins holiday camp at Clacton-on-Sea. On 13 September 1958, Cliff debuted on ABC TV's *Oh Boy!*, and currently his career has stretched over five decades. Gaining a knighthood, you could say that Harry Webb's future as Sir Cliff Richard superstar began at Ripley. The hall was demolished in 1996 and rebuilt along similar lines, reopening in 1997 as The Regal.

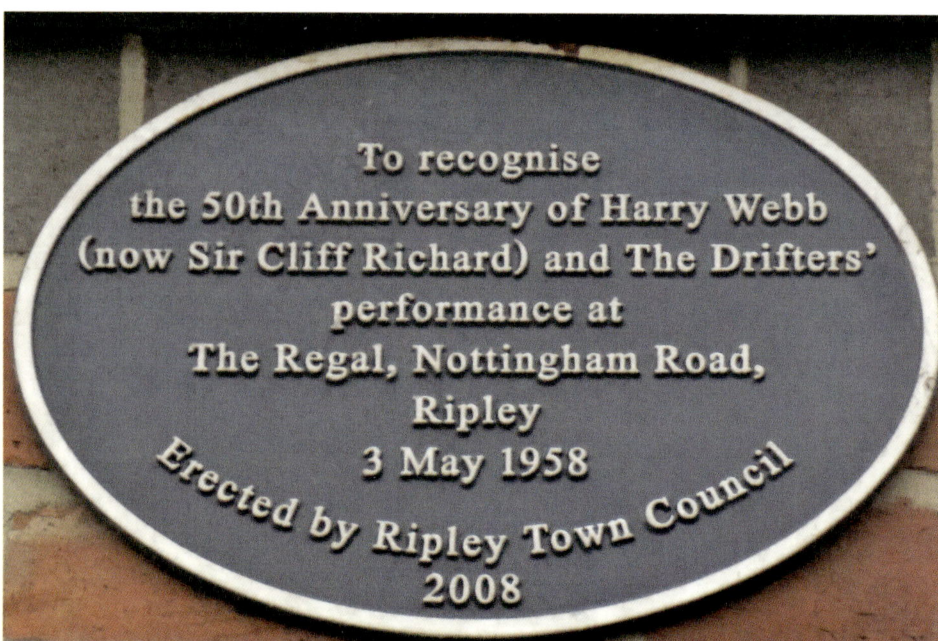

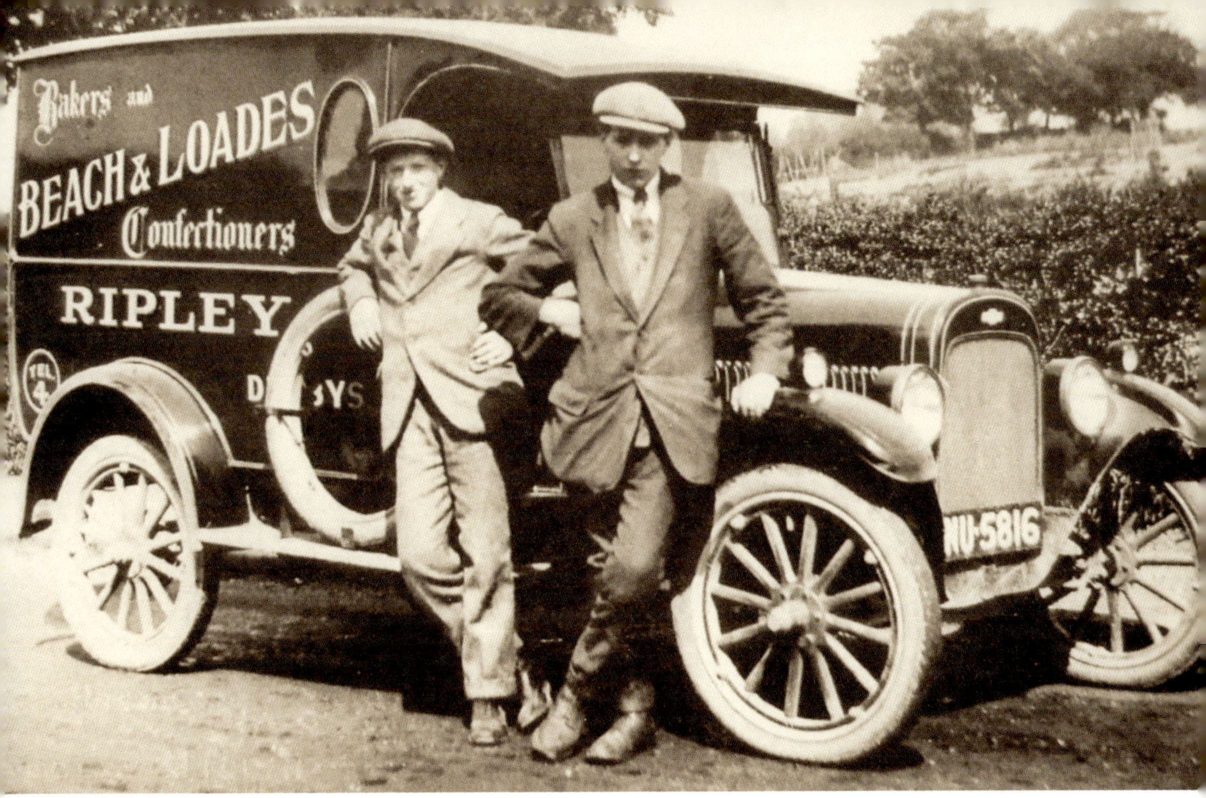

Beach & Loades

The partnership of two ex-miners and brothers-in-law Henry Beach and Herbert Loades began in 1918, when they bought Kay's bakery, off Dannah Street, Nottingham Road, and changed its name to Beach & Loades Bakery. The above photograph shows their delivery van in 1925. It became H. Loades & Son in 1937, and was taken over by Blanchards in the 1970s. The family had other interests in the town, including the Triumph Match factory at Codnor Gate, which they started in 1926, producing the Derby match. The factory burnt down in 1929, but was reopened as a stocking factory under the name Triumph Hosiery. In 1954, the company was purchased by Henry Haddon, who renamed it Haddon Textiles, and it was later purchased by the Mansfield Hosiery Company. It closed in 1975.

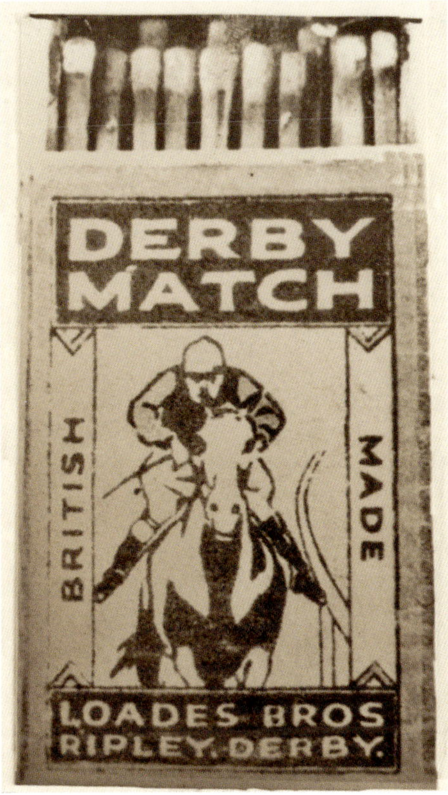

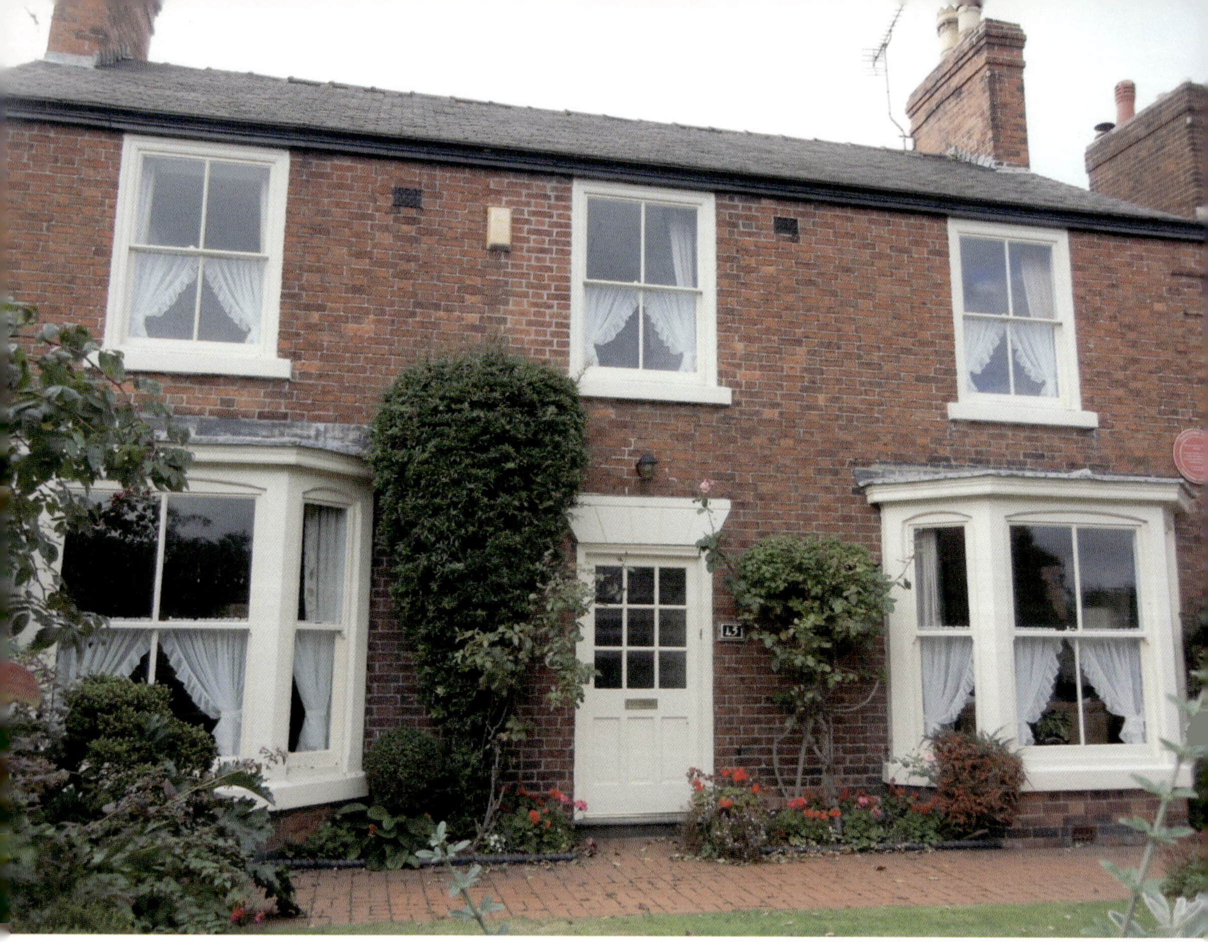

Barnes Wallis

There's a red plaque on Cromer House, No. 42 Butterley Hill (*above*), to national hero Barnes Neville Wallis (*pictured opposite above*). Barnes was born at Cromer House on 26 September 1887, and was the second son of Dr Charles Wallis and his wife Edith. They had moved to the town in 1886, when Dr Wallis joined the practice of Dr Allen at The Elms, Ripley. At school, Barnes excelled in English, science and maths, and at the age of seventeen, he took an apprenticeship in engineering before serving in the First World War. Between the wars, he worked on the design and building of airships, then moved on to commercial aircraft design, introducing many innovative features. England and Germany went to war in 1939, and in 1941, Barnes was working on a depth-charge designed to be dropped from an aircraft, ricochet across the surface water of a dam, then sink and explode underwater. This bouncing bomb was to attack the enemy at the Ruhr Valley Dams in the heartland of Industrial Germany. Practice runs were carried out on Derbyshire's Derwent and Howden Dams by Wing Commander Guy Gibson and his 617 Squadron, then the attack took place on 17 May 1943. The Dambusters' raid has gone down as the most dramatic and famous air strike in history, an event that has been well documented in books and films. Sir Henry Tizard, the scientific adviser to the Ministry of Aircraft Production, said that 'Dr Barnes Wallis, made the finest individual technical achievement of the Second World War'. He was awarded the CBE in 1943, and was knighted in 1968. He died in 1979, and the following year a memorial service was held at St Paul's Cathedral, London, attended by Prince Charles. Thirty years after his death, the Dambusters' raid was depicted in Ripley's well dressing celebrations with Barnes' daughter, Mary Stopes-Roe, as guest of honour. At the bottom of Moseley Street, adjacent to the Red Lion, is a recreation field named after Barnes Wallis.

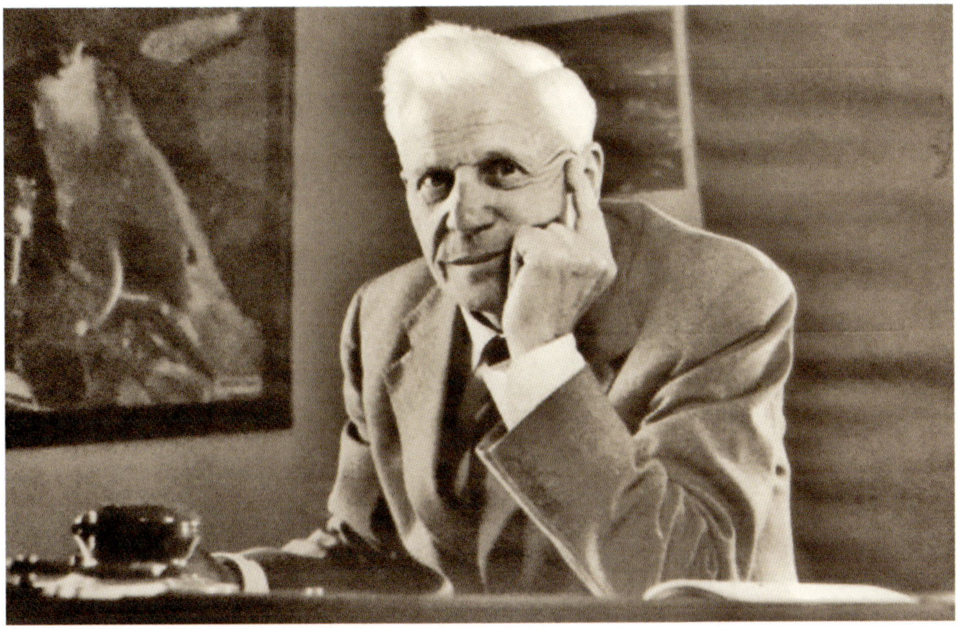

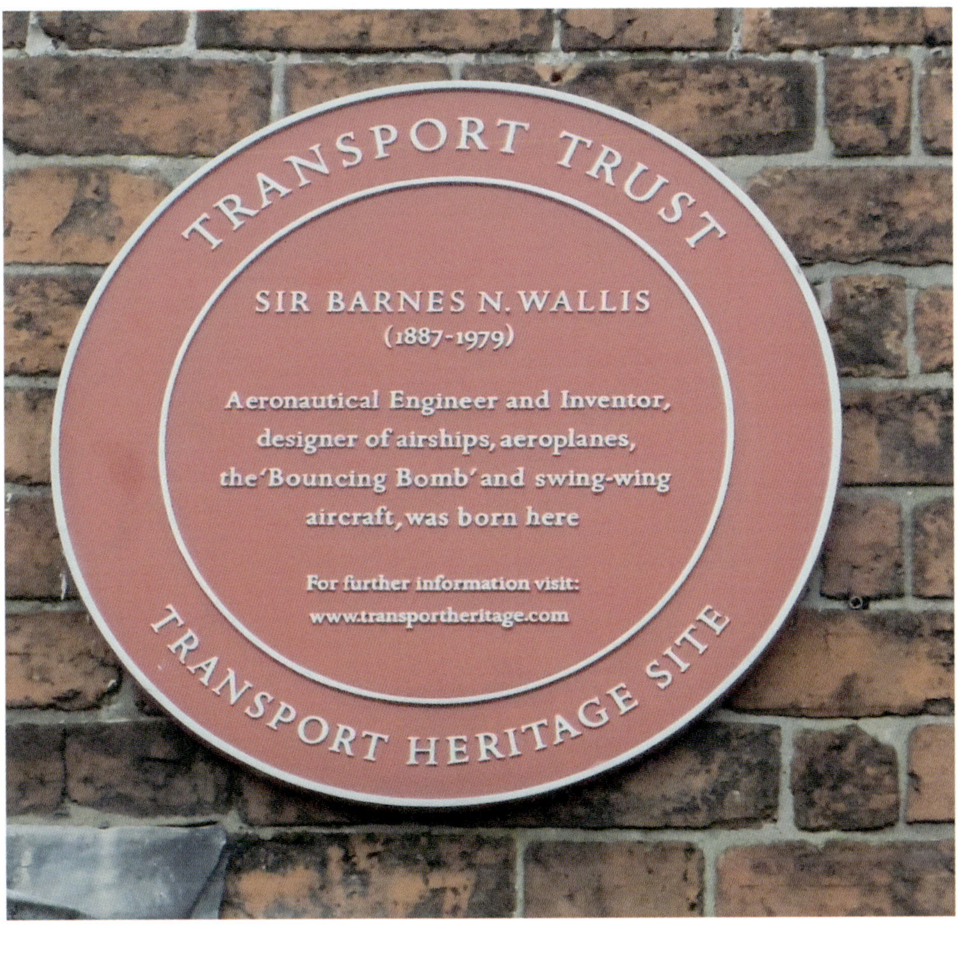
TRANSPORT TRUST
SIR BARNES N. WALLIS
(1887-1979)
Aeronautical Engineer and Inventor, designer of airships, aeroplanes, the 'Bouncing Bomb' and swing-wing aircraft, was born here
For further information visit:
www.transportheritage.com
TRANSPORT HERITAGE SITE

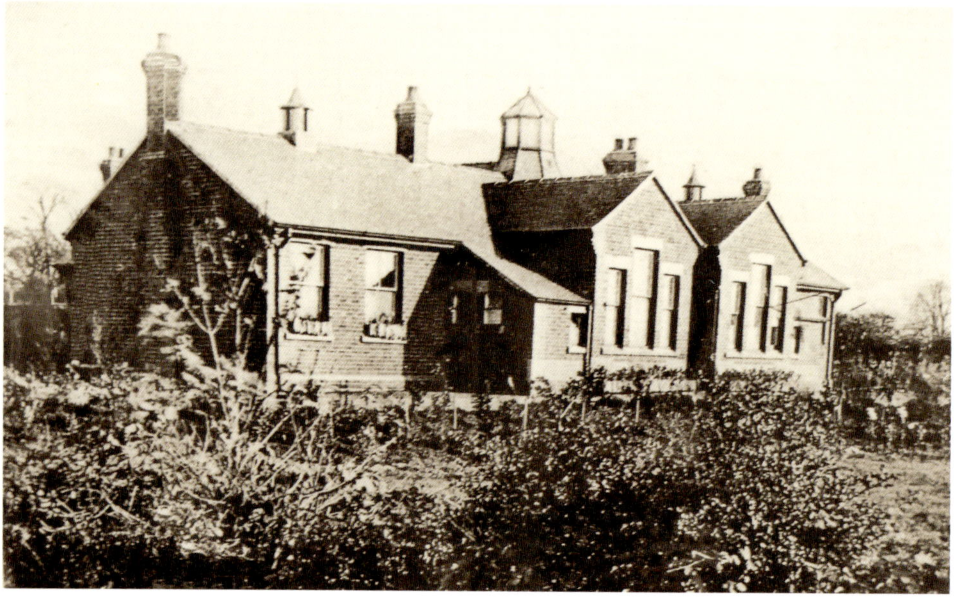

Cottage Hospital

Ripley Cottage Hospital was built in 1912 after Thomas Neal, a miner, was badly injured at Ripley Colliery and did not survive the road journey to Derby Royal Infirmary. The hospital was originally set up through donations from Ripley workers' wages. Its Sandham Lane site was extended in 1921, and the hospital celebrated its centenary on 7 September 2012. It serves the community for both inpatient and outpatient care, and the original building has been extended so much that it's hardly recognisable today. Ripley Hospital League of Friends was formed in 1955, and has remained a major fundraiser for over fifty years.

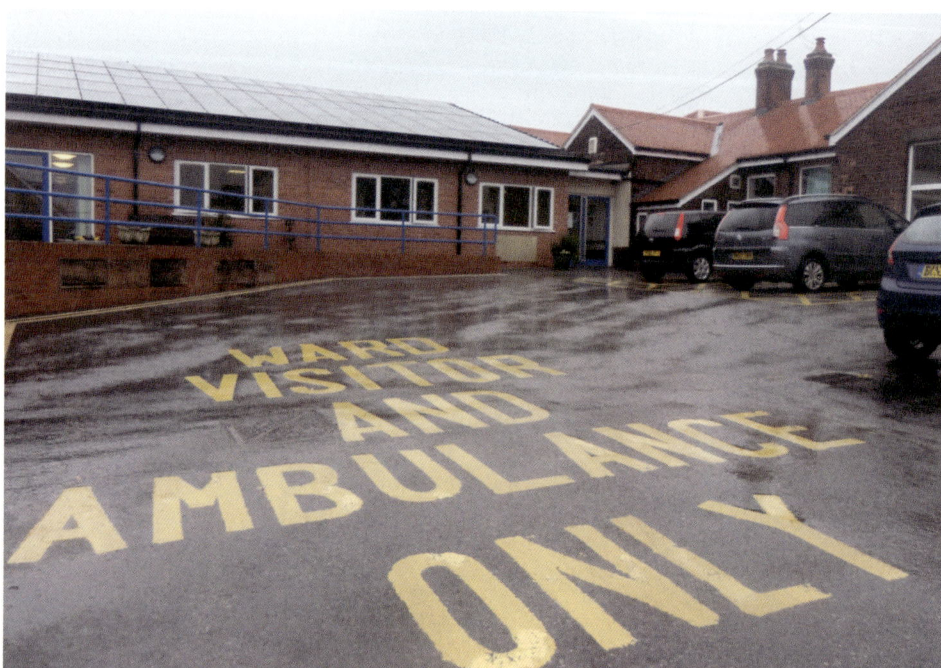

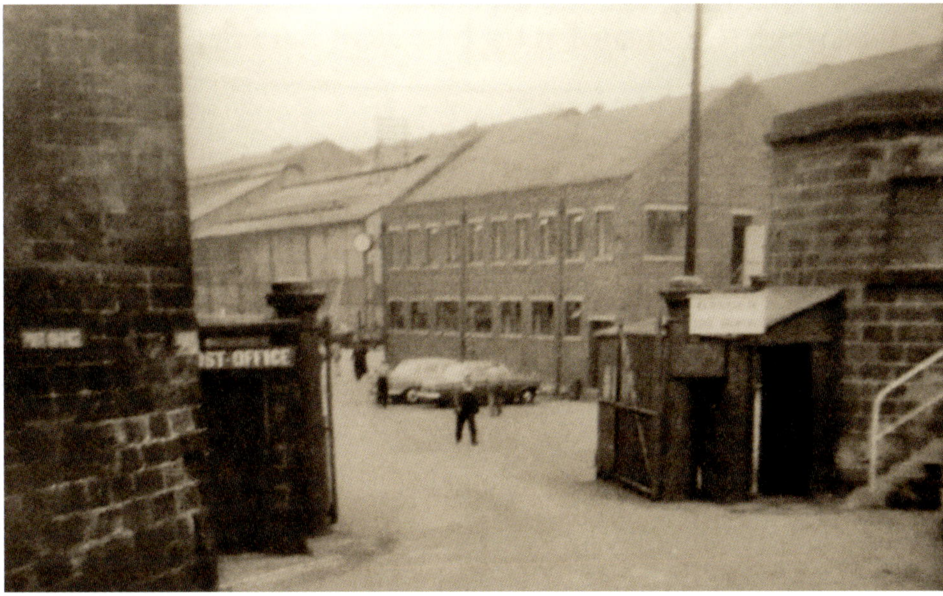

The End of an Era

In 1870, the Butterley Company was operating some 15 collieries, and employed 8,000 men in their collieries, ironworks and engineering sheds. At its peak in the 1950s, with ironworks and engineering sheds, a limestone quarry, lime-kilns, collieries and ironstone pits, the Butterley Company provided work for 10,000 people in and around Ripley, but Britain's industrial monopoly was slipping away. As the twentieth century came to a close, fortunes were changing. The Butterley Company that had existed in various forms for 219 years went into administration in March 2009. Many of the works units were demolished later that year, and the entrance gates were closed for the last time on a deserted yard. Parts that survive, like the quaint, hexagonal building on the right of the entrance gates, which was once part of the Butterley post office, are looking very sad.

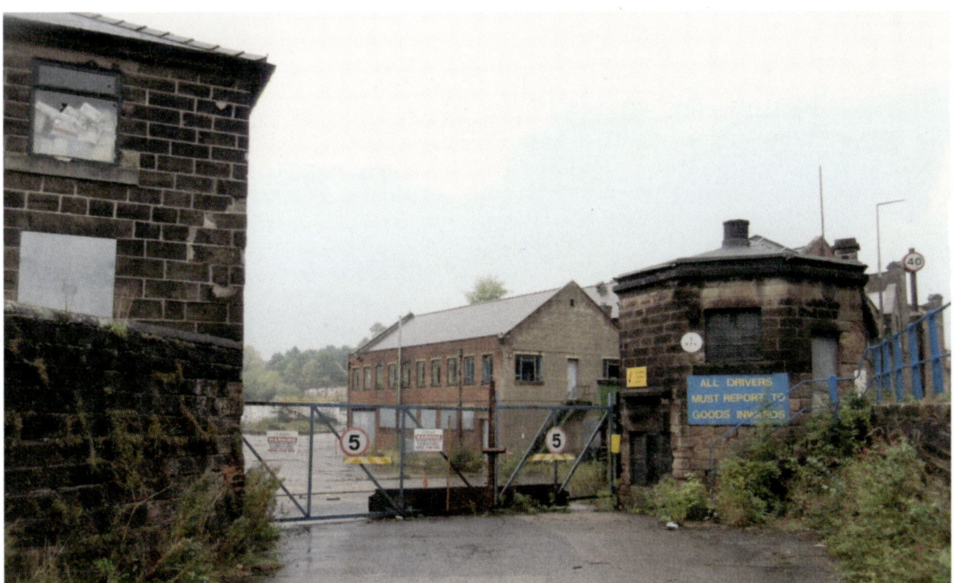

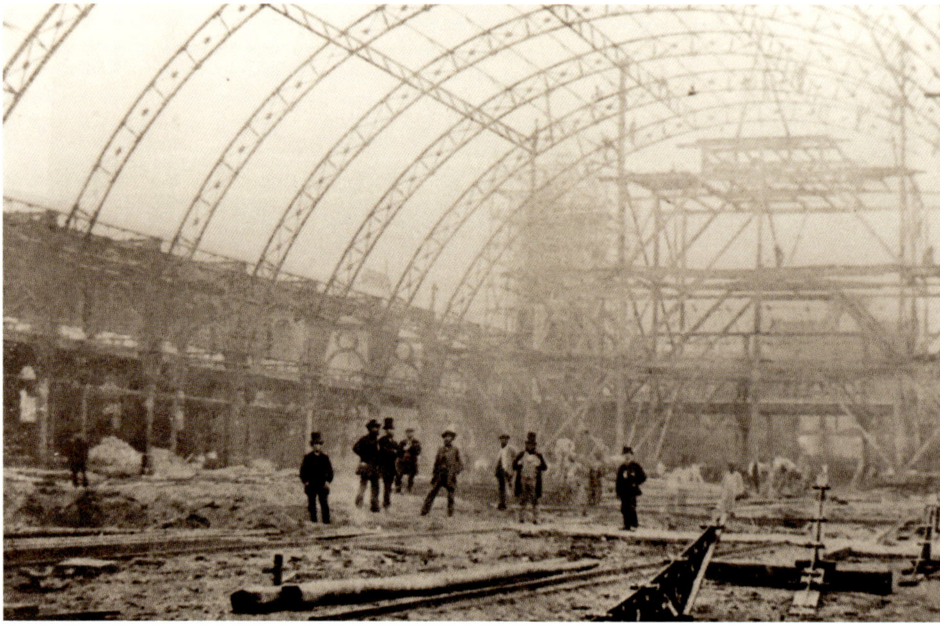

Ripley's Greatest Legacy

In the wall at the back of the abandoned site is the remains of the original No. 1 blast furnace, with an inscription on the stonework of the wall stating it was rebuilt in 1791. This was one of the blast furnaces that produced the products that made Butterley world renowned for its structural steelwork and heavy engineering projects, like the roof of St Pancras station, London. In the millennium, St Pancras station underwent a huge revamp, but retained the 1867 structure, a tribute to the enterprise, skill and art of those early Butterley engineers and constructors. In our photographs, the roof is being built, and 150 years later the bronze of Sir John Betjeman appears to be admiring the roof structure above him.

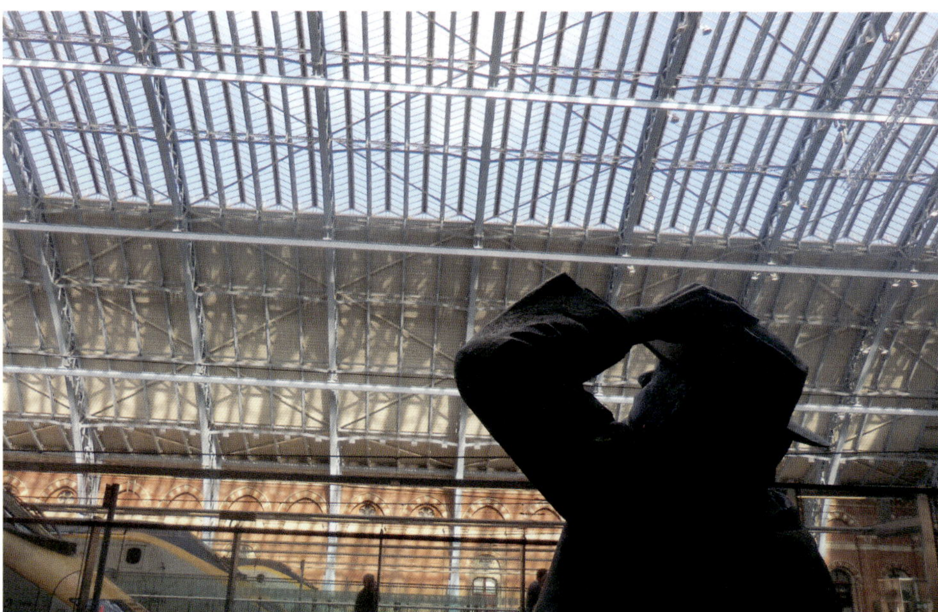

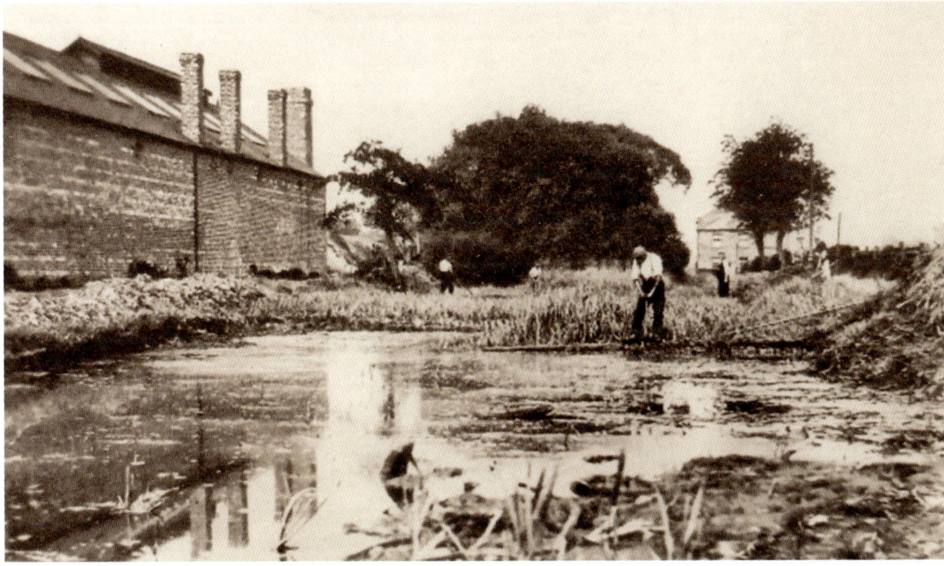

Preservation in Progress – Cromford Canal

The Cromford Canal that started the whole thing and brought prosperity to the Golden Valley was closed to through traffic by 1900 because of the collapse of the Butterley tunnel, and the canal fell into neglect. It was abandoned under the LMS Railway Canals Act of 1944, then taken over by British Waterways under the Transport Act of 1947. The 1960s saw the renaissance of canals as a leisure amenity, and there is a major campaign to reopen the 14½-mile canal between Langley Mill and Cromford. Five miles of the canal between Cromford and Ambergate, plus an attractive length through the Golden Valley, has been restored by the Cromford Canal Society, but work is ongoing. The photograph shows a primitive method of clearing the canal, with workers standing on planks laid across reed beds and digging them out with spades. The recent photograph looking down the canal at the Golden Valley shows how dense vegetation can take hold.

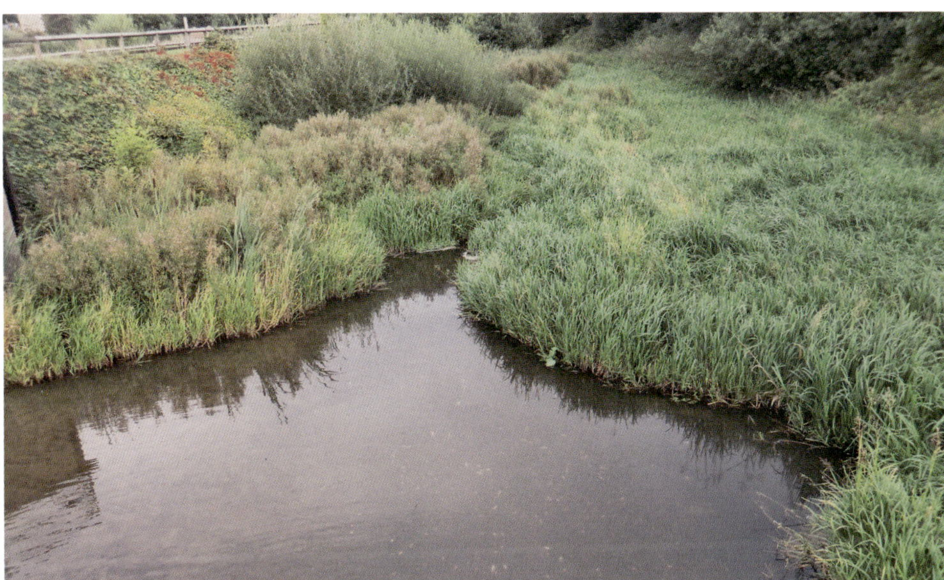

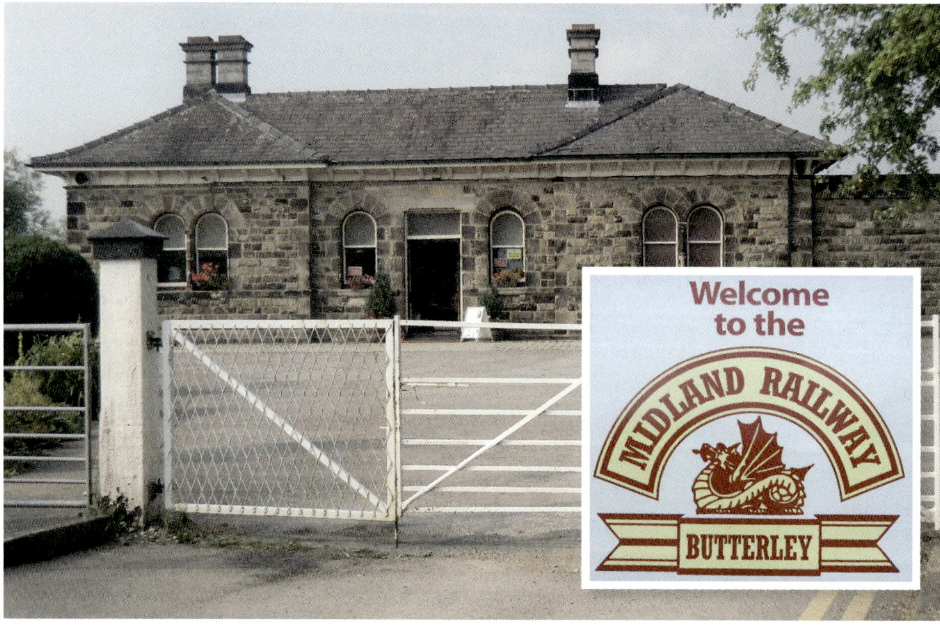

The Midland Railway Heritage Line

By the 1960s, the area was in decline. Railway branch lines lay abandoned and overgrown as the pits and the railways that served them closed. British Rail was removing track and selling it at scrap value, but the Derby Corporation bought a portion of the line between Ambergate and Pye Bridge for £45,467, and the Midland Railway Trust was born. At Swanwick junction, where a network of lines ran in all directions, a carriage shed was built and collecting began. Just past Swanwick junction was Butterley station, but the brick station building with its stone lintels had been demolished. However, British Rail donated the almost identical stone station from Whitwell (*above*) as its replacement, and at the same time, the smaller building on the opposite platform at Whitwell was removed and transported to be used as the station at Hammersmith further down the line. A large amount of equipment, locomotive and rolling stock was collected, grants and donations were received, and at Swanwick junction the facilities have been extended to include the railway's main workshop, with a locomotive repair depot, historic carriage/wagon repair facilities and a museum (*below*). With such significant backing, the line reopened as a heritage railway on 22 August 1981, and it's now possible to travel back to the age of steam through the Golden Valley.

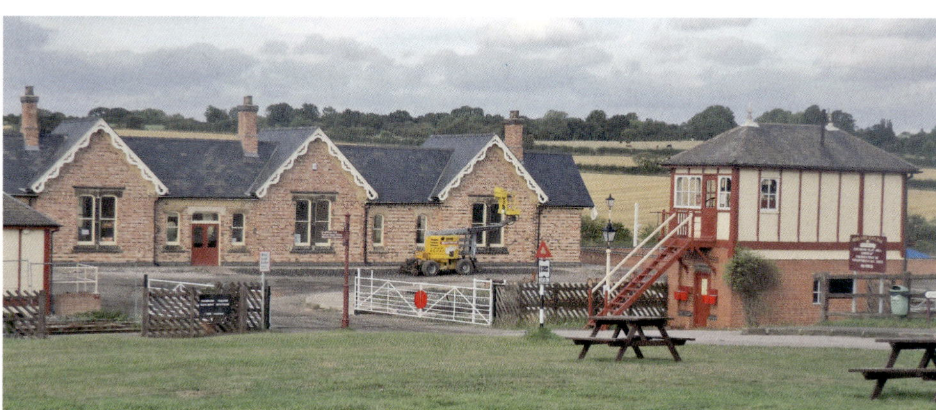